RETHINKING COMMUNITY FROM PERU

Illuminations: Cultural Formations of the Americas
John Beverley and Sara Castro-Klarén, Editors

RETHINKING COMMUNITY FROM PERU

The Political Philosophy of José María Arguedas

Qué está diciendo Arguedas Nación
Todos los sangres?
Hasta q' punto esta propuesta es abandonada
en los zorros?

- Ver debate Todos los Sangres
- Cornejo y Rama — Arguedas
        - leer Todos los sangres

Irina Alexandra Feldman

UNIVERSITY OF PITTSBURGH PRESS

Published by the University of Pittsburgh Press, Pittsburgh, Pa., 15260

Feldman, Irina Alexandra.
Rethinking Community from Peru: The Political Philosophy of José María Arguedas / Irina
Alexandra Feldman.
      pages cm — (Illuminations : cultural formations of the Americas)
Includes bibliographical references and index.
ISBN 978-0-8229-6307-3 (paperback: acid-free paper)
1. Arguedas, José María—Criticism and interpretation. 2. Arguedas, José María—Political
and social views. 3. Peruvian fiction—20th century—History and criticism. 4. Arguedas,
José María, Todas las sangres. 5. Ethnic relations in literature 6. Social conflict in literature.
7. Community life in literature. 8. Sovereignty in literature. 9. Indigenous peoples—Andes
Region—Politics and government. 10. Andes Region—Politics and government. I. Title.

PQ8497.A65Z647 2014
863'.62—dc23   2014012658

To Roberto

CONTENTS

ACKNOWLEDGMENTS

First and foremost, I would like to thank, infinitely, Horacio Legrás for his intellectual generosity, interest in my work, and unwavering support. My deepest thanks also go to Sara Castro-Klarén for enriching conversations, advice, and encouragement. I also thank the two anonymous readers of the manuscript for this book. Their suggestions were key to improving the final version of the present work. Many thanks to the Department of Spanish and Portuguese at Middlebury College and my colleagues for logistic help and inspiring discussions. This book would not have been possible intellectually, affectually, or practically without Roberto Pareja.

RETHINKING COMMUNITY FROM PERU

ARGUEDAS

Rethinking Community

But the survival of the Indians depended on making possible the impossible.
  —Horacio Legrás, *Literature and Subjection*, on the indigenous
  logic in *Yawar fiesta*

A true political act: it makes the impossible possible.
  —Slavoj Žižek, *Violence*, on the solution of the Israeli-Palestinian conflict

This book takes up the Benjaminean definition of "illumination" as "that image of the past which unexpectedly appears to someone singled out by history at a moment of danger," and envisions José María Arguedas and his work as the embodiment of this experience. He perceived himself as signaled out by history to be a "living bond" between the creole and the indigenous parts of Peruvian society.[1] He faced what was seen as the threat of imminent annihilation of the Quechua Indians and their culture at the moment of rapid modernization of mid-twentieth-century Peru. His belief in his mission to prevent, or at least to record, this process, which appeared as tragedy to him, made him look at the Peruvian present through the prism of the Quechua worldview,[2] rooted in the past and in the history of long duration, or as Arguedas's friend and one of the founders of the Liberation Theology Gustavo Gutiérrez put it, "en el tiempo de los sabios," "within the temporality of the wise."[3] The force of Arguedas's propositions lies in the Andean perspective that guides him in his representations of the Peruvian empirical reality, where the "Andean perspective" does not mean that the novels recover the original, intact, or authentic Quechua worldview. Instead, Arguedas emerges as a thinker who creatively processes various theoretical tools available to him through his vital and intellectual experiences: university education, Marxist thought of the 1930s and 1960s, and his own experience and study of the Quechua conceptual universe and language.

My analysis revolves around the concepts of community, political subjectivity, sovereignty, juridical norm, and revolutionary change. Arguedas's arguably most ambitious and controversial novel, *Todas las sangres* (All the bloods)[4] is at the center of this investigation, since it deals with the problem of nation building most directly. Study of his other novels, *Deep Rivers, El Sexto*, and *The Fox from Up Above and The Fox from Down Below* (*The Foxes*), which I examine in more detail in the last chapter, offers a panoramic rereading of Arguedas's fiction and elaborates further on the target concepts.[5] The originality of Arguedean political thought becomes evident when the textual analyses of the novels are introduced into a dialogue with the important political philosophers who address the problem of community, such as Walter Benjamin, Jean-Luc Nancy, Carl Schmitt, Jacques Derrida, Ernesto Laclau, Giorgio Agamben, Michael Hardt and Antonio Negri, Paolo Virno, Slavoj Žižek, and Álvaro García Linera.

According to Nancy and Agamben, the thought on community in political European theory has come to a halt. In our world, where the sphere of the political is profoundly intertwined with the sphere of economics, where the distinction between the public and the private spheres has eroded, it is almost impossible to imagine alternatives to the existing model of liberal democracy. At the dawn of the twenty-first century, political philosophers such as Hardt and Negri, Agamben and Žižek ask: How can the thought on community move beyond the horizon of a neoliberal democratic model? How can a political subjectivity and emancipatory alternatives be envisioned? What is the place of the popular in our political world? And, finally, what are the place and form of revolutionary and productive antagonism in further political developments of the world community, as we look at it from the second decade of the twenty-first century? How can the horizon of political possibilities be opened?

One characteristic that unites Arguedas's political thought and this heterogeneous group of philosophers is the feeling that "the liberal tradition no longer offers the intellectual resources to meet the challenges . . . of the modern world."[6] This is also the reason for the presence of Schmitt among the neo-Marxist thinkers. Schmitt's political thought has received renewed attention from philosophers from both the antiliberal Right and the Left between the 1980s and the present. Setting aside his daunting legacy of participation in the regime of the Reich, leftist thinkers like Benjamin, Agamben, and Žižek successfully mined his theory for the profound criticism of the legalism that marks the liberal democratic model. My use of

Schmitt's political thought will follow the lead of these critics of the model of liberal democracy who look to redefine the meanings of the concepts of political subjectivity, oppositional pole, antagonism, and revolutionary change for the politics of the twenty-first century.

My interest in writing about political concepts in Arguedean thought was triggered by my reading of *Mesa Redonda sobre Todas las Sangres* (Roundtable on All the bloods) of 1965.[7] At this event, the validity of Arguedas's representation of Peruvian reality in the novel was severely questioned by a group of progressive scholars. The most acute point of divergence between the discussants was the identity of the persons who lived in the Peruvian sierra. For Arguedas, the majority of people living in the Peruvian sierra and represented in the novel were Indians. For the social scientists, the young historian Henri Favre and important sociologist Aníbal Quijano, they were peasants, and presenting them as "Indians" implied a "historical disbalance" ("desnivel histórico") in the narration.[8] Two terms at play here, "Indians" and "peasants," defined the discourses of the discussants. Arguedas put on the table categories of a cultural, anthropological nature: for him the people of the sierra could be Indians, mestizos, or cholos. For Favre and Quijano the economic categories were prevalent. Therefore, they spoke of peasants, workers, and the feudal elites. The two positions enunciated different types of narrative projects—literary, scientific, and political—and also engendered different systems of expectations and readings of intentionality, where intentionality is understood as the association of certain types of behavior with a social category, defined as property of a social actor. Thus, for Henri Favre the fact that the subaltern persons were identified as Indians marked them as exploitable individuals. For Arguedas, this label did not carry this negative meaning but rather implied that they had certain cultural resources that gave them a sense of belonging, which the decultured workers did not possess. Thus, the Indians escape the alienating *tristeza* (sadness), while the other workers are subject to it and as a result sink into drunkenness and desperation. From their chosen categories, Arguedas and the social scientists interpreted differently the antagonisms between the social groups in the Peruvian sierra, and imagined very different outcomes for these antagonisms. Favre and Quijano envisioned class struggles, which could, theoretically, satisfactorily conclude in a project of a homogenization appropriate for nation building. Arguedas's hopes for articulation of the nation project were similar, but he read the antagonism between the Indians and the *mistis* as deeply rooted in the cultural heterogeneity,[9] inherited from the centuries of colonial domination. Consequently, Arguedas was torn by contradictions. Desiring for Peru to become a nation, he recognized that it was not a homogeneous society required for such a national project and acutely perceived the distinctly constructed subjectivities and sovereignties that were clashing within the Peruvian national territory. Our purpose will not be to solve these unsolvable contradictions but to signal the location of the problem, to find the loci of the antagonisms and the possibilities of negotiation between different modes of political existence represented in the Arguedean text.

Since Favre and Quijano, among others, understood antagonism, politics, and sovereignty differently than Arguedas, it resulted in the conclusion, on the part of these social scientists, that the novel was an ill-informed representation of Peruvian reality.[10] Arguedas wrote a note after the event that declared his intention to take his own life, which indicates that he took seriously these accusations, recognizing them as having some profound truth.[11] This episode could be read as follows: on one hand, both Arguedas and the social scientists had the nation-state as their ultimate object of desire. But Arguedas simultaneously also recognized the existence of an alternative project of community represented by the indigenous ayllu. Nonetheless, nationalistic projects require exclusivity, as they are based on the idea of the subsumption of individuality into the nation and the delegation of sovereignty and of monopoly on violence to the state. Possibly, the truth that Arguedas perceived in the other scholars' accusation obliged him to see that he was putting irreconcilable projects side by side: the defense of distinct sovereignty of the ayllu and the nationalist project. His fiction, I propose, is a continuous struggle to live and write through this contradiction.

In other words, Arguedas was elaborating a defense of the modern nation-state as a horizon of expectation, and also its simultaneous critique. Since *Todas las sangres* argued the Indians' right to a certain degree of political autonomy and cultural difference, Arguedas's position was read as subverting the national project and curbing its possibility to resist the invasion of transnational capital. What is worse, it was read as an idealistic desire to keep the Indians as happily exploited persons, precluding them from emancipation, which developmentalist theories optimistically promised as a positive and dignified outcome for all the wretched of the earth. That was certainly a terrible accusation for a thinker like Arguedas. But looking at this accusation from the distance of fifty years, it is striking to see that Arguedas prophetically announced the heterogeneous conception of the national community that emerges in our day in the neighboring Andean nation, Bolivia, embodied in the revisionist attempts that characterized the Constituent Assembly in the year 2007, and the redefinition of the Bolivian state as "plurinational." Far from undermining Bolivia's ability to stand up for its sovereignty in the face of transnational capital, President Juan Evo Morales Ayma's government both allowed and supported these legal changes and simultaneously lowered the external debt as never before. It is also continuously promoting however gradual attempts at nationalization, which relatively increase the country's claims to sovereign decisions in both economic and political domains.[12]

Let us consider Arguedean theorization in a sort of prophetic light, in relation to the current legal debates around the indigenous autonomies. In 2003, Bolivian scholar Enrique Mier Cueto phrased the project for Bolivia as a plurinational state as an imperative: "Bolivia in this moment of its history faces a historical challenge of establishing the basis for an intercultural co-living. This task requires before anything and initially, a *collective will* to co-live with the foreign, a will that, in order to be fructiferous in the future, should be based on a true *understanding* of the Other in all his strangeness and peculiarity."[13] This evaluation of Andean reality calls into dialogue two poles that see each other as radical others. But Mier Cueto's sentence is prescriptive rather than descriptive. In the process of the Constituent Assembly in Bolivia in 2006–7, such legal and administrative logistics of co-existing with the other as that of the existence of indigenous autonomies within the departmental autonomies had provoked many conflicts that spilled over from the institutional debate onto the streets, the situation that did not smooth over the years of Evo Morales's presidency, and which, in fact, remains patently recorded in the text of the resulting constitution itself.[14] The desired collective will remains a utopia in this historical situation: the reality presents a proliferation of wills instead of one will of the people. Ernesto Laclau theorizes that a modern, hegemonic nation is formed by the double movement of its components: a movement of difference and a movement of sameness.[15] The elements within a signifying chain have to forego their differences and recognize themselves as the same. This sameness is circumscribed by an absolute limit, which separates it from the other beyond this limit, defined as absolute difference. The sameness is not given but, rather, imagined and constructed, and demands an empty signifier that fills the gaps by pointing to the illusory fullness of the community thus consolidated. Any abstraction can serve as such an empty signifier, such as "liberty," or "progress." Articulation of differences to an empty signifier makes it possible to imagine a hegemonic relationship and a national community.

The hegemonic discourse of the Bolivian government cannot conceal that its hegemony is only that, after all (a hegemony), and not a utopian representation of the collective will of the whole population. And yet, in

Bolivia in the second decade of the twenty-first century, Arguedas's so-called crazy idea of multiple sovereignties found in *Todas las sangres* does not seem so utopian. Bolivian Vice President Álvaro García Linera and others theorize the possibility of an indigenous autonomy, which implies a local sovereignty of the Aymara, Quechua, or Guaraní community that does not cease to be a part of the Bolivian state, and which also continues holding on to its own sovereign right.[16] The Constituent Assembly approved the proposal of the indigenous autonomies as a part of the Estado Plurinacional de Bolivia (Plurinational State of Bolivia),[17] the new name with which Bolivia has rebaptized itself. This second revolutionary baptism recognizes as nations the different indigenous peoples that live on Bolivian territory and grants them historical and cultural recognition and rights. The new name of the country also marks a divorce from the legacy of the old Republic of Bolivia, established as a nation in 1825 after the Wars of Independence, which was blind to the possibility of someone being an Indian and a citizen of a modern nation simultaneously. In his analysis of the new constitution, the scholar Xavier Albó explains the peculiar phrasing of the concept of political subjectivity of the majority of Bolivians as "naciones y pueblos indígena originario campesinos" (indigenous original peasant nations and peoples). This concept, despite its lack of elegance from a professional jurist's point of view, gathers the autodenominations of the indigenous legislators who were working on the new *Carta Magna* side-by-side with professional lawyers.[18] The term emphasizes both ethnic and class adscription of these political subjects, thus bridging the gap that seemed unbridgeable in the discussion between Arguedas and the sociologists in the 1960s. As we have seen, José María Arguedas in the mid-twentieth century was forwarding this strong idea and was not understood by his contemporaries. But now, the contradiction that inspired Arguedas to think about suicide is a constitutional reality, albeit not in his beloved Peru, where we observe more timid advances in terms of indigenous rights.

I must address here, however briefly, this curious phenomenon. The Peruvian intellectuals of the twentieth century, such as José Carlos Mariátegui and Arguedas, and in the later decades Alberto Flores Galindo, Antonio Cornejo Polar, Nelson Manrique, and Gonzalo Portocarrero, have produced a brilliant corpus of historical, fictional, critical, and theoretical writing on the social reality of Peru and its indigenous population. Their texts abound in progressive, innovative insights useful for understanding a heterogeneous society of an Andean country, such as Peru or Bolivia. But in terms of constitutional implementation of these ideas, the Bolivian situation is quite different from that of Peru in 2013, which did not aim at a constitutional reform. In the Peruvian election of 2011, Ollanta Humala won, defeating a legacy of dictatorship associated with the Fujimori family; and although Gonzalo Portocarrero pointed out in June 2013 the political and economic improvements that Humala's government made, the Peruvian president's discourses were far from García Linera's radical propositions on the emancipatory power of twenty-first-century Indianism.[19] A Peruvian scholar, Marco Antonio Huaco testifies specifically on the case of the indigenous rights violations by the Peruvian state in the Amazonas Department, where the gold mining is harming the livelihood of the Awajun and Wampis indigenous peoples. In this situation, Huaco speaks of the "neoliberal anti-indigenous program" of the Peruvian state.[20] The situation in Bagua, the center of the conflict between the indigenous people and the state-backed mining companies, was especially conflictive and resulted in a massacre of the Awajun by the military police on June 5, 2009. Huaco underlines "the impunity of the political violence, which comes back, *this time* exclusively against the indigenous people."[21] Investigations were made, but the state officials covered up the military massacre, and the official discourse presented the indigenous protesters as the guilty party.[22] Why is there this continuation of a vicious circle of Peruvian politics that seems incapable and unwilling to step outside the confrontation between the Indians and the state? Bruno Bosteels offers a possible answer to this question, while speaking of "an obvious interruption of memory due to military coups and the catastrophe of neoliberalism."[23] Carlos Vilas and Richard Stoller diagnose, more concretely and putting the finger directly into the wound, that "the war between the Sendero Luminoso and the Peruvian State throughout the 1980s can be seen as a struggle between two poles of power for political-military control of disputed territory, with both sides' strategies based upon unusual levels of violence. Insurgency and counterinsurgency alike destroyed communities and forced inhabitants to take part in atrocities or to keep silent." They proceed to quote a United Nations mission report from 1991 that states, bleakly, that as a result of the atrocities, "the countryside, and to a lesser extent urban areas, presents . . . a panorama of conflictive destructuring of the socioeconomic realm."[24] Most certainly and sadly, one of the reasons for the lack of institutional or legal advance in Peru is the political violence of the 1980s, evoked obliquely by Huaca in his description of the Bagua situation, when he speaks about "this time," which refers to "that other time," when all the country was sunk in a bloodbath. Leftist politics are associated with terrible violence, just as is the neoliberal Right, and the population is too weary to commit to a program of significant change, afraid of the possibility of more violence.

It is not that in Bolivia there was no military dictatorship or neoliberal catastrophe. It is not even that the government of Evo Morales and García

Linera does not enter into conflict with the multiple indigenous groups that live on Bolivian territory, each one of them with their own interests, and forming the new oppositional pole in relation to the new Bolivian state. The conflict that has unfolded since 2010 between the Bolivian government and the Yuracaré community over the roads project through the lands of the Yuracaré Indians in TIPNIS (Territorio Indígena y Parque Nacional Isiboro-Secure) is an example of the political alignments always being contingent upon the alignments of power. The final decision to build the road despite the opposition of the eco-indigenist groups has earned Evo Morales an accusation of betrayal to his previous alliances; and yet García Linera sees even in this clash between the internal geopolitics and eco-indigenist arguments that these "creative tensions" contribute to the development of the new Bolivia.[25]

Moreover, García Linera, the ex-prisoner of a neoliberal government of the 1990s, is leading Bolivia as a second to the ex-coca farmer activist Morales. As a result of the symbolic presence of these two figures at the head of the country, the historical moments of repression, both of "long duration" and from the very recent history, are not hidden but evoked as a negative example. For instance, we see it in the film about the youth of Evo Morales, titled *Cocalero*,[26] which narrates the extreme violence that the coca farmers suffered at the hands of the repressive neoliberal state. In order to understand the meaning of these evocations, it is useful to turn to Slavoj Žižek's reflection about the ethical attitude of today's thinkers on the matter of the Jewish Holocaust. For Žižek, as for many others, it is, of course, unethical and "disgusting" to forget, or to deny this profoundly tragic event of European and world history.[27] What is paradoxically even less ethical is a legal declaration that prohibits one from questioning the facts of the Holocaust, because such a "legalized" official memory exempts individuals from reflecting on the event and becomes another perverse form of oblivion. It especially becomes perverse when the reference to the Holocaust justifies violence in the name of so-called Western values. The Slovenian philosopher tells us that the only acceptable and necessary manner of dealing with the fact that the Holocaust did take place in the modern history of Europe is to evoke it as a negative example, as if saying: this is what was done to the Jewish people; let it never happen to anyone else, ever again.

In Peru and Bolivia, in order to start thinking about the new possibilities of including the indigenous communities and individuals into the political fabric of the modern nation-state, one must negatively evoke the American indigenous Holocaust. Before thinking about the possibility of the pluricultural community, Bolivian intellectuals (García Linera, Luís

Tapia, Oscar Vega Camacho, Pablo Stefanoni, among others) recapitulate on the especially painful moments of history when the state massacred its people, whether they are conceptualized as Indians, campesinos (peasants), or *obreros* (workers). Essays on the 1990 Miners' March for Life (Marcha Minera por la Vida), the War of Water (Guerra del Agua) of 2000, and Bloody October (2003) proliferate in the La Paz publishing house Muela del Diablo. To begin to think of a new kind of national and yet multisocietal community, it seems that first it is necessary to exorcise the demons, to recall the moments of acute antagonism, to remember the victims of those clashes, and to mourn them. For the same reasons, in Arguedas's novels the representation of antagonisms and their deadly outcome plays as much of a vital role as negotiation. The moment of hard self-adscription to an identity is as important as the flexible management of ethnic labels. Moments when characters decide to die for a cause are key to understanding Arguedean thought. I am thinking of the characters of Rendón Willka and Anto, whose deaths in *Todas las sangres* are most ideologically conscious.[28] Anto and Rendón can certainly negotiate the identity they present on the outside: as an example, Anto passes from being a *pongo* (serf) to *vecino* (townsman) to mestizo. Rendón appears as *indio* or cholo or *ex-indio* or mestizo. But both die for something nonnegotiable, beyond their self-labeling.

Arguedas's novels have been generally considered from the point of view of identity criticism, emphasizing the culturally malleable, negotiable identities of the characters.[29] These readings revealed, importantly, the real heterogeneity against the previous scholarly desires of imagining Peru as free of postcolonial fissures. Standing in opposition to homogenizing discourses, Arguedas's novels have been of interest to this tendency in identity criticism. But I want to emphasize again that they are also important for identity politics, in other words, for strategic self-adscription to a discriminated ethnic group with the purpose of defending its ground in an open antagonism with the state. The invention of such an identity can work as a location from which to place a demand on the state, but it can also work in order to mark the ultimate political division into friends and enemies, according to Carl Schmitt's theory, if the state is unable or unwilling to receive such a demand.[30] This ultimate political moment occurs at the end of *Todas las sangres*: when the negotiation fails, the soldiers, representatives of the state, shoot Rendón Willka, and the indigenous communities all over the sierra rise in a general rebellion, *yawar mayu*. It is certainly important to see that in Arguedas's last novels identities are fluid, constructed, negotiated, and changing, as Melissa Moore demonstrates. But it is also important to see the moments when the constructed nature of these identities becomes irrelevant, as it deals with the question of life and death. True, within the novel they are only fictitious deaths of the characters. But these novelistic deaths reflect real deaths that happened because of persons taking a stand with a certain reduced, essential political identity at a certain decisive moment.

The relevance of Arguedean fiction to the understanding of such a political moment can be further advanced with a brief example of a passage that we will analyze in detail in one of the following chapters. Let us hear Rendón Willka's last words before his execution: "Our heart is made of fire. Here and everywhere! We have come to know fatherland, at last. And you will not kill fatherland, sir."[31] This enigmatic claim that the Indians ("we") "have come to know the fatherland at last" puts into play categories that escape either culturalist or economicist theoretical tools. Here we are talking fundamentally about the possibility (or not) of being a citizen, while participating in a cultural-economic way of life of the Indian communities, their particular subjectivities and their modes of political existence. This is a properly political question. Is it possible for the people who carry on the way of life determined by communal values and systems of production, functional within a separate sovereignty, to establish a satisfactory relation with the state, which pretends to hold the monopoly on sovereignty and violence? Rendón Willka's words respond positively to this question, but his physical death makes this relation problematic. This book will engage this problem and will attempt to respond to the question: How is it that the Indians come to know the "fatherland," if they continue to stand in front of the firing squad, without trial? And how is it possible at all to narrate a relation of this nature; how is it possible to write a novel about a community thus constituted?

In particular, Arguedas's last two novels, *Todas las sangres* (1964) and *The Fox from Up Above and the Fox from Down Below* (1971), address the question of whether the modern democratic nation-state is the best model of political organization for a community, and more so in a world of increased globalization. Because of this radical ideological content, both books received a mixed response upon their publication, and only in the 1970s began to be recognized for their literary and theoretical innovation.[32] And yet, the power of these narratives resides precisely in this radical content. In fact, the creative task of the poiesis, understood as the power of creation, and that of theory coexist in Arguedean fiction. It is symptomatic and revealing that the speech of the characters in *The Foxes* had once been dismissed as incomprehensible by Mario Vargas Llosa.[33] Arguedas writes in a language that juggles a representativity required of realist literature and also creates, in an infernal battle with the language, new words and expressions that acquire a conceptual and theoretical dimension. Estelle Tarica, for instance, studied the complex meaning of an expression Arguedas uses, "decir limpio" (clean speech), a concept of writing that expresses the essence of things and can only function when the enunciator is "clean" from negative passions, such as rage or resentment.[34] As Frederic Jameson suggests in his reflection "On Jargon," both political theory and poetry call for a language that is removed from the transparency of common sense and everyday speech. In Arguedas's case, both of these modalities of enunciation, theory and poetical prose, imply an intellectual battle with language and concepts, in other words, the immense effort of thinking and creating a new way of seeing and representing the world. Therefore, a text that has both a theoretical and a poetic aim, as is the case with Arguedean fiction, is often obscure and comes to speak of the kernel of the problem only obliquely. Additionally, Sara Castro-Klarén observes that the power of Arguedas's fiction lies in the creative process itself, conceptualized in *The Foxes* through the Quechua concept of *camac*, the creative power of the *huacas*.[35] The necessity to conjugate the creative poiesis and theory is the key reason why Arguedas, a trained anthropologist, turns primarily to fiction in order to represent the Peruvian reality "as he has lived it"[36] and to develop a conceptual system that allows him to think of future alternatives for the political and cultural life of Peru. The reason why the present study is primarily concerned with his novels is precisely because this novelistic mode of enunciation illuminates, creatively, the concepts from the sphere of political thought and political practice. But how does this difficult fiction acquire the dimension of a creative and theoretical reflection?

The poiesis in Arguedas works in a twofold manner. First, language is certainly one of the battlegrounds where the Quechua-Spanish cultural and conceptual encounters occur. The textual analyses in the present study explore the theoretical fertility of the language gap between Spanish and Quechua. When the indigenous characters in the novels, such as Rendón Willka, speak, they do so in Quechua-sounding Spanish. Arguedas invents a new language for these characters, where simple words, like "sadness" or "rage," become laden with new political meanings. New terminology to speak about community and about oneself as a subject emerges in this invented speech, as it becomes one of the sites where the new concepts materialize. For instance, when Arguedas uses such a simple adjective as *"triste"* (sad) to describe a miner, this word acquires the meaning of "a worker alienated from the modes of production" whose nonbelonging to a community deprives him of a possibility of effective resistance to exploitation.[37] The Arguedean expression condenses the semantic richness of the Quechua word *"khuyay"* (sadness) in Spanish translation (*triste*) and the political content of Marxist preoc-cupation with alienation of the working class.

Second, the last two novels, *Todas las sangres* and *The Foxes,* subvert the form of the novel through the irruption of the Quechua narrative modality, as Martin Lienhard has shown in his seminal study of *The Foxes,* and as Arguedas's personal friend, the sociologist Nelson Osorio, testifies in the documentary *Arguedas, hermano compañero, compañero de sangre. The Foxes* simply does not follow the rules in terms of construction of char-acters, narrator, or plot. But, as Horacio Legrás observes, the characters of the previous and supposedly more classical novel *Todas las sangres* are problematic as well since the reader often does not understand the motiva-tions for their actions.[38] Their extreme independence from the narrative voice implies that the narrator almost disappears from this novel, letting the characters speak freely and embody their ideological standpoints. In *The Foxes,* the narrative voice disappears altogether and divorces itself from the *relato* (storyline); it emigrates into the diaries that intercalate chapters where the dwellers of Chimbote narrate their story.[39] The result of these subversions of the novelistic form is what Antonio Cornejo Polar calls, when speaking about *Todas las sangres,* a "choral novel."[40] Similarly, Martin Lienhard reminds us how useful it is to read Arguedas's fiction with the tools offered by the theories of Mikhail Bakhtin, especially his idea of a dialogical novel.[41] In such a novel, it is impossible to deduce the ideological position of the narrator because the characters dialogue freely and each character voices a different ideological standpoint and different way of seeing the world. This dialogical form and the ideological multi-plicity it implies is brought to an apex in Arguedas's last novels, as Cornejo and Legrás show. The result is a space where the enunciations of different standpoints proliferate, allowing for different expressions of concepts to take place.

In *Todas las sangres,* the dialectic movement of the narrative strives to put the characters with different ways of seeing the world into dialogue with one another, and such is the case for the indigenous leader Rendón Willka and the industrialist Don Fermín.[42] This dialogue betrays the inten-tion of the novel to find a common ground and to reach a certain degree of representativity of the national reality. The dialogues in *Todas las sangres* stage the desired negotiations between the contending parties. The nega-tivity emerges, nonetheless, as the novel finishes not with a negotiation but with the execution of the hero, Rendón Willka, by the military police. Contrary to what happens in *Todas las sangres,* in *The Foxes* the charac-ters hardly dialogue, as the imperative search for negotiation, common ground, or a social contract ceases to be central to this text. For instance, at the beginning of *The Foxes,* mad Moncada preaches at the marketplace, voicing publicly his version of the sociopolitical present and future of Peru and Chimbote.[43] The reader is privy only to some disparate responses to his preaching, which come from transitory characters, which never again reappear in the novel. Moncada's speech is a proclamation more than a dialogue. In the absence of the possibility of any kind of articulation, in *The Foxes,* as Horacio Legrás concludes, the recognition as a possibility finds its limits, both aesthetic and political. Thus, the questioning, advanced in *Todas las sangres,* of the modern nation-state and of modern democracy reaches its extreme phase in *The Foxes.*

This critique is not purely negative, however, and Arguedean fiction offers partial, at times tragic but functional models to follow, both for the task of emerging as a responsible political subject and for the task of creating a community. The radical attitude of finitude is the defining quality of such characters as Rendón Willka of *Todas las sangres* and Bazalár of *The Foxes;* this attitude is the key for the emergence of a political subject into which Arguedas deposits his hopes for the future. This attitude that transpires in Arguedean fiction is akin to Jean-Luc Nancy's elaboration on the importance of finitude-attitude, and to Jacques Derrida's theorization on "radical atheism that denies the desirability of the transcendent and situates all value in what is mortal and passes away."[44] A lax community, akin to Hardt, Negri, and Virno's idea of multitude is formed on the basis of the subjectivities that emerge from this tragic and honest finitude-attitude. The convergence of this community is based on solidarity, unhinged from any hope for a transcendent whole that somehow would compensate the suffering of earthly existence.

Since 2003, and in the light of Arguedas's centenary in January 2011, there has been a renewed interdisciplinary interest in his work.[45] For instance, in the special issue of *Revista de Crítica Literaria Latinoamericana* in January 2011, William Rowe and Martin Lienhard renewed the discussion on the subversive, revolutionary nature of *The Foxes.* At the Congress organized by the Universidad Católica in Lima in 2011, many prominent scholars spoke of the present applicability of the author's work and ideas. Importantly, Estelle Tarica spoke of the practical use of Arguedas for the Peruvian Commission for Reconciliation as a reference for the committee's task of working through the reconciliation process of post-terrorist Peru, trying to recover from the trauma of 80,000 deaths caused by the Shining Path and military violence.[46] Gustavo Gutierrez, similarly, specifically addressed the question of Arguedas's presence beyond his death and beyond academia, as a conceptual inspiration for young people to continue their reflections on the possibilities of emancipatory thinking, speaking, and acting.[47] These scholarly contributions inform my study and serve me as a model because they are deeply rooted in careful textual analysis and make use of tools offered by literary criticism, while at the same time produce ideas that go beyond the sphere of literary or academic reflection.

This book enters into debate with both canonical and recent criticism on Arguedas, namely, the works of Angel Rama, Antonio Cornejo-Polar, Martin Lienhard, Horacio Legrás, and Estelle Tarica, among others. All these studies appreciate the faithfulness of the Arguedean fictional account to the profound truth of the Andean reality. Taking an almost scientific approach to Arguedas's social novels, they suggest that Arguedean fiction demands an interdisciplinary approach. My reading rejects Angel Rama's promise of successful transculturation in Arguedas's novels; instead, the multiplicity of political subjectivities that are analyzed in what follows is better understood through Cornejo-Polar's concept of heterogeneity. The continuing relevance on Arguedas's work as ethnographer, novelist, and public figure, as evinced by the recent publication of his complete anthropological works in Peru and continuing publications about his work, has been a driving force behind my research.[48] Furthermore, this book establishes a dialogue with the theory of postcoloniality and subalternity proposed by the Indian Subaltern Studies Group and its Latin Americanist counterparts.[49] Contesting the unfortunate perception that theory can only be produced at the "center," Arguedas's literary and essayistic production is evidence of important theoretical thought produced on the "periphery," namely, in the Andes. In this manner, and theoretically, this book proposes a dialogue between theory and anthropology produced in the Andes and the European philosophical tradition. In short, the book works through the following three tasks: to offer a new reading of Arguedas's fiction; to revise the idea of how a creative and theoretical thought is produced; and to elaborate and sharpen a number of specific concepts from political theory in an Andean context and beyond, putting Arguedean theorizations in the framework of political thought from the twentieth and the twenty-first century.

In order to understand the locus of enunciation from which Arguedas produces his political thought, I turn to studies in Andean anthropology and history—for example, the work of Gary Urton, Frank Salomon, Peter Klarén, and Arguedas himself, among others.[50] The anthropological accounts illuminate the frequently obscure enunciations in the novels, written in Quechua-influenced Spanish and involving the Andean cosmological or religious concepts. For instance, the second chapter of my book demonstrates that the relationship of an individual to their death is essential for their self-definition as a subject of a community. In this case, I turn to anthropology in order to shed light on the often oblique language used by Indian characters to speak about their vision of afterlife; thus, I hone in on the concept of finitude, proposed by Nancy and further elaborated here, as a key to understanding the Andean proposal on community and political subjectivity.

Although this book is fundamentally a work of literary analysis, history also offers fundamental background support for this study. The reader will need to keep in mind certain pivotal moments of the development of the Peruvian state, as he or she explores the problems addressed in the analysis of the novels.

Frustrated Ideals and Attempts at Homogenization

In a recent blog entry analyzing pitfalls of Ollanta Humala's presidency, the sociologist Gonzalo Portocarrero writes: "El gran problema de la sociedad peruana es la brecha entre las leyes y las costumbres, la escasa vigencia de la ley y la debilidad de las instituciones" (The great problem of Peruvian society is the gap between the laws and customs, the scarce presence of the law and frailty of the institutions).[51] This is one of the central problems addressed in the following chapters.

After the Wars of Independence (1810–25), the liberators and legislators such as Simón Bolívar wished for laws that would overcome the differences created by the dual colonial regimes of the "republic of Indians" and the "republic of Spaniards." Nonetheless, the liberators were inspired by the European ideas of nationhood and citizenship, based on ideology of the liberal subject, a citizen whose recognizable features are provided by property ownership and literacy. Bolívar's ideas were divorced from the Peruvian reality, where the majority of the population was indigenous and did not fulfill any of the classical citizenship requirements.[52] Consequently, despite the liberal nature of the first constitutional text of 1823, the colonial division was reinstated and played a major part in dealings between the state and the peasant communities. For example, the colonial indigenous tribute (*tributo*) was rebaptized as an indigenous contribution (*contribuición indígena*) and was reinstituted in 1826.[53] Bolívar's dream was a republic without Indians as a separate cultural element. It was a dream that had very real pernicious results for many indigenous persons as their communities were legally abolished in order to homogenize the population and make the Indians available to be subsumed into the nation. But despite the legal abolition of the ayllus, the homogenization did not occurr. In this new situation, the indigenous people ceased to be subjected to the colonial state, but they did not become citizens of the republic as they were not granted equal status with members of other socioeconomic groups. The relations of production remained semifeudal. As a corollary to this situation, the political liberal equation of "one person equals one vote" never became functional because the vast majority of Indians remained Quechua monolinguals, who did not read or write in Spanish, and the nation-state could not imagine having more than one official language or to incorporate orality as part of voting practices. The indigenous peoples' social subjectivity remained in a shady area of subalternity, neither inside nor outside the political horizon of the state.

Politically, the Indians continued to be an element foreign to the creole nation, and they also were perceived as such by creole ideology. Toward the end of the nineteenth century, when Peru lost the War of the Pacific (1879–84), the defeat was blamed on "too many Indians" populating its territory.[54] The racist discourse grew stronger over time,[55] ideologically separating the country and its people by regional, ethnic, and class categories, where the coast was associated with the elites and the Spanish heritage while the Andean sierra was stereotypically equated with the exploited and culturally and linguistically distinct Quechua population. In Flores Galindo's vivid example, in the Peruvian army the esprit de corps was nonexistent because the soldiers were mostly Indians and mestizos recruited by force, while the officials came from the newly formed Lima aristocracy and had nothing in common with their men, not even language.[56] In this situation, a national consensus was impossible because there was no means of communication on the level of language, ideology, or customs between urban elite and middle class, on one hand, and the indigenous peasants on the other.[57] As a result, the model of hegemony, based on consensus and communication, was not working for Peru, as we learn from narratives like Flores Galindo's or *Todas las sangres*. What becomes evident as we read the novel is that a colonial model of nation building, which conceptualizes the articulation of a national body and soul as a result of imposed practices, does not seem to work for Peru, either. Neither consensus nor repression can cancel out the heterogeneity of the social texture.

The historical truth is that indigenous peasants could not overcome segregation even after their participation as so-called citizen-soldiers in the War of the Pacific. As Florencia Mallon tells us, although the Junín peasants fought against Chilean invasion under Mariscal Cáceres and claimed citizenship rights at the end of the war, they were called "bandits" and stayed as they were before the war—unincorporated into the nation. The Lima elite did not see themselves united with the Andean population—neither by the category "Peruvian," nor by any other category. Disdain and fear, as opposed to consensus, marked the attitudes of the Peruvians of different classes, ethnic groups, and regions toward one another.

This soicoeconomic, cultural, ideological, and ethnic gap was not bridged during the twentieth century. The populist governments of the 1920s and 1930s proposed to negotiate these internal differences and forged an alliance with the radical middle-class sector, which sympathized with the cause of the Indian peasantry. The government took up an official *indigenismo* ideology, and the constitution of 1920 recognized Indian ayllus and created a government institution where the Indians could legally claim their land titles.[58] Augusto Leguía's reformist government (1919–30) tried to curtail the local power of the *gamonales* (landlords), making the state more present in the provinces. This encouraged indigenous peasants' mobilization in defense of their interests. The autonomy of these mobilizations alarmed the central government and soon it retreated from its pro-Indian policies and anti-gamonal actions, repressing the Indian movement. The rule of the gamonales returned to the provinces and remained largely uncontested until the 1950s, the decade in which the action of *Todas las sangres* begins. This pattern will occur repeatedly during the twentieth century, such as in the government of Fernando Belaúnde Terry (1963–68), which professed populist rhetoric and subsequently harshly repressed Hugo Blanco's uprising at La Convención.[59] Even as late as 1990, Carlos Iván Degregori underlines the strong presence of the *gamonalismo* legacy in the sierra when he analyzes Sendero Luminoso's relative success in securing the peasants' support in the Andes in the 1980s. According to Degregori, Sendero Luminoso appeared as a "new patrón, hard and unflexible but 'just.'"[60]

This situation was further aggravated by the actual exclusion of the indigenous population from the democratic rituals. Although the repeated suffrage reforms of the nineteenth century theoretically included all persons of legal age into the voting practice, it did not substantially influence the inclusion of the Indian peasant population. The vote was open and public, and the local authorities manipulated the peasants unabashedly until the 1930s.[61] The rhetoric of official *indigenista* ideology persisted among Lima intellectuals, but it was far from effective in changing the reality of the remote highlands.

In the mid-1960s, the Peruvian state was forced to consolidate at all costs its national imagery, and we begin to see the realization, however problematic, of hegemony in Peru. Or was it a bloody imposition of state domination on reality, which refused to obey theory? Although the internal contradictions of Peruvian society did not diminish, the increasing presence of external forces produced the need to recognize Peru's unity despite the differences within the country. The increasingly popular mobilization expressed in the labor and peasant movements announced the now undeniable political presence of the Quechua and Aymara Indians. The consolidation of civil society was brought about by internal migrations and an increased urban population along with a boom in literacy and the university student population, which now included working-class students and recent migrants from the highlands. In the year 1965, the Shining Path appears on the scene and the Peruvian military effects the first bloody repression of highland guerrilla movements. José María Arguedas publishes *Todas las sangres* the year before, in 1964. The national imagery might have been consolidated; it might have opposed the imperialist encroachments; but the imagined homogeneity of the nation was still a utopia. Historically, the Peruvian flag that the peasants waved as they occupied the lands of the hacendados[62] is evidence that they had some idea of the power of national rhetoric and the legitimacy it offered. But it did not protect them from bullets when the hacendados accused them of disrupting the peace, also in the name of the nation.

In *Todas las sangres,* the use of the national imagery by the Indians marks the gap between the ideal of the inclusive nation and the violent reality. Although the Peruvian flag does not serve as an effective shield against bullets, the Indians keep hanging on to it.[63] We also see the centrality of the Peruvian flag as a symbol in the words of an old Indian mayor, after the *subprefecto*[64] arbitrarily attacks and wounds him: "The wound does not matter. . . . Other thing matter [*sic*], *subprefecto*. I, Indian mayor, elementary school third grade. We the community Indians will be respect [*sic*]. We will know how to read. The community Indians, we are so, so many. With the Peruvian flag we will firmly stand."[65] In this quote, the indigenous mayor uses a reference to the national flag, the embodiment of the idea of the nation, to oppose the physical violence exercised by a representative of the actual Peruvian state. Using Quechua-influenced, tortuous Spanish, the Indian constructs a sort of chain of equivalences between the *comuneros,* community Indians, their capacity to read and *ser respeto* (literally, "be respected"), and the Peruvian flag. We might say that in this speech the representative of the ayllu declares one of the main facets of Arguedas's proposal for the future of the Peruvian nation. The comuneros should be citizens because they are the majority, "so, so many"; they are the physical bodies that compose the nation; they will learn how to read and make political decisions; they will be Peruvians. But they will not shed their cultural specificity and will not abandon their status as comuneros, Indians organized in an ayllu. In an oblique reference to the Indians' exclusion from the rituals of democracy in the nineteenth-century constitutions, the capacity to read is underlined here as a passageway to citizenship, but it does not mark the erasure of indigenousness. Furthermore, in the reverent words of the old Indian, the reference to national imagery overrides the arbitrary violence of the state's servant, from which he just suffered. In other words, this statement saves the idea of the nation despite the reader having just witnessed the corrupt face of the state apparatus, which works and wages this arbitrary violence, paradoxically, also in the name of the nation. Nonetheless, this proposal of a literate Indian who is still an Indian contradicted the mainstream progressive Peruvian thought of the 1960s.

The Peruvian social sciences discourse of the time shared an important point with Simón Bolívar's ideas: it hinged on the idea of necessary homogenization for successful execution of any nation-building project. The idea was to eliminate Indian comuneros, not as living persons but as a culturally separate social group, a heterogeneous element. Within this logic, the Indians necessarily cease to be Indians once they learn how to write and begin to participate in the political life of the country. In the context of this ideological horizon, the scandal of the indigenous mayor's declaration is that it asserts that the Indians can simultaneously keep their loyalty to the indigenous community and also acquire recognition as citizens. This simultaneity, as we will see, is the original kernel of Arguedas's political thought: the categories, which would appear mutually exclusive, are shown to be compatible, however problematically, in the reality reflected in *Todas las sangres*.

Arguedas, for his part, claimed that "the contradictions [represented in the novel] are those that naturally exist in our country, the *different ways of seeing the world*. The great ambition of my book was, precisely, to show this multiplicity of conceptions, according to the degrees of proximity to the world in fury."[66] The novel's goal is to theorize the simultaneity of being a literate Indian-Peruvian, which we saw illustrated in the old Indian mayor's discourse. In this proposal, the Peruvian flag does not protect the Indians, and yet, paradoxically, it remains a symbol of promise for the future of cooperation between two heterogeneous modes of collectivity: the ayllu and the nation.

We could say that the seed of disagreement at the roundtable event is found in the different readings by Arguedas and the social scientists of cultural codes. As a consequence, the category of the political is understood differently by the debating theorists, which makes a dialogue about political reality and its representation almost impossible. For Arguedas, cultural and historical factors determined the people's behavior, even more so than economic factors. Culture, or what Arguedas calls "the way of seeing the world," was the foremost political dimension of human actions on individual and social levels. On the contrary, Quijano's and Favre's classically narrow concepts of the political prevented them from seeing the profoundly political dimension of some of the aspects of Arguedas's novel. Consequently, the text was read as politically irresponsible, as an escapist and false representation of reality—in a nutshell, a reactionary vision. However, in *Todas las sangres* we note the same "widening of the borders of the political"[67] that Horacio Legrás observes in Arguedas's earlier novel, *Yawar fiesta*. In this interpretation, the articulation of the impossibility for the cultural aspects to be absorbed by hegemonic politics does not mean an apolitical reading but, rather, signals the opening of the sphere of the political,[68] which lies at the heart of the Arguedean revision of the concept of the political itself.

In a reflection on the Bolivian War of Water, or Guerra del Agua, the Bolivian sociologist and current vice president Álvaro García Linera observes the same effect of the widening of the political field. This time around it occurs not in a textual universe but in the reality of the political action on the streets of the city of Cochabamba in the year 2000. The following extensive quote, written in combative and metaphorical language, demonstrates the real political implications of such an amplification of the political field:

> Against the extension of the spaces of the capitalist exploitation or the desert of expropriation, arose a high tide of new politics of the vital necessities, around which the people not only organized to dispute the conditions of survival, reproduction, and even [the processes of] production in rural areas, but also *the recomposition of the political life.* The high tide has *modified the borders of the political. The spaces of the political have widened and extended,* at the same time as this movement leaves empty a series of political institutions, such as the party system. The plebeian politics has overflown the liberal spaces, where the people are no more, and only are said to be represented [or present].[69]

The widening of the field of the political is contingent upon the emergence of what García Linera calls the "multitude form" of the popular organization, which opposed the Bolivian state's pretensions to sovereignty through hegemonic politics mixed with plain exercise of force. Political philosophers Negri, Agamben, and Virno,[70] from whom García Linera borrows the term, elaborate upon the concept of multitude as a collectivity that cannot be described as a people that is constituted as such through their fundamental relation to the nation. In what follows, I will engage this concept to understand the representation of Peruvian reality in *Todas las sangres,* which widens the field of the political in its description of collectivities that are far from coming together as a homogeneous "people."

CHAPTER 1

SOVEREIGNTY AND AUTHORITY IN *TODAS LAS SANGRES*

Todas las sangres is a fascinating book. It is a Dostoyevskian drama and a social novel that combines the exploration of the internal motives of the characters and the wide diagnostic of the Peruvian social reality. It tells the story of arrival of the transnational mining company, backed by the state, to the town of San Pedro in the Peruvian Andes. The main characters are both individuals and larger-than-life social types. For instance, the hero of the novel, Demetrio Rendón Willka, is a Quechua who left his ayllu for Lima, studied there, and shares the ideas about political organization and economic advancement with his fellow Indians and other non-Indian characters. The industrialist Fermín Aragón, an ambitious nationalist, supports the mining company until it becomes clear that he is being cheated in the deal. The Christian fanatic Don Bruno Aragón, his brother, first appears as a figure of the colonial order, an abusive landowner, who, as the novel progresses, increasingly collaborates with the indigenous ayllus to secure their economic and political integrity in the face of the violence displayed by the Peruvian state in defense of the mining project, which meets resistance from the disparate dwellers of the sierra around San Pedro. Apart from the individual characters, the state, the hacienda, the ayllus, the town of San Pedro, the Lima slums, and the mine all can be said to have a characterlike existence of their own in this complex text.

As the historical excursus in the introduction suggests, three factors limit the sovereignty of the Peruvian state: the competing sovereignties of the ayllu and the old-time landlords; the confusion of the political and the economic spheres of action; and the infringement of the other states on the political decisions within the Peruvian territory, a feature of its neocolonial condition. From the standpoint of political philosophy, *Todas las sangres* can be read as a criticism of these specifically Peruvian ills, and also as a questioning of the structures of modern democracies in general. Here we will analyze how different social formations and characters within the novel negotiate the supposedly absolute limits of state sovereignty.

To introduce the reflection on the dispute of sovereignty, it must be noted that the sleek formula "legal country versus real country" is not particularly descriptive of the historical situation in the Andean countries. The dichotomy of this formula presupposes the residence of law (and, consequently, sovereignty) only on the side of the state. But, as we are about to see in *Todas las sangres,* there are other modalities of law and sovereignty that work within the indigenous community and within the hacienda. The different nature of this power and legality can be understood when we explore how the concept of authority works, or does not work, within the logic of sovereignty of the ayllu, of the hacienda, and of the state.

In *Todas las sangres,* at Don Bruno's hacienda and in the ayllu, the exercise of power lies with the figures of authority: Don Bruno and the *varayok's,* the staff-bearing indigenous mayors. In the Peruvian state, on the contrary, the exercise of power is unhinged from the principle of authority, and partly for this reason degrades into pure relation of imposition and domination. Now, this claim that "different sovereignties" can coexist within the territory of a state can appear almost scandalous. How can sovereignty, which is classically defined as the attribute of the state,[1] coexist with other sovereignties within the same national territory?

In the modern world, the sovereigns are states and their sovereignty theoretically should be defined vis-à-vis other states.[2] But the Peruvian state as represented in *Todas las sangres* fails to acquire this dimension of a sovereign. As we work through the aspects of the classical definition of sovereignty, we must wonder whether subjects accept transferring part of their sovereignty to the state. In an ideal situation, the state would enjoy a monopoly on violence because the activity of justice has been previously transferred to it by the citizens. The sovereign must be the one who declares that a given situation is stable enough to have law and authority; the sovereign is "granted" authority and in turn "grants" the stability of the law to the subjects. The Peruvian state in *Todas las sangres* does not present the characteristics of such a sovereignty, while other formations, the hacienda and the ayllu, exemplify a modality of sovereignty other than the formula for the modern state. For instance, Don Bruno in *Todas las sangres* is clearly granted the capacity to grant and phrases this movement in metaphysical terms, as if saying, "I am the lord by the grace of God, and I am responsible for my Indians before him." This "granting" does not emanate from the people (the Indians) but from God. This difference is our starting point for drawing out the profiles of different sovereignties competing on Peruvian territory and on the pages of the novel.

In Brian Milstein's reflection on the classical definition of "kingly" sovereignty as theorized by Bodin, the will of the sovereign is the source of law. God grants the power to the sovereign and the sovereign is responsible to God alone. The law, coming from the will of the sovereign, does not bind the sovereign, who is above the law.[3] Enlightenment thought, especially represented by Kant, rejects this voluntarist theory of sovereignty and "detaches sovereignty from divine will." In this line of thought, "right is no longer the emanation and manifestation of the awesome will of the sovereign. . . . The sovereign himself is the subject of reason. . . . The immanence of right is transferred from sovereignty to citizenship." The citizen's first attribution is "lawful freedom, the attribute of obeying no other law than that to which he has given his consent." This postulate of Kant's is in direct opposition to Bodin's theory that one cannot bind oneself by a law that one creates. For Kant, the law emanates from the citizens, gets subsumed into the sphere of the state, and the citizen obeys the law that is born from his own political subjectivity. As a consquence, the foundation of authority in such sovereignty is not as mystical as in the kingly kind of sovereignty, for something that has human origins is much less awesome than something that emanates from the divine.

In our approach to the sovereignties of different orders in *Todas las sangres,* Don Bruno's sovereignty in his hacienda fits the model of kingly sovereignty, as he is granted by God the power to grant. Bruno is also not bound by the laws he creates and which condition the lives of his serfs. The sovereignty of the ayllu functions differently, exercised through a type of direct democracy in an assembly of the entire community, but the varayok's, its figures of authority, share one important trait with Don Bruno. Their power and authority are also granted by supernatural beings other than Don Bruno's Christian God: the Andean divinities or Apus, the mountain spirits. This fact imprints a special characteristic on the type of relationship these public servants have with the community they serve and represent. Also, this reference to the divine produces a certain recognition between Bruno and the Indians, which is absent when these characters interact with the more "modern," or simply more secularized characters of the novel. The Peruvian state's problematic sovereignty, which theoretically should be working within a Kantean model, is deprived of the mystic element that sustains and makes effective the exercise of power and authority in the cases of the varayok's and Bruno.

Giorgio Agamben claims, following Hannah Arendt, that authority as concept had disappeared from the modern world, or has degraded into the concept of authoritarianism.[4] This postulate points out another difference between the sovereignties of the Peruvian state, on one hand, and Don Bruno's and indigenous varayok's, on the other. As Agamben explains, *auctoritas* in the Roman law was a term difficult to delimit. Unlike *potestas,* which was a legally defined power, auctoritas was not delimited by law but rather was a diffuse concept very connected to a physical, individual person. In this sense, auctoritas was a nebulous kind of power where the public and the private converged. In Agamben's example, Cesar Augustus had the same potestas as the other magistrates but was superior to them in auctoritas.[5] But what is this "something extra" of authority? Agamben's analysis underlines that the principle of such an authority is not coercion but something akin to loyalty, which is not delegated by the people to the lord but emanates from the physical body of rule and gets "infused" in the people. The "body of rule" can be an individual like Augustus of Agamben's example or the character of Don Bruno in *Todas las sangres,* or a collective body like the Roman Senate or the indigenous cabildo of the Arguedean universe.

Conjugating Agamben's claim with Milstein's argument, we can propose that the degree of mystical foundation of authority depends on the source of a sovereign's power. If kingly sovereignty is conceptualized as originating from God, this explains its mystical nature: "mystical" does refer to the divine origins, after all.[6] Agamben's example is revealing, in this sense: out of the twelve Caesars, only half were recognized as divine— those that brought the most glory to Rome.[7] Augustus was one of these divine Caesars, his authority emanating from his person, imprinted on him by the divine origin of his power. The divine is thought of as something that resides beyond human understanding and thereby comes the impossibility to define clearly the limits of the concept of authority. The name of Don Bruno's hacienda in *Todas las sangres,* La Providencia,[8] is telling. Providence, divine will, is the source of Don Bruno's power and authority, and his obsessive references to his social position of domination as a result of the divine decision underline his consciousness of origin of his power. Bruno did not choose to be a lord over his serfs, but he occupies the position into which God willed him to be born.[9] Don Bruno reads this fatality as a mark of profound responsibility for "his Indians." The conceptual connection between the God-granted authority and active responsibility emerges when we compare the figures of Bruno and the indigenous varayok's.

The varayok's, Indian figures of authority, act in direct reference to their spiritual guide, the mountain called Padre Pukasira (Father Pukasira). When we meet Adrian K'oto, the first Indian *cabecilla,* or leader, he is consulting the mountain through the traditional offering of the coca leaves.[10] As ethnographic studies show, the legitimacy of the leaders in the Andean cultures generally comes from social, political, and religious spheres, not separated in the Andean epistemology as they are in the Western cultural approach. It is worth quoting extensively Bolivian jurist Enrique Mier Cueto's comment on this matter in order to understand this special kind of legitimacy in the Aymara ayllu:

> At the meeting of the communal assembly, not only the physical persons are convoked to participate in a decision, but through the rites (with coca leaves and with ritual offerings) the divinities of the Ayllu and the forefathers (beings with supernatural powers) are made present . . . ; both types of beings [divinities and forefathers] are considered a part of the community and therefore have a right to vote, which they exercise through the particular signs in the rituals, and consequently the couple [which is about to accept a position of leadership in the community] has the approval not only of the persons, but also of the divinities. . . .
>
> This communal authority, therefore, has power rooted in a complex political and religious legitimacy, its power being granted by the human and by the superhuman, *and this origin of power makes of this social legitimacy a strongly cemented condition.* This power, doubly structured by the religious and the political, in reality seems dual only to the foreign eyes, and in the Aymara cultural context this power is unitary, and its separation in this context, even for analytical purposes, is inexact.[11]

The scenes of organized meetings in the Quechua ayllus in *Todas las sangres* mirror the socioethnographic account and analysis presented by Mier Cueto. In the novel, the two scenes that focus on the figures of authority to be discussed here are, first, the presentation of the character of Don Bruno in the assembly in his hacienda;[12] second, the moment when the Indians from the Paraybamba community elect new authorities, in a communal assembly.[13] In the textual analysis of these scenes we will see that Bruno and the varayok's have authority as their common denominator. They inspire certain loyalty in the people when they face them, which the state fails to do.

Before turning to our examples, let us briefly comment on this failure. The state's ghostly presence can hardly inspire any feeling other than nebulous fear. Rather, when its agents, soldiers, or assorted representatives of government bureaucracy appear on the stage, we see them using violence. We see soldiers shoot the working Paraybamba Indians, annihilate the hero of the novel, Rendón Willka, and neutralize Bruno, both authority-holding leaders. The arbitrariness of the state agents' actions is a symptom of the state's lack of authority over its citizens and even over its own servants. The state authorities are doubly unpredictable, not only because of their disposition to infringe on the law to their own benefit, but also because they do not know what the state expects of them and cannot rely on any defined rules of conduct. They must improvise, even if they are not, in their essence, "bad people" or "corrupt officials," and their improvisations usually come down to immediate use of force. But why does the Peruvian state fail to consolidate not only authority but also a unified sovereignty, as any state is expected to do?

Kant's definition of the role of the citizen can help us find an answer to this question. In the concept of the state that has dominated political thought from the Enlightenment on, the sovereign state is an agent of the right that preexists it; in other words, the state must obey both the principle of reason and law that emanates from the citizens. The citizens, on their part, only must obey the law to which they have given consent. These are the basic precepts of democracy, the theoretical horizon, which dominated Peru in the 1960s. But in the postcolonial situation the Indians' participation in the democratic ritual was very limited. Therefore, the sovereignty of the Peruvian state could hardly be said to emanate from its citizens. In fact, only a reduced number of persons establish the law in the Peru of *Todas las sangres;* it seems that the represented state formation is an oligarchy that only claims to be a democracy. In the novel, the serfs of the haciendas simply do not exist politically outside the hacienda to which they belong; their entire being is subordinated to the sovereignty of their respective lords. In the words of Adalberto Cisneros, a repulsive but incredibly lucid character of the novel, "The Indians only have their village or their master, but we the lords have fatherland: Peru."[14] But then, only the lords are the citizens of this "fatherland," which makes for about 5 percent of the country's population and does not constitute a popular base required for a functional democracy. Consequently, the Indians' existence can be more or less infused with physical suffering, but it is irrelevant for the Peruvian state, which has no relation with these persons whatsoever. The Indians, either the ones that belong to the haciendas or the ones who live in free communities, do not exist politically. But what happens when these indigenous communities decide to claim their right to full citizenship? The state is surprised by the emergence of these persons out of their political nonexistence, and the reaction of the state police forces always ends up being that of crude repression. To put it in historical-theoretical terms, when faced with the Indians, the state expresses its sovereignty in the radical sense Carl Schmitt had given to this concept, by deciding on friend-or-enemy status of a person or a group of persons.[15] An extreme example from *Todas las sangres* serves as an illustration: when the sergeant kills Rendón Willka without trial or proof of any crime, couldn't we say that he treats him as an enemy? Why does it become possible to execute a man, a Peruvian, in this manner?

In a political sense, what Millstein calls "internal sovereignty" obeys the same principle as "external sovereignty." Just as the state can decide against whom it can go to war, so it can single out its internal enemy, whom it declares the "public enemy," outside the law.[16] This category refers to a strictly public domain, as it conceptualizes "enemy" not in terms of personal repulsion but in terms of political division.[17] Rendón Willka, for instance, is very conscious of this ability of the state as he reflects on the flexible use of the term "communist": everybody who opposes the state is thrown into the same pile designated as "communists."[18] This term designates the absolute other, the "natural" enemy. This movement, which makes it possible to temporarily suspend the law on the national territory, is analyzed by Agamben as a "state of exception," a strong concept criticizing modern democracies. This is exactly the legal gap that permits the execution without trial of the discontent Peruvians, like Rendón Willka.

Todas las sangres thus engages with political writings on the nature of democracy itself. In the case of Peru in *Todas las sangres,* the state marks the Indians, and ultimately anyone who opposes its economic or political interest, by the sign of the absolute difference, which ends up justifying the use of force, to which the state recurs at the moment of confrontation. Upon defining the Indians as enemies, the Peruvian state erases the distinction between internal and external confrontation, treating the confrontation within its own territory as if it were a confrontation with an outside force, another sovereign. The negotiation becomes impossible because this kind of definition establishes the confrontation as natural and inevitable. As Schmitt explains, "the enemy exists only when, at least potentially, one fighting collectivity of people confronts a similar collectivity."[19] Of course, the problem with the situation in *Todas las sangres* is that instead of similar collectivities, such as states, disputing their sovereignty, we see on one side rifle-armed military police, and on the other side unarmed Indians. This problem is aggravated even further because the confrontation with a political enemy, as Schmitt observes, can reach extreme degrees of inhumanity in the treatment of the enemy, due to the rhetoric of absolute otherness that tends to dominate such conflicts. In the rhetoric of the Peruvian state in *Todas las sangres,* the Indians appear as "secret," "mysterious" "sorcerers" opposed to the ideals of rational choice that should dominate a modern public sphere. The Lima press reports about the destruction of the town of San Pedro, rhetorically clumping together under the label of "communists" the Indians, the impoverished whites of the town, the artisans, and anyone who opposes the state-protected mining company.[20] In the press, the category "communist" is sufficiently diffuse, imprecise, and abstract to apply to anyone, as Rendón Willka had noticed. This rhetoric opens the dangerous gap where innumerable corpses of private, politically nonexistent persons can fall. It gives them, negatively, their political existence.

The reference to the mining company brings us to the two other key factors that undermine the sovereignty of the Peruvian state in *Todas las sangres:* the intertwining of the political and the economic spheres and the limitation of the sovereignty of one state by another state as a consequence of the neocolonial situation. Carl Schmitt tried to rescue the political as an independent sphere and criticized the general tendency to mix spheres in his 1932 essay that defines the sphere of the political. *Todas las sangres* can also be read as a criticism of this tendency, as the novel portrays the negative effects of the invasion of the transnational company Wisther and Bozart into the Peruvian territory. In the meeting of the mining company directors, "Zar," the president of the company, explicitly states that the engineer Cabrejos, the local administrator, "will dispose of sufficient power to confront them [the Indians who live near the mine and whose lands are being expropriated] *in the political and in the economic issues.*"[21] The nickname of the supreme manager, "Zar," makes reference to absolute monarchy, czar, thus suggesting that the reach of this businessman's power is practically unlimited in any sphere of life. In explicit reference to the economic management of the political powers, Zar states that "the minister already has obtained the decree of the expropriation of lands, which were indispensable for the installation of the processing plants."[22] As we learn later in the novel, such expropriation of land in favor of private persons or entities is unconstitutional. And yet, it is applied by force of the Peruvian *national* army and police. The international economic pressure is present subtly and undeniably—at the meeting of the directors, "only one foreigner was present" who "remained silent during the entire session, but was the first one to approach the president and congratulate him."[23]

From all these symptoms, we can diagnose the failure of the Peruvian state to gather the minimum requirements for the status of sovereign, either externally or internally. In fact, the separation into "external" and "internal" is profoundly mined in this nation, where the persons living within its national borders are treated as political enemies and where the foreign influence is decisive at the moment of determining the political categories of friends and enemies. *Todas las sangres* can be read as a reflection on the erosion of the conceptual and real borders that existed (or should have existed?) between the inside and the outside of the national frontiers, and between the economic and the political. The novel faithfully reflects the global tendencies that severely limit the sovereignty of economically dependent nation-states like Peru. Here I must evoke the suggestive reading of *Todas las sangres* by Antonio Cornejo-Polar. According to Cornejo, Arguedas creates a common front against imperialism and overrides the internal contradictions between bosses and workers, Indians and the lords. My reading does not negate this interpretation and recognizes the common front as the text's object of desire. But, in a complementary manner, we must observe that from Arguedas's description of Peruvian reality emerges a state that is too disarticulated and co-opted by the transnational capital to firmly stabilize such a common front and to consolidate hegemony.

Don Bruno, Rendón Willka, and the indigenous varayok's stand as opposing examples to the failure of the state. The separation of the spheres of the political and the economic power, and the subordination of the second to the first mark these figures that consolidate local sovereignty and are infused with authority. The melancholy narrative voice describes Don Bruno's hacienda and the indigenous towns of Paraybamba and Lahuay-marca. These smaller human collectivities, the hacienda and the ayllu, are represented as visions of plenitude, of certain unity, clearly marked by borders and lacking dissent on the inside: they are functional sovereignties.

This positive parallelism in representing the free Indian towns and the hacienda is surprising at first, since the reality of the social and legal relationship within the hacienda is that of domination by the lord, Don Bruno, over "his" Indians. Nonetheless, in the descriptions of this hacienda, the image of the *pisonay* tree,[24] which grows in the patio of Don Bruno's hacienda, is projected onto the hacienda itself: it is "illuminated," "purified" from the social reality of domination by this natural image of the tree. In the first description of the hacienda, we read that "the sun was shining, playing on the flowers of the great solitary *pisonay* in the patio."[25] In Don Bruno's conversation with his Indians that follows, the narrative voice returns once and again to the description of the tree, which participates in the conversation. For instance, the tree reacts positively when Bruno ceases to act as a violent master and enters into a dialogue with the Indians: "the *pisonay*, then, opened its flowers which darkened while he [Bruno] was threatening [the Indians]."[26] The tree opens its flowers, mirroring the surprising, incredible way of communication that opens between Bruno and his Indian serfs.[27] When the reader imagines the hacienda, his or her inner eye sees the tree, surrounded by the carpet of red flowers on the ground. The unity of the hacienda is reflected in the stable, recurring tree image. The pisonay is like a promise of this totality and clarity of immediate identification of the Indians, Don Bruno, and nature, despite the power hierarchy, which marks the relationship of Bruno to the indigenous workers.

The image of the cross on the recently built bridge that connects La Providencia with the lands of Paraybamba, the indigenous village, is another symbol of stability and unity. Its lengthy and majestic description stays with the reader, making us forget the miserable shacks where the Indians live. "Don Bruno abruptly stopped. The bridge seemed not only solid but also beautiful. A red cross presided over the narrow and savage river, projected its shadow of Christ's passion on both sides of the current."[28] The cross dominates the imagery of Paraybamba village, fulfilling the same function as the tree in the description of the hacienda. The "whole" images of these smaller human formations allude to the unity and functional sovereignty that provides this unity, which the Peruvian state lacks. The state has no pisonay tree, no cross on the bridge, no concrete external borders that separate it from the imperialist incursions from the outside, and no unity of its subjects. The state, enslaved by the pressures of international capital, does not subordinate the economic to the political. By playing out this counterpoint, the novel proposes that the organizational characteristics of the smaller human formations, ayllu and hacienda, should serve as a model for functional sovereignty on the larger scale of the Peruvian nation. This is Arguedas's political advice for effectively protecting the fatherland's ever dwindling, infringed sovereignty in the face of external threats.

Mystic Aura against Surplus Value

Don Bruno enters the stage as an embodiment of the class of *gamonales*, traditionally perceived in Peruvian scholarship as the chief oppressor and a "natural" opponent of the indigenous population. *Todas las sangres* revises this postulate, upheld by the Peruvian intellectuals from José Carlos Mariátegui to Aníbal Quijano, as it represents the figure of gamonal as a possible ally of the Indians in their struggle for inclusion into the Peruvian nation. Further, the narrative underlines the similarities between the formations of hacienda and ayllu and explores them as a theoretical ground on which the projection of the sovereignty of the Peruvian state can be built.

Historically, the origins of the gamonales as a class and the nature of their power justified the constitution of a "black legend" of gamonal in the Peruvian historiography. The gamonales emerged as a result of dissolution of the colonial institutions after the advent of the republic. The three pillars of colonial administration, the priest, the *corregidor* (sheriff) and the *curaca* (indigenous nobleman) lose their power. In the resulting power vacuum, the landowners' power is augmented as they add the local political power to their economic power rooted in land possession. Their power, still resting on the idea of "natural lord" inherited from the colony, became almost infinite on the local level: they could even mobilize "their" Indians and wage a small-scale war on the neighboring haciendas.[29] At the same time, these landowners spoke Quechua, lived on their property and administered it directly. They mixed, according to Flores Galindo, racism with paternalism, constituting profoundly ambivalent relations with their serfs. No legal frame regulated these relations, and the gamonal could pass from protection to abuse with legal impunity.[30] By the mid-twentieth century, when Arguedas situates his narrative, the power of the landowner was often defined by custom alone, unchecked by any law, due to the weak presence of the state forces in the highlands. In *Todas las sangres,* Don Bruno represents such a gamonal, whose status in relation to the Indians and to the Peruvian state is ambivalent and requires a close reading in order to be understood. We can start our discussion of Bruno and the structure of power he represents with a general statement: We will talk of a moribund sovereignty of gamonal, whose political influence was dwindling in mid-twentieth-century Peru. We will reflect on Arguedas's requiem for the kind of "kingly" sovereignty represented by Don Bruno—and I say "requiem" because the narrative treatment of the character sounds like a glorifying funeral music. Beyond poetics, the parallels between sovereignty exercised by Bruno and that of the indigenous authorities force us to reflect on the theoretic implications of these relations.

With every description of Bruno, the reader contemplates his impressively presented figure, culminating in an exclamation of one of the secondary characters: "He is an Archangel!"[31] The connection between the ideological positions of the narrative voice and Don Bruno has been hinted at by critics, from the roundtable to Cornejo Polar, to Melisa Moore, but this link asks for a deeper exploration. It is a bit uncomfortable to recognize the fascination with a figure of gamonal on the part of Arguedas, a scholar and writer whose dedication to the cause of the Quechua Indians has always been underlined and put in the forefront. But what can we deduce from this fascination?

In fact, what at first looks like incongruence is quite logical. Bruno is a character who painfully evolves from a "flagellating" old-timer to the prophetic words, "ya no flagelarás," "you will never flagellate again," pronounced by his wife Vicenta.[32] Bruno uses the traditional means, his social status, to emancipatory ends, that is, for the liberation of his serfs, which causes his repudiation by the power bloc. Bruno, in a sense, is a surprising, hopeful symbol of a Peru that evolves from the abusive colonial structures toward a formation that recognizes the existence and participation of the Indians as Indians. The refusal on the developmentalist critics' part to recognize Bruno as a political option can be explained by their desire to cancel, forget, and cross out the colonial past of modern Peru. Arguedas, in his recognized sympathy for Bruno, proposes that Peru must evolve as a nation from its real historical condition, including its colonial past. In the trajectory of Bruno the colonial structures self-cancel from within their own logic of power.

Beyond the obvious point of convergence between Arguedas and Bruno in their emotional compromise with the indigenous worldview,[33] there are also other aspects. The narrative voice of *Todas las sangres* is fascinated with spectacular displays of power based on authority. Don Bruno's corpo-reality is the antipode of the ghostly state. The violence that comes from him has a concrete, palpable, and therefore vulnerable, authorship: Bruno is responsible for each whipping he orders. On the contrary, the force deployed by the state, as we will see in the chapter 3, comes from a diffuse source, impossible to locate. The descriptions of Bruno Aragón and majestic references to the indigenous varayok's are examples of the fascination with solid bodily presence of the figure of authority.[34]

Bruno is a surprising kind of revolutionary who acts according to the traditional principles of power. He holds a kind of absolute power within his feud, which includes the power to "re-speak" the law of his hacienda. His internal and external sovereignty can be neatly reflected by the classical definition of sovereignty: he has internal control, and he uses his right to wage war on external enemies. From this position of power, Bruno grants "his" serfs the right to trade with the other indigenous communities, gives them land, and finally frees them. Bruno's reforms overflow the limits of his feud, infecting the feuds of other landlords who bet on supporting the mining company. Bruno recognizes just as much as his practical and supposedly progressive counterparts that the time of haciendas is over. But, instead of collaborating with the new powers, the mining company and the state, he prefers to seal his fate of social, and probably also physical, demise. He is thrown into jail and labeled alternately as a "feudal" lord, or as a "communist" supporter of the Indian resistance. Why doesn't Bruno collaborate like everyone else?

Bruno carries to the ultimate consequences his traditional position of a sovereign, and the reason for this resides in two concepts: authority and responsibility. His behavior is determined by a factor that for Arguedas is stronger than economic determination: his "way of seeing the world," or in other words, the cultural traits that define his personality. What are these traits? As a product of his birth and the society where he is born, Bruno is a traditional "kingly" sovereign within his feud; he is the law personified, unbound by any previous law, and responsible only to God, the source of his power. The narrative voice establishes from the beginning Bruno's position as a traditional gamonal: "Since the advent of the Republic, each landlord was the [local] 'Spanish king.' They dictated the laws, and the law was followed only to the degree that suited the lord."[35] In the first scene in La Providencia, we watch Bruno exercise his sovereign power as he orders physical punishment of his overseer Carhuamayo.[36] But the speech that Bruno pronounces after whipping Carhuamayo builds a complex conceptual chain around his action. The divine source of his authority has a consequence, the weight of which is probably even greater than that of human law. Bruno calls it "responsibility," and this idea is his major moving force in the narrative. Let us first analyze the scene that represents Bruno as the abusive and all-powerful sovereign, and then revisit one of the scenes of "madness," when his sovereignty self-consumes in the flames of responsibility, compelling him to progressively liberate his serfs.

The first scene is a spectacular display of "kingly" power, set up as a ritual following a strict order, established by tradition. "With the first rays of sun," the Indians entered "in order" the enormous patio in front of the lord's house; the lord (*patrón*) appears on the elevated porch. Adrian K'oto, the head of the Indians, stood in front of him accompanied by thirty inferior indigenous authorities. "He kneeled first, and then, in certain order, as if forming a wave, all the rest of them kneeled" in front of Don Bruno.[37] This is the scene: the lord is on the elevated porch, and in front of him is a mass of Indians performing a ritual that supports the display of Bruno's immediate power. *Todopoderoso*, "all-powerful," is the word that describes Bruno's aspect at this moment, a word that usually designates the Christian God. This performance by Bruno has its audience: the Indians that are standing in front of him. In a moment, Bruno (the lord, the king, the actor) will start his performance of making laws and executing them.

Jürgen Habermas, in his study of the transformations of the public sphere, narrates the emergence of the bourgeois public sphere in England and France in the eighteenth century. Although his study is very place and time specific, his observations about the nature of the *publicum* of the European Middle Ages are useful for us here.[38] Habermas calls the "representative public sphere" the structures that were active in the Middle Ages. Then, the logic of representation worked very differently from the bourgeois idea of the public sphere. "As long as the prince and the estates of his realm 'were' the country and not just its representatives, they could represent it in a specific sense. They represented their lordship not for the people, but 'before' the people."[39] In the Middle Ages, the performance of lordship is connected directly to and depends upon a successful representation of virtue, which must be embodied, for instance, in behavior guided by what became known as courtly virtues.[40] This embodiment of virtue, in turn, alluded to the invisible presence, that of God.[41] Habermas talks of an "aura" of power that emanates from the lord that testifies to the existence of the higher being with his physical presence. The corporealization of this kind of power is the key: the physical behavior of a nobleman, his gestures, clothing, and speech, are all a requirement in the representation before the people. This kind of publicity, though, does not constitute a sphere of political communication.[42] The medieval publicum, within this concept of *representatio,* was defined only negatively, as the inverse of the lordly status, as a passive receptor of the spectacular representation, which had no means to enter the dialogue with the sovereign power. But there is one thing the medieval lord and the publicum have in common: convergence of the "public" and "private" sphere. All the powers of the lord emanate from a unitary source, which can be conceptualized as a private domain. Bruno is a subject within whom the public and the private are inextricably linked. It becomes especially evident because the English liberal formula "private vices, public virtues" does not apply to Bruno at all. His lust and his sexual behavior is the central topic of his discourse before his serfs and also a central impetus for his public decisions, the ones that affect his serfs. At the same time, the individuals that compose the publicum are private persons who have no means of acting politically, similar to the serfs on Bruno's hacienda, who are passive receptors of the will of their lord, at least at the very beginning of the novel.

Descriptions of Don Bruno closely reflect Habermasean concepts of a spectacular public sphere. Bruno manifests *before* his people the presence of the divine power that made him lord. His own physical person is the corporealization of this power. The narrative voice describes his gestures, clothing, and physical appearance exhaustively, almost obsessively, in much more detail than those of any other character. For example, in one of the first descriptions, the narrative voice says that "his blond beard gave him the air of an outraged angel, of a vision sent down from heaven,"[43] underlining again Bruno's connection to the divine. Bruno's appearance seems to be crucial to who he is, and to what he represents: he is special because he looks special and vice versa. His appearance seems to coincide with his essence and foreshadows the radical political shift that he will undergo as the novel progresses, from abusive lord to liberator. The reflection of Bruno's moral strength, first hidden and then revealed, is especially evident in this description: "Amongst so many mestizo people and those wearing indigenous headgear, he, so blond, with such blue and peaceful eyes, had the appearance not of a gamonal devoured by lust but of a notable believer, whose innocence radiated."[44] The narrative voice presents Don Bruno in these admiring words. As the narrative progresses, the reader finds out that what seemed to be the first "superficial" description turned out to be the foreshadowing of a profound truth about this character. Bruno is, in fact, an "admirable believer" whose "innocence" or pursuit of it makes him move away from his negative personal conditions that his angel-like appearance denies: that of "gamonal," possessed by "lust." At the end of the novel, he escapes his social status and suppresses the erotic passions he considers "dirty."

Apart from manifesting the incorporated coincidence between appearance and essence, Bruno also has the "aura" that Habermas grants to the kingly sovereign. According to the narrator, "Don Bruno was transfigured in the presence of the 'small' landlords. Despite his poncho, all the aura of his countenance and his attitude dominated the living room: he looked truly impressive."[45] The narrator is fascinated by Bruno because in his figure we see a correspondence of the aesthetic and the moral, a sort of happy concurrence of the good and the beautiful, however problematic both of these categories might be. Once we turn to the discussion of the indigenous varayok's, it will become evident that their exercise of power is equally effective as Bruno's, and for the same reasons: incorporation of power that implies responsibility and infuses its bearer with an "aura" of respect. At the same time, the Indian mayors represent a different modality of the good and the beautiful. The important aspect here is that the narrative voice admires both of these modalities, thus canceling out the radical ideological opposition between the gamonales and the Indians, firmly upheld by the social sciences in the 1960s.

Let us look back at the scene in the hacienda to trace Bruno's progressive revelation of his true essence, which is announced in his physical descriptions and then embodied in his political actions. Bruno's first speech in front of his serfs already starts to problematize the narrator's description of this character as a "kingly" sovereign, as if the character were subverting the narrator's intention. His speech is an extended order to his serfs to go serve in his brother's mine, without payment, of course. But Bruno's reflection on Christian virtue, which he must represent, betrays his doubts about his own sovereign power. In other words, his belief in the divine origin of his power clashes with his capacity to perceive the inevitability of historical change. Bruno cannot believe anymore in his own sovereignty because he cannot believe that it will work eternally; and if his authority is divinity based, it should appear and be eternal. Discarding the belief in timelessness, Bruno also has to discard the idea of postmortem reward for the Indians for obedience and suffering, which they owe him according to his Christian-shaped beliefs inherited from the colonial past and which Bruno cultivates in them by inviting Franciscan friars to preach at the hacienda. At the moment he recognizes the timely nature of his power, he also recognizes historicity of his own and "his" Indians' suffering. Bruno begins to act within a vision of history and move away from the perspective of timelessness that motivated him before.

Bruno suffers; we may say that moral suffering is the definitive trait of this character. He sees himself as contaminated by lechery and power, guilty of raping the hunchback girl and of inflicting suffering on his serfs. He is lord by divine will, and therefore his responsibility for the bodies and souls of the Indians obliges him to make them suffer so that they do not stray from the right moral path and receive their reward in the afterlife. The Indians' suffering is different from Bruno's: unlike the lord's moral burden of choice for himself and for his serfs (since there still is a room for choice in the God-driven universe), theirs is a suffering of harsh living conditions. It is a physical suffering, while Bruno's is moral. In order to explain his own suffering, Bruno capitalizes on the idea of responsibility for the spiritual well-being of "his" Indians. If we turn his conflicting principles into two simple formulas, on the one hand, he says to himself, I am rotten and dirty because I make people suffer. But, on the other hand, responsibility is my suffering, and, conversely, suffering is my responsibility. I take responsibility for the transitory suffering of "my" Indians, so as to ensure their well-being in the afterlife. However, Bruno starts to doubt these precepts as he sees his Indians change. His own change is manifest when he progressively contributes to diminishing the Indians' suffering on this earth, and not in the afterlife.

During the entire novel Bruno looks for a way to cleanse himself of his two sins: rape and abuse of power. Since the suffering he had inflicted was physical and direct, he looks for a physical and external suffering as a punishment. He finally finds his desired punishment in the lousy (literally, full of lice) prison, which brings him redemption from class guilt. At the end of the novel, Bruno is imprisoned by the state officials for his subversive actions, namely for freeing the Indians and thus aiding their revolt. But it is important that he *volunteers* to go to jail, thus finally finding penance for all the abuses he had caused to women and for all the suffering he inflicted on the Indians "of his property" (*de su perinencia*). The voluntary nature of his action truly elevates Bruno to a rank of self-sacrificial figure, emulating the sacrifice of his model, Christ.

But in Bruno's imagination his burden extends further. He blames himself for having lent his Indians to Fermín for work in the mine, thus contributing to the destruction of the town of San Pedro and to the unnecessary deaths the development of the mine had caused. Bruno especially laments his part in the death of Anto, the old faithful servant who dies defending his land that the mine annexes: "I defied God! I gave my Indians to Fermín. I brought the machines, which are turning into dust the cornfields, blessed by all the Virgins. I made disappear into air the body of Anto, the father of my father."[46] This quote shows a complex associative chain of Bruno's guilt: his lust and rapes drive his father, Don Andrés, mad; he, Bruno, does not care for his father while he is sick; and further he contributes to death of Anto, who takes care of the old Don Andrés de Peralta. It is as if through his lament for the death of the old servant, a scandalous action in itself, Bruno expiates the abuses the Indians had suffered at the hands of the feudal lords during the four hundred years of their subjugation. To use the terminology borrowed from Fernand Braudel, Bruno carries on his shoulders guilt of very long duration.[47]

Our description of Bruno's internal psychological factors is not gratuitous, because these contradictions are externalized in concrete political changes and reforms in the lives of the serfs. In the paradigmatic scene in the hacienda, after the narrator describes Bruno as a classical "kingly" sovereign, Bruno's own words and actions question his social position. Violating the established custom, Bruno allows the foreman of his serfs, Adrian K'oto, to speak to him and to criticize his recently executed order.[48] The Indian tells him that the overseer Carhuamayo, who just then had been flagellated following Bruno's orders, is innocent. And Bruno believes him! It seems that K'oto was testing the waters with this first challenge to Bruno's decision. Next, unbelievably, K'oto places a demand on Bruno. His cautious response can be paraphrased like this: we will go to the mines, *if* you let us trade with the free community of Paraybamba, which is dying from starvation.[49] The conditional "if" in K'oto's speech is almost imperceptible; it is almost unheard, because what the man is doing is unheard of! What he is demanding is a big deal: to open up the frontiers of the feud, whose closure guarantees the sovereignty of Bruno's power. Bruno's concession can be read as a magnanimous gesture, a key aspect of a sovereign's behavior; but it is also more than that. To begin with, he publicly recognizes his serf, Adrian K'oto, as a man of speech: "Speak to me!—the lord shouted at him.—You have permission!"[50] Bruno "shouts" at K'oto; it seems he does not believe his own public decision to let his serf speak to him, because this is also unheard of. In short, it takes two to tango: both the lord and the serf are bending the rigid custom that builds a wall of silence between them. The amazing thing is that they are bending it in the same direction.

How is it possible? The Indian's arguments convince Bruno because they are phrased in the language of Christian mythology, the discourse shared by the two men. Bruno welcomes this aperture to dialogue, which, he senses, will contribute to his own elimination as an element of social structure. The omniscient narrator tells us that "the lord was doubting. The cabecilla was interrogating him with humility that made his guts freeze."[51] If the serf is speaking with "humility" to Bruno, why should the lord feel that his "guts froze," the image suggesting a vague fear? Why is he afraid of a man who is humbly speaking to him? It should be emphasized that maintaining the conversation with the Indian and letting him negotiate places the lord in such a new situation that he does not know what to do next. He prompted this situation, but the readiness of his interlocutor to also change the rules of the game throws Bruno off. The narrator signals the drastic nature of the moment by qualifying both characters as "perplexed" with the new situation: "los dos andaban extraviados." This unifying expression, "los dos" (both) narratively connects Bruno and Adrian K'oto, establishing a clear parallel between the lord and the serf, prefiguring their alliance for the change in the same direction. To jump to the end result of this incredible conversation at the end of the novel, let us look at one of novel's final images: "in the prison of the provincial capital, Adrian K'oto was embracing don Bruno."[52] This is what happens when people start talking: they find enough in common to end up in the same jail, imprisoned for similar charges, driven there by the same motivations. The embrace is a mute gesture of solidarity; but first, words were necessary to bring Bruno and Adrian K'oto to this gesture.[53]

Many creole characters (as opposed to Indians) qualify Bruno as mad because they cannot decipher his behavior; for example, his brother Fermín does not blame Bruno for the attempt at fratricide by labeling him "loco."[54] Each stage of Bruno's "madness" pushes him further to subvert the tacit alliance between the power blocs (the old landowners and the mining

company), in favor of his pact with the Indians. This behavior leaves perplexed both Bruno's social equals and the Indians, but the Indians decipher him at the end, while the creoles prefer to simply dispose of him as
a bothersome element. For example, at a cabildo with Paraybambas, the
Indians surround Don Bruno and watch as a young girl approaches him,
about to throw herself at his feet. And he says, "Get up! Do not kiss my
feet. I am not a God anymore."[55] He then has a conversation with the girl
(talking again!) and lets her go. Carhuamayo, the mestizo overseer, cannot
process Bruno's behavior: "Carhuamayo had heard the dialogue, feeling
somewhere between surprised and perplexed. The lord was changing; he
was 'half going mad.' He was suppressing the women's reverence and did
not let them kiss his boots. Why?"[56] In this quote we must note not only
Carhuamayo's confusion, but also the important shift that Bruno's word
"anymore" reveals. It summarizes the change of Bruno's status from the
first scene in the hacienda, when he enters with the air of "todopoderoso"
(almighty). This change is so much more revolutionary, as it extends not
only to Bruno's serfs but also to other Indians, the members of the free
and poor Paraybamba village. Furthermore, it extends not only to indigenous authorities, who were traditionally respected, but also to any Indian,
including a young girl. Bruno does not want to be God *anymore* for any of
these persons.

But Bruno's "ravings" have just begun. He listens to the story of Paraybamba's suffering due to abuses of the nouveau riche Adalberto Cisneros,
whose father took away the Paraybamban lands through smart machina-
tions. What follows is a complex scene, which culminates with Bruno and
the Indian varayok's performing an indigenous ritual punishment on Cisneros by stripping him naked and sending him for a walk in the frozen
mountains. This scene and the dialogues among Cisneros, Bruno, and the
Indians deserve a detailed reading, as it is very revealing of the concepts of
power and sovereignty discussed here.

Bruno listens to the old Indians who came to revere him at his hacienda and report on their subhuman living conditions. All of a sudden,
Bruno declares to the varayok' who just finished his disaster report: "Old
man! I have much land. I will give you Tokoswayk'o, the whole strip of land
on the side of La Providencia, so that your people can plant there." And
the Indians' reaction: "The old man was looking at Don Bruno, as if he
were suddenly hit on the back of his head. All the villagers had the same
expression."[57] After this, Bruno travels to the community's village in order
to organize an assembly and make a communal decision on terms for use
of the land he had just given to the Indians. There, Cisneros shows up in
person, with the idea to confront Bruno Aragón de Peralta and defend

what he considers, according to the law of the Peruvian state, his lands and rights over the Indian village. A number of facets of this encounter underline salient features of both a personal and political nature in the trajectory of Don Bruno.

He knows that the other members of his social class see him as deranged. After he intervenes in Paraybamba and defends the Indians against the abuses of Adalberto Cisneros, he tries to explain his actions to his overseer: "Carhuamayo: more than once you looked at me as if I had lost my mind. That is how we, the ones who have *great responsibility,* present ourselves among men, who do not know how to do anything else but obey; that is how we appear when the road of good and evil is obscured before us."[58] Bruno makes reference to his responsibility, the origins of which we have located in the "mystical" foundations of his sovereign authority. This responsibility is the conceptual hook that enables us to understand his actions. Bruno makes radical decisions, which align him progressively with the Indians, instead of supporting the power bloc where he supposedly belongs. The moment of decision for Bruno is "when the road between the good and the evil" becomes blurry, that is to say, Bruno formulates his political decisions in terms of ethical opposition. His ethics are rooted in the Christian mythology, whose language he shares with the Indians. In the worldview shared by Bruno, his serfs such as Adrian K'oto, and the Paraybamba villagers, the ethical and political categories override the economic considerations. For this reason, Bruno wants to give away his land to the Indian community: he is more interested in being on good terms with his God than in economic profit. The narrative voice underlines many times that most of Bruno's lands are unused for production; they are vast and Bruno loves them platonically for their beauty. Similarly, the Indians in *Todas las sangres* want land only for self-subsistence; they want to work land in order to eat and survive, not to produce surplus value. Thus, in a parallel manner, the logic of accumulation of capital is foreign to both Bruno and the Indians, which is why Bruno is seen as archaic by the other members of the ruling class, such as his brother Fermín or other landowners, who are ready to follow the tendency of the modern world to subordinate all aspects of human life to economic profit.

The punishment of Adalberto Cisneros is highly revealing, underlining the similarities between Bruno's and the Indians' worldview and clarifying the conceptual gap that separates them from Cisneros and the Peruvian state, the priorities of which reside in economic interest. Bruno's actions manifest the points he has in common with the Indians, such as the value of authority and justice as seen in the mutual recognition and respect between the newly elected indigenous mayor and Don Bruno. This respect is for the essence of the person who emanates the aura of authority, and not for his material possessions: for one's public and political, not economic, status. They oppose Adalberto Cisneros, who understands the logic of the state in however corrupted a way because, in his words, the police back up his power because he bought the senator.

Bruno and the Indians recognize each other's authority, backed up by the narrative voice. Even before choosing an official mayor, Bruno prays together with the oldest Paraybamban in front of the cross and, in the ritual of choosing the indigenous authorities, kisses the Peruvian flag that decorates their insignia.[59] The Indians, for their part, believe in Aragón's intrinsic superiority over Cisneros because he is a true "great lord," while Cisneros is a "greedy cholo" ("*cholo*" here could be translated as "nouveau riche," although usually this term also carries the meaning of a racial mix). The narrative voice supports this idea: "The villagers saw . . . that Cisneros did not have the expression of an all-powerful lord but another one, maybe the one that *corresponded to his true nature: of a mestizo thief who cannot face a true lord*."[60] The narrator affirms the intrinsic, essential difference between Bruno and Cisneros. From the moment Cisneros appears before Bruno and the Paraybamba villagers, Bruno sets about to demonstrate the illegitimacy of the other man's claim to the title of the higher estate, despite Cisneros's newly amassed wealth. Aragón de Peralta uses a criterion inherited from colonial times for distinguishing the "great lord" from a "cholo," by asking, "Can you say 'Credo' in Spanish?" When Cisneros admits that he is incapable of praying in Spanish, being a Quechua monolingual, Bruno concludes, "You are no lord, then, friend Cisneros."[61] Bruno makes Cisneros admit his ignorance in public before the assembly of the Indians, theatrically representing the difference between himself and his adversary. This theatricality of representation is central to our investigation, represented in this concrete example by Bruno and Cisneros.

Habermas, exploring the difference between the representative public sphere and the bourgeois public sphere, defines the difference between a nobleman and a bourgeois by their relation to the concept of representation. The nobleman can represent himself in front of the people. His power is displayed publicly in his person, whose second (or maybe first) nature is the know-how of the social ritual. The bourgeois is a private individual—he does not represent anything.[62] The nobleman "has a right to seem; the latter [the bourgeois] is compelled to be, and what he aims at seeming becomes ludicrous and tasteless."[63] According to Goethe, who witnessed the transition from the representative to the bourgeois public sphere, one can ask a nobleman, "Who are you?," but one should only ask a bourgeois, "What do you have? What possessions, what knowledge?" This is because

the nobleman has an essence, an immobile core, but the bourgeois personality is always "erratic." Bruno's question to a Cisneros acolyte, an Indian
who appears in nontraditional clothing and claims to be a *vecino*, a "white
villager," illustrates this preoccupation with capacity to represent that is
conditional on the immobile core identity: "And who are you? What do
you represent?"[64]

As we begin to see, Bruno and the Indians operate within a concept of
representation different from the one predominant in the liberal democracy. The authority of Don Bruno and the varayok's must be represented
publicly. For example, before the burial of Bruno's mother, the narrative
voice underlines that "the people of the town saw him [Bruno] riding
through the streets at the majestic trot of the stallion."[65] The majesty of
Bruno's person is very much supported by the majesty of his horse, as it
contributes to his theatrical appearance. The narrator fixes his admiring
eyes on his horse Lucero, just as he admires Bruno. When the two (the
horse and the horseman) enter Don Lucas's hacienda, Bruno stages his
entrance carefully: "At noon, with ferocious sun, entered Don Bruno into
Don Lucas's hacienda."[66] He enters "with the sun," like a natural phenomenon, and the punishment he brings to the cruel landowner is as inevitable as nature's wrath: Bruno shoots Lucas in front of the other man's
serfs, proclaiming publically that he is punishing him for the inhumane
treatment he gave to the Indians. The abused Indians recognize in him
something more than human, just by laying their eyes on him: "¡Arcángel,
Don Bruno!," they shout.[67] Thus, the body of Don Bruno, just like that of
an absolute monarch, is infused with the superhuman aura of authority,
which makes his vengeance acquire a political surplus. Bruno's execution
of Lucas is read by the Indians as a political act, going far beyond a private
act of madness or vengeance. Furthermore, Bruno does not delegate the
responsibility for this act to anyone. His authority carries the immediate
responsibility as its corollary. Peruvian state officials, uninterested in these
subtleties, take Bruno to jail for this act.

The two brothers, the developmentalist Fermín and "pre-modern"
Bruno, clash over the meaning of representation at the burial of their
mother. For Fermín, the representativity of a public sphere is an antique
remnant. Fermín feels ashamed at the ceremonious behavior of his
brother, echoed by the equally ceremonious attitude of the Indians, when
Bruno is about to entrust his mother's corpse to the ayllu. Fermín asks
him to "stop the farce," but Bruno replies, "The Indians do not make
comedy! I do not make comedy! We live and we die!"[68] For Bruno and the
Indians, the representation and its essence coincide. The narrative voice
describes the varayok's in the attitude of the same theatricality as Bruno,

paying special attention to the Indians' dignified postures, their scepters (*varas*), and their outfits (as we have seen with Bruno, in the representative public sphere the physical representation of power is important in all its ritual details, clothing, and gestures).[69] The narrative voice admires on more than one occasion the "impersonal"—more than human—expressions of the Indians' faces as they act as public authority. The insignias of their power are very important, as they are a physical symbol of authority. While holding his vara, the Indian emanates that aura observed around the person of Don Bruno. In Paraybamba, Bruno makes a ritual saving of the varas from the houses of the undeserving Indians, Cisneros's collaborators. The varas are "alive" as they wait for the Indian authorities, suffering torture on the rack.[70] The vara is like a part of the body of the varayok'. Rendón, when asked by a fellow worker to come and have a drink, excuses himself: "estoy envarado" (I am carrying a vara).

The two poles of the representative authority of the two estates, the Indians and the antiquated great lords, recognize each other in solemn rituals. Bruno, in his interaction with the indigenous authorities, again perpetuates mutual respect and recognition. For example, "The mayor gave the pistol to Don Bruno. The lord kissed it and hung it on his belt, under his poncho. Then, the Indian started to walk away . . . and occupied his place behind the lords. The copper rings and the polychrome designs on his vara were shining in the light."[71] The theatricality of this representation becomes evident as gestures, clothing, and symbolic objects (the gun and the vara) become the center of the description.

Another way in which Bruno and the Indians oppose Cisneros and Fermín is their belief in the preeminence of political identity over economic status. The dressed-up Indian cannot respond to Don Bruno's question, "What are you, what do you represent?" Bruno immediately condemns him socially and morally: "Falsified Indian, devil's excrement, you have money because you have stolen from your brothers."[72] This Indian's conduct is reprehensible, because, in fact, Bruno sees any accumulation of capital beyond the needs of subsistence as a "*robo,*" robbery. To call someone the "devil's excrement" is to say more than "a bad person"—it is a person who transgresses the basic precepts of admissible conduct for a determined worldview. For Bruno and the Indians, "excremento del diablo" is someone who tries to rise socially through acquiring wealth at the expense of neighbors, or "brothers," in Bruno's words. Here we arrive at the cornerstone of the alliance between Bruno and the Indians: they oppose the logic of accumulation of capital for the purposes of private benefit and the social ascension that goes with it. Echoing this characterization, the Indians condemn Cisneros as a "greedy cholo" more than once in the novel.

Interestingly, Cisneros's lands are legally his, within the logic of the positive law: his father had acquired them through an astute manipulation of the Indians' precarious economic conditions and the Peruvian legal system. Adalberto Cisneros is actually proud of being a self-made man. He embodies an American dream story: ruthless, violent, and ambitious, he could be a hero of a Hollywood western. But within the vision held by Bruno, the Indians, and the narrator of *Todas las sangres,* his accumulation of capital is plainly rejected because legality within the positive law does not cancel its negative effects on the Indian community of Cisneros's acquisitions.

When one of Cisneros's friends asserts that he is not a cholo anymore because he is "now a great lord of [hacienda] Parquiña," a young Paraybamban retorts, "Even so, always cholo."[73] The difference between these two positions is, again, in the adverbs: "now" versus "always." For the Indian, the estate is a perennial quality: one is born as a great lord, an Indian, or a cholo. Within this logic, a good representative of an estate is someone who does not fake being of another estate. But how do we know if someone really is a great lord or not? The knowledge or absence of knowledge of the social ritual within the theatricality of the representative public sphere betrays them. So, Bruno discovers Cisneros's true nature because the man does not know how to pray in Spanish or how to greet properly. "Your mule," Bruno tells him, didactically, "if it could talk, would know how to greet [properly], because one can see that it is of good breed [*es de buena casta*]."[74]

Our reading suggests surprising things. First, we diagnose one of the sources of the failure of the nation-state's sovereignty in Peru: multiple sovereignties. Second, reading *Todas las sangres* as a political proposal does not suggest that this state of things, namely, the presence of "premodern" sovereignties, imbedded into the social framework of a state that wants to be modern, is negative for creation of a community. The novel rescues the concept of authority from its authoritarian implications, which this concept has acquired in the historical development of the modern nation-states, as Arendt and Agamben suggest. Besides, the novel's representation of the hacienda and the ayllu rescues these formations from being discarded as merely retrograde or abusive. In fact, we learn here that authority that remains in force within the ayllu and within Don Bruno's hacienda unhinges political power from economics and from the necessary engagement in the logic of capital. Authority and the mystic "aura" it grants to Bruno and the varayok's is profoundly political in that its sphere of action is *only* a creation of community. This is the kernel of resistance to the logic that moves men like Adalberto Cisneros or Fermín Aragón, who understand the principle that governs the modern state, which collapses the divisions between the spheres of the economic and the political.

Authority, as it is inextricably tied to the notion of responsibility, is charged with regenerative energy. In Agamben's study, the Roman notion of the *autor* was directly linked with the notion of "augment," to "perfect the act" as it stemmed from the sphere of the private law, where paterfamilias could validate the act of a minor.[75] Bruno augments, and thus politicizes, the act of the Paraybamba village taking back its old lands and expelling Cisneros, despite the fact that the nouveau riche was their legitimate owner within the positive law and within the authorityless logic of the modern state.

Nothing in the novel suggests that Bruno as a social subject or that hacienda as a social formation has a chance of survival—it is a declining, dying sovereignty, and both the narrative voice and Bruno himself know it. But the novel rescues the political nature of Bruno's administration of power through the rhetoric of fascination, poetic representation of his character, and underscoring his image as a figure of authority. The ayllu emerges, nonetheless, as a solid structure, where power also works within the logic of authority, and whose political power grows as the novel progresses. And if the power of authority and responsibility, which separate the spheres of the political and the economic, even saves a gamonal from being wholly abusive, it certainly has emancipating power within the ayllu. How does it work? It works by protecting the particular sovereignty of the ayllu from the state's homogenizing military and ideological excursions and by politically augmenting the ayllu's acts toward the outside.

CHAPTER 2

ANDEAN COMMUNITY

Beyond the Limits of Death Demand

> We are here entirely, for the fatherland; for Wisther there will be no spirit.
> The body without spirit, it is devoured quickly by mine, by sadness, by
> drunkenness.
> —Rendón Willka in Arguedas, *Todas las sangres*

n *Todas las sangres*, the bond between individual and community is
established fundamentally through the conceptualization of relationship to the divine and the transcendental, as the example of Don Bruno
evinces, in the previous chapter. Jean-Luc Nancy theorizes the relationship between political subjectivities and death in a complementary vein.
Both Arguedas and Nancy, one in the field of what is problematically called
"fiction," and the other in the language of philosophy, criticize the European model of nation building by reflecting on the concepts of finitude and
transcendence. A dialogue between these two lines of thought, each from
a different origin and genre, distills the subjective position from which to
think of the new visions of community.

Nancy criticizes the European national projects built on the principle
of essentiality, the maximum embodiment of which was the Third Reich.
Such a nation sees itself as a solid unity, where each individual person must
be subsumed into the common body of a nation. In this vision, death of the
martyrs is essential for the construction of community because it solidifies
the national collective body, canceling the singularity of each person and
subsuming the dead hero into the transcendental and eternal substance of
"people." In such a community, death is the ultimate work of community
building, which is done on the threshold of earthly existence but with its
vector directed toward eternity. In Nancy's reading of *Mein Kampf,* the

Aryan's duty is to sacrifice himself or herself as an individual for the sake of the Aryan race.[1]

For Nancy, "the political is the place where community as such is brought into play."[2] The end of the political is the problem that moves Nancy's theorization, as, in our days, all the aspects of power seem to be reduced to economic or administrative, technocratic or managerial categories. Nancy argues that the thought on community must be renewed in this situation in order to prevent this death of the political, which would lead to the tyranny of economics and technocracy. Nancy concludes that the thought on community has come to a halt,[3] and this is why we cannot think of options beyond the dubious neoliberal notion of "democracy." He calls this phenomenon a disease of "immanentism" that affects Western thought on subject and community. In Nancy's own words, "the thinking of community as essence is in effect the closure of the political. . . . Being-*in*-common has nothing to do with communion, with fusion into a body, into a unique and ultimate identity that would no longer be exposed. Being-*in*-common means, to the contrary, *no longer having, in any form, in any empirical or ideal place, such a substantial identity, and sharing this (narcissistic) 'lack of identity.'* This is what philosophy calls 'finitude.'"[4]

This conceptualization of a common front that does not presuppose a solid union or common identity echoes the proposal put forward in *Todas las sangres,* the text that strives to draw out a community alternative to the classical thinking on the essential national project. As I discussed in the first chapter, *Todas las sangres* describes multiple communities that wage distinct sovereignties on the territory of the Peruvian state. Each one of them establishes different relations to death and finitude, relations that are both collective and individual. A particular relation to death and afterlife engenders different political subjectivities within those communities. From this point of view, the ayllu and the Peruvian nation are the two entities where the political subjectivities function differently due to the divergent relation to death and afterlife.

The lax bond that *Todas las sangres* works out as a project of a new community can be thought in terms of finitude, which is the only vehicle that binds a singularity to a being-in-common, according to Nancy. In the key definition of the concept of finitude, Nancy explains that the revelation of a person's finitude occurs at the moment when he or she realizes that their own self is not equal to himself or herself and that he or she is not a finished, closed-off entity. One cannot say, "I am dead" and cannot speak of one's own death nor birth. This reveals that each individual being is finite, and there is no afterlife, at least not in language. The community serves to give us our death and our birth. The relationship with the community as giver of birth and death is the conscience of finitude. Consequently, the way individuals confront the ultimate experience—death—determines the possibility for envisioning a community that is based on something other than the Hegelian "spirit of the people." The Andean concept of the death experience and what follows it, as presented in *Todas las sangres,* provides a ground from which the thought on being-in-common is achieved.

Todas las sangres develops a "nonproject" for Peru, a term I borrow from Nancy's essay on "The Inoperative Community." In Nancy's words, "a community is not a project of fusion or in some general way a productive or operative project—nor is it a project at all."[5] Nancy opposes this idea of community to the Hegelian idea, which has figured collectivity as project, and figured the project, reciprocally, as collective. Nancy suggests that it is possible to think of a community constructed by moving away from the philosophy of subject and by thinking of alternative *singularities.* Reinterpreting the classical dyad, Nancy envisions a nonnation of nonpeople. Arguedas's Andean perspective, worked through in *Todas las sangres*, offers the readers practical illustrations on how to move toward this ideal that Nancy contemplates. Moreover, what is prescriptive in Nancy is descriptive in Arguedas. In other words, the novel offers a working model to follow. Concretely, the Indians' experiences of physical pain and death, their vision of afterlife, and their concept of work are the hinges on which the new proposal revolves, teaching the reader a very concrete lesson: we must move away from the essential thought on community by confronting in all honesty our own finitude. Only then will our thought on community be able to move forward, beyond what Christopher Fynsk calls the "tired concepts."[6]

Against this Western, Christian-rooted preoccupation with transcendence, in *Todas las sangres* quite a different view of death and afterlife is offered by the narrative voice and the ayllu-allied Indians. This concept of death has everything to do with this life, and not much with eternity. As a very important part of the earthly experience, which is the substance of history, the suffering and deaths of the Indians are often evoked in an act of memory. The narrator tells us, revealingly, "The Indians of the Providencia feared the mountain Apark'ora; its mine shafts were believed to be damned. In times not long past hundreds of Indians were annihilated in the mine. A murky memory remained from those times, like of the great plagues that passed over the Indian villages like fire."[7] This excerpt suggests that *Todas las sangres,* as well as the entire Arguedean corpus, carries the burden of many corpses. It is a text of mourning for the Indians who died in a centuries-long holocaust. Painful remembrances surface here and there in the narrative. The mythical terror that the Indians feel when they hear the name of the mountain Apark'ora reflects the historical memory of the annihilated victims—of real people and of real corpses that exist outside the novelistic universe. Large numbers, "hundreds," of the victimized dilute the individuality of these persons. And yet, the personal mortality of each Indian becomes the pivotal point of the novel with the hero Demetrio Rendón Willka's death by firing squad. As a result, complex dialectics of subjectivity emerge from the conceptual bond of death and community.

Nancy's critique of the European national projects is our first conceptual reference that guides the analysis of these dialectics. But the dialectics of relation to death and afterlife in *Todas las sangres* are complex and require a varied toolbox for their analysis. As the opposing pole of thought on death and community, the Bolivian political scientist Álvaro García Linera presents a practical appreciation of martyrdom as a tool for effective consolidation of a communal unity of what he calls the "twentieth-century proletariat," embodied in the Bolivian miners' syndicates—doubtless, the very idea that Nancy abhors. García Linera believes in the usefulness of such a martyrdom, although he is interested more in the practices of resistance than in those of nation building. As he expresses it, "generally, the blood and the dead in the popular myths leave an unresolved debt that demands of the further generations a compensation; it is an *active convocation to a search for unification,* which would satisfy in the imaginary . . . a symbolic replacement of the sacrifice of life that could have been one's own."[8] *Todas las sangres* inscribes the thought on death and community dialectically, between Nancy's and García Linera's opposing theorizations. What do we learn from Arguedas's theorization? Is blood necessary to cement any community, or is the community built on death ideologically deformed, crippled for the future?

In response to these questions, I will interpret Rendón Willka's death by firing squad by reading this character as straddling between different systems of subjectivity and functioning within different sovereignties, as discussed above in chapter 1: that of the indigenous community and that of the state. His death will have different meanings from the point of view of the indigenous community and from the point of view of a wider type of national communality. Apart from Rendón's personal departure, I also consider collective deaths in the novel, which remind us of historical deaths of the hundreds of indigenous persons. What is dying, transforming, and surviving in *Todas las sangres?*

Importantly, the disappearance of Indians as persons is paralleled by the narrator's preoccupation with the survival, adaptation, and transformation of ayllu as structure. Arguedas ethnographically documented that the ayllu

has not disappeared in the mid-twentieth century, and then incorporated
this fact into the novelistic narrative. Some of the ayllus disbanded, but
some, like the communities of the Mantaro valley,[9] presented the opposite
case where their horizontal relation with the capitalist system of production
strengthened some traditional practices and consequently the identity of
the community's members and their sense of belonging.[10] For Arguedas,
the case of Mantaro was a positive model, the manner for the ayllu to survive and to serve as a social formation that would improve the lives of the
Indians. According to Ángel Rama's seminal, although at times problematic,
theorization, an ayllu like those of the Mantaro valley guaranteed a higher
standard of life and simultaneously protected the Indians from deculturation. Arguedas used Mantaro communities as a model for a strong community able to survive; and in *Todas las sangres,* Lahuaymarca represents
such a community. Although for Arguedas the case of Mantaro supported
his belief that the ayllu had a future, it was still hard for him to oppose the
interpretation of the historical trajectory predominant in the 1960s, which
saw the Indians' deculturation as inevitable and desirable.[11] As a response
to this deterministic condemnation, Arguedas developed a sort of anticipated mourning. This sadness transforms the fear of deculturation into the
imperative to think of other possibilities. It is as if the picture of the Lima
shantytowns, or of the mining town painted in *Todas las sangres,*[12] posits a
question: Is this depressing picture the only way? Are there no alternatives?
Can the positive traits of the slums or the mining town be salvaged and
bettered? Is the Lahuaymarca ayllu destined to disappear like other communities in Andahuaylas and Apurímac? Will Rendón's brothers become
"sad" like the many migrant workers of the mining town?[13] Conceptually,
the indigenous community inspired Arguedas to more controversial and
creative thinking by the very fact that the social sciences of the 1960s were
condemning it to sure death. Importantly, it is not that Arguedas's contemporaries were blind to the fact that the ayllu still existed in the sierra. But
for them the ayllu represented economic structures more or less integrated
into the capitalist system of domination. The roundtable on *Todas las sangres,* which was mentioned in the introduction, put to Arguedas a question
that was not easy to escape: Was he not presenting a picture of a happy community while it was made available for exploitation by the capitalist forces?
What kind of community was he trying to preserve, and for what purposes?
Along with the preservation project of the ayllu, in *Todas las sangres* there
is also a project for another kind of community, altogether new.

In fact—and taking up Nancy's critical terminology—we see here confronted two essential community projects, that of the nation and that of
the ayllu, which stand in radical contradiction precisely because of their

essentiality. The essential thinking on the process of consolidation of the Indian community is strategically necessary to preserve the common Indian front, in a movement similar to the one described by García Linera, where the memory of the martyrs solidifies the subaltern resistance. In order to place demands on the emerging state, the Indian community must construct a political subjectivity from which to make this demand. Indian subjectivity confronts the national sovereignty that pretends to engulf the indigenous community and dissolve it into the homogeneous mass, ready to be subsumed into the nation. At the same time, the common national front is, in fact, very necessary in order to oppose the infringements of the transnational capital. Thus, the essentially postulated Indian community opposes the essentially proposed national community, while both emerge as an urgent necessity in the novel. Can there be a solution for this double necessity? In the next conceptual step, Arguedas develops a new vision of a national front that is nonessential. While the two first options can be thought as essential because they deal with imaginary homogeneous material (only "simply" Peruvians or only Indians), the third option cannot be essentialist because it recognizes and deals with a heterogeneous makeup of the Peruvian society. Let us trace these complex dialectics.

Nancy's idea of loosely articulated singularities is useful for thinking about this sort of national community in *Todas las sangres* because it allows for heterogeneity and consequently saves the ayllu from being diluted in the nationalist idea. In the novel, the nonproject depends on negotiation between two especially strong discourses on coexistence: the national discourse whose main exponent is the industrialist Don Fermín Aragón and the ayllu-inspired options voiced by the hero of the novel, Demetrio Rendón Willka. For other characters, such as Bruno or the poor whites of San Pedro, it is impossible to imagine themselves as a part of a larger whole beyond the strictly local level, where their modes of communality are deteriorating progressively.

Don Fermín Aragón, landowner and miner, thinks money and thinks Peru. For this pragmatic capitalist, smartly managed profit is the answer to the problem of postcolonial cultural heterogeneity and material misery in his beloved country. For him, the profits will yield proletarization of the Indian peasants, will finally integrate the sierra with the coast, and will place Peru in the world market, not only as a pool of natural resources but as a competitive partner. Fermín wishes for Peru to become a homogeneous nation, which is the reason he sees the Indians and his own brother Bruno as culturally and ideologically retrograde residue that aborts Peru's progress toward this bright future. His plan of action is the following, as he explains it to his wife and ally, Matilde: "Do you think that we still have a right to own serfs? Do you think that the serfs constitute a productive force? They are dead weight. . . . Now I need them. . . . I will exploit them mercifully and thoroughly. . . . But, later, when I will be sufficiently strong and out of reach of those who want to devour me, I will liberate the serfs. My plan is ready. Bruno must die."[14] Fermín summarizes his plan in the death sentence for his own brother, Bruno, who represents the old-time colonial and Christian values, standing in radical opposition to Fermín's capitalist and modernizing projects. This plan, therefore, requires a violent erasure of the old structures defended by Bruno, namely the hacienda and the ayllu. As a result of his modernizing efforts, Fermín believes that progress will arrive in his native town of San Pedro: "we will give them a power plant, schools, a soccer field, businesses."[15] He, Fermín, will save Peru from its backwardness—not because he is an idealist but to benefit individually from the bettering of society as a whole. Ruthless as Fermín might seem at first, he is a man possessed by an idea who does not give up when the transnational company Wisther and Bozart usurps his mine, and continues fighting for self-sufficient Peruvian industry. He gives up the sierra as the focus of his activity and opts for the coast where he can have certain economic autonomy. But Fermín keeps his lands in the highlands, industrializes his hacienda, and uses the revenues from his coastal business to modernize the sierra. His alliances, beyond his individual interests, lie with his native region, and on a larger scale, with Peru. Although represented as a malign, pitiless character at the beginning of the novel (for example, he says that "old people should not live" while speaking of his own father[16]), Fermín comes to incarnate an ideal industrialist for Arguedas, the least of the necessary evils.

Fermín repeats Rendón's words when accusing the engineer Cabrejos: "you the chemically pure ones . . . have been defined by Rendón: you threw away your soul."[17] He enters in alliance with Rendón Willka, despite the fact that an ideological ocean separates them, because they have the same enemy: the transnational mining company. Actually, Rendón expresses this alliance in an enigmatic and profoundly dialectic language typical for this character: "Don Fermín is like me, only from the other side."[18] What does it mean that he is "like me but from the other side"? The dialectics of negotiation between Rendón and Fermín reveal the profoundly Andean structure in the narrative of the novel. As Frank Salomon comments on the patterns of Andean social relations as projected in the pre-Hispanic myths, "the inseparability of complementarity from conflict is implied to be a motor force in the mutability (what one would call the historicity) of west Andean society."[19] Fermín and Rendón stage the conflict that is the force of history. Reading Rendón's words as political, one can say that

Fermín's vision of Peru as a homogeneous nation stands in contradiction with Rendón's idea of a nation that incorporates Indians as culturally distinct elements. Nonetheless, both Rendón and Fermín share their concern for Peru in its struggle with transnational capital, and both voice their belief in the power of work as a tool of resistance. Fermín conceptualizes the process of building a nation as a project of unification achieved through industrialized labor. The operability and usefulness of all the elements involved are, consequently, his first concern and interest. Rendón and other Indians, similarly, propose a mode of work that consolidates the Indian community and which, if incorporated smartly into the nation, could benefit Peru as envisioned by Fermín. The narrative voice welcomes the possibility of such an outcome.

Since the negotiations between Rendón and Fermín are staged within the Andean dialectics of coexistence and conflict, the multiple interests they articulate are constantly played against each other. Rendón's alliances, similar to Fermín's, are "layered," albeit in an inverse order from those of the industrialist landlord. His first commitment is to the Indians from his community, but his commitment on a larger scale is to Peruvian nationhood. In the epigraph to this chapter, he tells Don Fermín that the Indians will be fine working for a Peruvian industrialist, expressed in a conceptual reference to "fatherland," but will degrade if sold to a transnational company: "We are here entirely, for the fatherland; for Wisther there will be no spirit. The body without spirit, it is devoured quickly by mine, by sadness, by drunkenness."[20] Around this quote, in the pivotal scene when the metal is discovered, an ample alliance is formed, unbelievably. Although in the beginning of this scene the engineer Camargo says that "Peru belongs to the enemies, I think. We are all born enemies"[21] (in reference to the profound abysses that crack postcolonial Peruvian society), the rest of the scene contradicts this pessimistic assertion. Fermín, Aprista[22] worker Antenor, and Communist worker Portales echo Rendón's words, expressing their desire to protect the mineral riches from the transnational capital.[23] Is this a momentary alliance formed in the face of a threat, or does it promise a stable common front?

This scene suggests that a being-in-common is still possible in the Peruvian society, despite the fact that violence marks the original contact between the different communality models. This makes *Todas las sangres* into a nationalistic text, in its own way. At the same time, Arguedas's own defense of the ayllu seems to contradict his proposition of that wide common front, but he dialectically recognizes its necessity if a point of resistance to imperialism is to be found. The problem with this common ground, though, is that it is not democratic at all: those with money and power always tread on the dispossessed. Is there a way to overcome this tendency? Is there a mode of existence that can promise horizontal relations, and at the same time project a collectivity large enough, beyond the reduced local level, to resist the imperialist invasion?

Rendón's declaration is a contradictory response to these questions, and here a short excursus into the intricacies of the Arguedean language is obligatory. His enigmatic expression that reads in Spanish "estamos *enteros* para el patria" (we are here entirely, for fatherland) should not be taken lightly as a Quechua-like distortion of Spanish, because these distortions charge the Quechua-dressed-up-as-Spanish with multiple and more complex meanings. "Enteros" can come to mean "completely, with all our communal heart," or simply "all of us," or "each one of us entirely devoted to the cause," or "entire community, as a unity," "equal, undivided hierarchically among ourselves," or possibly all of these at once. Within our reading, this expression acquires a special importance because it can refer to the essentiality of the Indian community as a unity, each individual Indian fully subsumed and identified with his community and consequently, in the next conceptual step, with the project of working for the fatherland. But this essentiality stays at the level of the Indian community, while the nation, on the contrary, emerges as built on the alliance of the atomized, differentiated political singularities (the capitalist, the Aprista, the Communist, and the Indians). Within this solution, it seems that the projects of the Indian community and the national community cease to stand in radical opposition and instead complement one another in their common task of opposing the transnational capital. Reading through the model of community offered by the ayllu in *Todas las sangres* will help us understand this problematic interaction between different levels of communality and to develop further our understanding of how the individuals' relationship to the experiences of work and death determines their political subjectivity and their mode of participation in community.

The Ayllu, Finitude and Community

The Lahuaymarca ayllu represents in *Todas las sangres* an unabusive, horizontally structured communality, which has land as means of subsistence and which resists culturally and physically the arrival of industrialization in a power vacuum, the result of the traditional landowners' and elites' loss of power, while the new power structures fail to fill the void. Lahuaymarca has its brother-antipode, the community of Paraybamba, which had lost its lands to the expansion of the latifundio. As a result, it does not have the means to survive, the reason "mothers kill their newborn babies," and has no resources to have "neither authorities nor ritual celebrations."[24] In other words, Paraybamba cannot reproduce itself either physically or symbolically. The cases of these two communities mark the key point: land ownership and its defense is a cornerstone of survival for an indigenous community. As I mentioned above, the difference between Lahuaymarca and Paraybamba parallels Arguedas's ethnographic studies, illustrating his thesis about strong and weak communities.[25] The strong ones have been exposed to the influence of Western culture, been culturally and economically mestisized, and developed the antibodies against expansion of capitalism. They can avoid disintegration, deculturation, and alienation. The weak ones are the more isolated communities, which could not resist the rapid expansion of capitalism that occurred in Peru in the 1940s through the 1970s, and virtually disappeared. Illustrating this dichotomy in the novel with the cases of Lahuaymarca and Paraybamba, Arguedas accurately portrays the liveliness of a strong community like Lahuaymarca. He also projects a hopeful story of rebirth for weak communities like Paraybamba.

Lahuaymarca works as a community because it guarantees its own self-subsistence and self-reproduction in a material and symbolic sense: it, literally, works. It has land, resists the attempts to usurp this land, produces leaders, and plays a political role in the region. It educates Demetrio Rendón Willka, the hero of the novel, with communal contributions.[26] Functionality of community depends on internal coherence and on its capacity to face violent confrontations with the old-time landowners of San Pedro and industrialists who want to use the Indians as a cheap labor force in the mine.

Faena, a ritualized kind of work done for free for the benefit of the community, is the cornerstone of this communality. On the basis of this ritualized work, Rendón Willka, when appointed overseer in the mine, manages to ensure that the mine does minimum damage to his fellow Indians while collaborating with Don Fermín on his, Rendón's, terms. Far from becoming alienated proletarians driven by an abusive overseer, Rendón and the Indians form a horizontal communality, where Rendón's authority rests on his status as a *varayok'*, a staff-bearing indigenous authority. The work in faena is conceptualized as a competition with a purpose of showing one's dexterity, remunerated not with money but with admiration of the fellow workers.[27] These fellow workers, we should add, have something else in common: the sense of belonging to a community, which in turn gives them strength to work and saves them from sinking into sad drunkenness.

The Indians' work inspires admiration among the skilled workers of the mine, as they comment, that if one works with the Indians' attitude, work ceases to be martyrdom.[28]

This conception of work is reinforced with the numerous references to the Indian concept of life after death, where positively experienced work continues to occupy center stage. The dead Indians go up the mountain K'oropata, where they build an endless fortress under the supervision of Saint Francis. Afterlife is not an inverse of earthly existence, as in Christian beliefs, but the continuation of physical life, the meaning of which is entirely dependent on work for the benefit of the community. Arguedas's anthropological study on post-Hispanic Quechua myths testifies to the predominance of this conception of afterlife in the Quechua worldview, and even the name of the mountain K'oropata echoes the name of the mountain Q'oropuna, where the dead go in Puquio's ethnographically recorded myth.[29]

More recent ethnographic and anthropological studies reinforce Arguedas's findings. Sharon Kaufman and Lynn Morgan, in their survey of classical and recent anthropology of the beginnings and ends of life, document how the different cultures conceptualize the moment when life ends, which is largely determined by this society's concept of what happens to someone after the physical death of the body.[30] More locally specific, in his study on the meaning of death in the Andean *cosmovisión* (a term, as we mentioned in the introduction, that could be translated either as "philosophy" or "worldview"), Víctor Bascopé Caero underlines the difference that separates the view of afterlife in a Quechua ayllu of Cochabamba, as compared to more urban or mestizo sectors of Bolivian society. He says, specifically, that in Andean communities death is considered to be a part of life and is not regarded as a tragedy but, instead, as an important conclusion and culmination of an individual's life on earth. Death of the physical body is not a definite ending but a continuity of being within the "universal totality." For instance, after physical death it is believed that the person resides among the physical, geographical community of the ayllu for another three years and then moves on to reside in a wider geographical terrain.[31] This ethnographically documented concept of afterlife is represented and explained in the novel and determines the way Indians live earthly existence and how they manage the social reality that surrounds them.

According to Nancy's theory of finitude, this picture of the Indian community of the living and the dead is a vision akin to an essential community, since the Indians are not hard materialists and indeed believe in life after death. Nonetheless, this Andean idea is different from that of the Christian tradition of thought on death and life after death, which is necessary to obtain true essentialism. The Christian worldview imagines a reality beyond reality, where the essence of the community endures, subtracted from the erosion of time. Besides, it sees death as a passage from an unimportant, temporary earthly existence to the truly important eternity, a philosophical position that has very concrete consequences on how a person might choose to live his or her life. As we will see illustrated in what follows, the indigenous idea of life after death does not establish this type of hierarchy between history and eternity, between this life and the next one. This is the key difference between the two worldviews, which has very concrete practical and political implications.

The concept of "work of death," of sacrifice for the community as the ultimate obligation to make a "voluntary gift," does not function in the Indians' vision of afterlife as it does in Nancy's analysis of the nationalist rhetoric. In the Indians' worldview, as represented in *Todas las sangres,* neither is death understood as sacrifice, nor is the afterlife seen as a reward or punishment for earthly existence, nor as a sort of deposit of the timeless values of the community. At the moment of their death, the Indians simply move from one neighborhood to another, from the valley to the top of the mountain. The dead Indians do not become subsumed into the body of an imagined community but, instead, remain as atomized singularities even after having crossed the threshold of death. It is true that working their land and building for the benefit of community is the type of work that cements the community. But death itself, the passage, does not emerge as work. Work *in* death, or the fact that the dead continue working just as when they were alive, turns out to be quite different from what Nancy calls the work *of* death.

The vision of work *in* the afterlife underpins the Quechua conception of work not as martyrdom or sacrifice, as it is for the non-Indian workers but the substance of existence itself.[32] We must note that either in the ritualized work mode of faena (in this life) or in the building of the endless fortress (in the afterlife), work is not just the means but also an end in itself. The surplus this work produces is the political substance of the ayllu: the individual subjectivities and the communality. First, without dissolving the singularity of each Indian, work becomes a site where each Indian shows off his or her dexterity in front of fellow Indians. Second, work produces a sense of belonging to the community itself, in what can be called a *horizontal destitution,*[33] conceptualized positively in Arguedas, contrary to the negative meaning of the word "destitution" in English. Namely, in the concept of ayllu that *Todas las sangres* puts forward, all the Indians are poor and all of them are working. They all, ideally, progress together and do not come to know the individual ambition. Work, the substance of existence, is the very source of their happiness, and neither Indians nor their leaders want or try to avoid working. This is one of the reasons why the relationship between Rendón Willka, the other indigenous authorities, and the rest of the Indians remains always horizontal and not abusive, unlike what we witness in the case of the non-Indian representatives and officials. The second practical reason is the rotational nature of the ayllu government, where the members of the community by turns fulfill leadership roles.[34] By having very present the perspective of the afterlife and being alert to a possible sudden death, the consciousness of the ultimate equality between all the Indians is preserved, independently of who is serving as a temporary authority. The community is conceptualized as giver of birth and death to each member, and the knowledge of this fact is made present in the everyday work routine through the incorporation of the ritual aspects of the faena. Arguedas emphasizes the parallel nature of the ritual of work and burial by describing the two painstakingly throughout the novel and emphasizing the inclusive and participative aspects of these events. As a result, to put it in Nancy's terms, each Indian is constantly conscious of his finitude, always reminded that community is the giver of his birth and death. The behavior of the Indian varayok's, the staff-bearing authorities, illustrates this particular mode of relation between each individual and the community.

Communal authority of the staff-bearers works in Lahuaymarca as a protective shield in the face of outside forces, using the mechanism we call "deferring authority." Melisa Moore makes a similar observation, although without developing it further, stating that it is the ayllu that allows the Indians to elude or to delay the authority of the state.[35] Different concepts of subjectivity clash when ayllu meets the state and not only the state but also the aristocrats of San Pedro or the engineer Cabrejos—that is, anyone incapable of imagining subjectivity outside strict individuality. Thanks to the conceptualization of subjectivity laden with conscience of finitude, the varayok's establish a horizontal relationship with the other members of the community, a relationship that functions outside of the model of political representation. Because of this conceptual shift, the staff-bearers escape the pitfalls of mediation and uncertain relation with the electorate that the representational model implies. They also avoid the temptations of abuse of power, which befall all the non-Indian authorities in the novel, like the *subprefecto* or the non-Indian town mayor. The staff-bearers lead a communal council, where every member of the ayllu is present in a continuous exercise of direct democracy. The council orders the ayllu internally and protects it from the mining company's encroachments. This protective mechanism of deferment surfaces in this exchange between the ruthless engineer Cabrejos and Rendón Willka:

"You are in charge of the Indians?"

"You knowing, master. Don Bruno is in charge of the Indians of the hacienda, also in their souls. The council is in charge of the Indians of Lahuaymarca."[36]

In Rendón's response we read a negation of personal, individual merit and responsibility, characteristics that Cabrejos expects to find in him as a representative and a leader of the Indians. Confused by this response, engineer Cabrejos concludes that Rendón is not, in fact, anyone's representative or caudillo, and therefore must be politically innocuous. Rendón is able to deflect the authority behind his actions to the communal authority—an abstract notion, at the end—thus rendering his own person insignificant in the eyes of his opponents, which opens up a space for his political activity.

Let us not fall into the trap Rendón sets up for Cabrejos and his other enemies: It is not that he creates a sort of persona that covers up his true doings, fundamentally different from what he shows to the outside. Neither is he a sort of savvy impostor who poses as an Indian when really he is not. Rendón's response that he does not have a right to order can be read as a lie by Cabrejos, as we confirm that Demetrio's personal activities influenced the Indians' mobilization. Specifically, we learn that Rendón's educational activity opened the serfs' eyes to the fact that existence without lords and overseers is a real possibility. Toward the end of the novel, a nameless liberated serf of cruel landowner Don Lucas declares that his fellow serfs are organized and know how to self-govern now that their old master is dead: "We will harvest, we will take care of it. Don Demetrio has taught us, and also his delegates."[37] And yet, to teach (*enseñar*) someone how to harvest is quite different from ordering or being in charge of someone (*mandar*). We see Rendón repeatedly in a council with other indigenous authorities in Lahuaymarca, other ayllus, and in the mine.[38] He certainly brings back from Lima certain conceptual resources, which he shares with the other indigenous authorities. But if "mandar" means an authoritarian kind of power, concentrated in the hands of one individual, then there is no textual evidence of Rendón acting as a person ordering the Indians. "Guiding" could be a more appropriate word, but neither Cabrejos nor the Peruvian police are interested in these subtleties, and the only thing they eventually come to believe is that Rendón organizes the Indian resistance in some way they do not understand since he is neither a delegate nor a representative nor an authoritarian caudillo. What, then, is he? Positively, we can interpret Rendón's response as a declaration of the limits of his power due to the concept of subjective finitude operative in the Indian community. The subjectivity of a staff-bearing authority like Rendón is inextricably linked to the experience of community, and consequently his relationship with the rest of the community members is articulated very differently from the Western model of political representation.

As I mentioned in chapter 1, Giorgio Agamben suggests that the concept of authority has practically disappeared from the Westernized world,[39] where everything this concept had to offer is assimilated into the notion of authoritarianism. On the contrary, the principle of authority is still active in the Indian community. In fact, the authority of the varayok' can be understood better through Agamben's etymological exploration of the term "authority" than through the Western idea of representation. In Roman private law, *auctoritas* was an institution that meant to "augment," in the sense of giving a legal dimension to the actions of a minor. The head of a household gave a legal and public dimension to the actions of the members of his house, the dimension that their actions lacked without this mediation. In this sense, the authority of the varayok' relates to the community much as a paterfamilias is related to those belonging to his household. The application of the concept of the Roman private law to the Indian community is revealing in itself as it suggests that within the Indian community the separation between the public and the private sphere does not work in the Western sense, as I observed at length in chapter 1.

The "shield-like" quality of the varayok's' authority goes beyond Rendón Willka. In another scene, the (importantly) nameless characters of the varayok's of Lahuaymarca announce to the impoverished non-Indian townspeople of San Pedro that the Indians will not work for less than two soles a workday. The townspeople protest, but it is beyond the varayok's purview to change the decision, because it is "the decision of the common council."[40] The San Pedro whites feel powerless and decide to torture the oldest varayok's. The Indians reply that torture does not matter because they cannot change the decision of the ayllu. Here we see the varayok's employ a method similar to Rendón's in his conversation with Cabrejos: the individual person does not take responsibility for a decision when confronted with an outside adversary, emphasizing the function of their individuality as a mere extension of the communal will, which cannot be changed in the absence of the entire and direct presence of that community. The structural differences between the Western and indigenous models of government prove functional as weapons of resistance because non-Indians do not understand the possibility of this kind of authority and do not know how to deal with it.

We should underline that the indigenous relation with their authority is not a model based on representation at all. The varayok's perform as representatives when they talk to the agents foreign to the indigenous community, as if translating the indigenous mode of operation to the outside. But the freedom of their decision is curbed when they are delegated to the outside of the community. They are mere carriers of the decisions but not their makers. Nancy's consciousness of finitude is not only present here tangibly but is also brought to its logical, everyday consequence in the practical behavior of the varayok's. They seem to remember at every moment of exercise of their authority that it is the community that gives them their birth, their death, and—here is the Andean addendum to Nancy's initial proposal—their power to deliver a communal decision and to work as translators between the Indian community and the outside.

The Indian community members do not pass over their authority to the varayok's as the voters do with a representative, and yet the authority is infused in the varayok's. The five men, when defending the community's right to salary, speak the community's will while standing in front of the general assembly of the Indians, the town whites and mestizos, but they do not have the power of decision for the community when far away from it. Sovereignty over the community is not transferred to them as a part of their status, as in the case of the parliamentary model of representation. To express the same effect through another concept: the fundamental difference is that this altered relationship of representation seems not to affect the subjectivity of the representing subject as it happens in the case of state institutions in the novel, such as the courts or the police. Even though staff-bearers are the chosen authorities—for their experience or age or status—there is still a debt to the community that engages the limit of their existence. Despite the varayok's authority-infused status, in order to agree on a decision, all of the ayllu must be present.

The difference between the liberal democratic model of representation and the one operative in the indigenous community represented in *Todas las sangres* can be further explained if we think, following Ernesto Laclau, that in modern parliamentary societies representation is never a reflection but is a reciprocal action through which the leader both represents and informs the body of represented people. This setup yields the freedom of manifestation and decision of the leader, and less so of the people. In the case of the Indians, the indigenous authorities' freedom is curtailed, in part, precisely by the absence of a discourse on the individual, self-sufficient subject. Consequently, the subjectivities of the varayok's do not acquire the excess of empowerment, as in the parliamentary representation model. This emerges as the key reason why the indigenous authority appears as the only dignified and unvillified instance of power on the pages of the Arguedean novel.

Now we must ask if the Andean alternative singularity, born from a particular relationship with the afterlife as represented in the vision of K'oropata, engenders a model of relationship with the authorities that could work in a larger, unessential community. In other words, what can the attitude of Arguedean Indians offer on the theoertical plane? This contribution is at least twofold. Shockingly for the reader, and in the words of the five Indian elderly varayok's, for them "torture does not matter" when they defend the decision of their community. Their courage in the face of a danger to their individual person is practically infinite. So, first, the authority and integrity of the varayok's depend on individual valor when it comes to the threat to the physical self.

The second contribution has to do with the consciousness of experience that conceptualizes itself as the radical opposite of representation. Let us remember the words of Don Bruno, who identifies completely with the Indians' conceptual universe: "The Indians do not stage farce. I do not stage farce. We live and we die!"[41] In this declaration, pronounced by the majestic Bruno, we read the defense of the elaborate traditional ritual of Indian burial, which is being performed to give Bruno's mother, Doña Rosario, access to the Indians' community in the afterlife. This burial, naturally, appalls both the traditional aristocracy of San Pedro and all the new social actors who favor social ascension. Doña Rosario's descent to the Indian universe signals the movement *opposite* to the one that the progress-oriented Fermín envisions for himself, his family, and Peru. But for the Indians and for Bruno, "to live and to die," enacted in the ritual, stands in radical opposition to "staging farce," or staging of any kind. "To live and to die," here, is the positively marked, meaningful pole, while "staging" marks its meaningless counterpart. Keeping in mind that Jürgen Habermas traces the concept of representation to its origins as a theatrical representation, Bruno's rejection of the "farce" extends to the political conception of this category. Living and dying, for Bruno and Rendón, are the real thing, while playing a good delegate (or "representing") is a comedy. Bruno defends the Indians' rituals, contrasting them radically with the new rituals of the representative state, which is trying to gain ground in the sierra. Burial, just like work, is thus not an act of representation for the Indians and Bruno but the very essence of experience, insofar as it is an effective political action of building a community. On the opposite side, for Bruno, the phantasmal authorities of the new order with his own brother Fermín as their leader, are the ones who "stage farce," trick the highland people, and brandish their power marked by a complete lack of legitimacy.

The varayok's, Rendón, and Bruno declare a similar attitude to pain and death. It is not a glorious relation. K'oropata, the mountain where the dead keep on working eternally, is not an object of desire: it is not a radical betterment of one's earthly existence nor a hellish vision. It is not that one has to offer one's death as a gift to the community, because the community does not really need it; in fact, the community will do everything possible to avoid it. In a parallel example outside of the fictional universe, Carlos Ivan Degregori shows in his study of the indigenous communities' experience of facing the Sendero Luminoso in the early 1980s, that the Sendero's tendency to punish the thieves and adulterers with death was where the indigenous peasants drew the limit of their acceptance of Sendero. "Punish, but do not kill" was their proposal to the guerrilla, because, in an economically precarious community, every person capable of working *in this life* is very valuable for communuity as a whole. "Who will take care of their families?," the peasants asked when opposing Sendero's extreme violence that undermined the very subsistence of their precarious economies.[42]

But when the death arrives, the community has to aid its members in death through a ritual that ensures that one will arrive at the top of the mountain K'oropata. Finitude of the Andean subject, as we see it emerging in the novel, does not refer to the fact that activity and life stops after an individual dies. Rather, in a sense very strictly tied to Nancy's original definition, finitude in the Andes refers to the necessity of the direct and clear bond between an individual singularity and community. Only then can the transitional moments of birth and death be made functional. Only then, in the Quechua worldview, can the dead offer help to the community of the living Indians, which is the only surplus that community gains from death in this vision of the afterlife.

In *Todas las sangres,* the dead participate in the communal rituals, as when the dead youths are remembered during the harvest ritual. In the words of the narrative voice in the novel, "in this manner, in the *k'achua* hymn they remembered the young men who died over the past year, they paid homage to them and made them participate in the celebration."[43] The ritualized work on earth reincorporates the dead so as to make the living community stronger, while the ritualized work in the afterlife builds a bridge that connects them to the living. On K'oropata, the dead even have days off to help out the loved ones when they are in trouble. The dead, along with the mountain spirits, the Apus, also participate in the election of authorities and help Adrian K'oto in his inquiry about the immediate future. We could say that the living Indians work and the dead Indians work, and both do so for the benefit of community.

Manifestly absent from this picture is what Jean-Luc Nancy loathes in the concept of "work of death," namely, the sacrifice at the moment of death itself, or the transformation of the whole life experience into sacrifice. Nancy denounces that in the Western philosophical tradition, the possibility of the community's creation is contingent upon the sacrificial deaths of the community's martyrs, especially embodied in the dead soldiers. This is the case in the formula "they died for their country," where the maximum realization of an individual, a soldier in the particular case, is death for the sake of a community, and where death is seen as work—the work of building a community. Jonathan Sheehan, in his study of sacrifice before the secularization process of European modernity, shows that the idea of personal secular sacrifice as a work of building a community is not new but was present as early as Greek and Roman historiography, which praised the heroic death of centurions who inspired their own soldiers to go into a hopeless battle by offering them the example of their own, willed sacrifice.[44] Similar to Nancy, Sheehan criticizes the idea of a sacrifice *demanded* by a modern nation-state of its citizens, emphasizing that a sacrifice—a concept that evolved from religious domain into the secular—needs to be an act of free will in order to carry the moral weight associated with this concept.[45] As Sheehan summarizes this critique, "the free and subjective choices in honoring their God are reoriented toward the nation, which now monopolized claims on virtue. This is the most malignant face of secularization, where sacrifice sits gnomelike inside the machinery of the modern state, secretly choreographing its violence."[46] Nancy's analysis (from the philosophical perspective) and Sheehan's (with a more historical take on the same issue) lead us to conclude that the logic of sacrifice has been perverted in modernity, and as a consequence Nancy calls to end sacrifice altogether, as a practice and as a possible horizon of expectation.[47]

The ethnographical studies and *Todas las sangres* show that the Quechuas' conception of afterlife and, consequently, their attitude regarding the moment of death—either violent or from natural causes—does not reflect this harmful demand for personal sacrifice derided by Nancy. As a consequence, the moment of death is only a necessary passage, given to the singularity by the community, but it is not seen as work demanded by or useful to the community. Instead, the ritual incorporation of the dead youths in the community of working Indians through k'achua hymns works as an alternative community-building mechanism to the demanded sacrifice. The ritual of memory and mourning, practiced by the singing of these hymns, actively brings to the fore, for the living

Indians singing the hymns, the consciousness of one's own physical vulnerability and dependence upon others at the moment of one's birth and
death. Judith Butler suggests that a community built on the activation
of this consciousness is one that is more likely to avoid the principle of
domination.[48] This is so because at the moment we realize the vulnerability and mortality of our own physical body in this body's inevitable
dependence on others, we recognize that the other is sharing the same
condition. Thus, the ritual incorporation of the dead in the community
emerges in the scenes described in the novel as an effective and potentially more egalitarian alternative to the logic of demanded—and thus,
devalued—self-sacrifice.

As in the case of the elderly varayok's, the Indians in the novel demonstrate the consciousness of their own finitude not only in their vision
of afterlife but also in their attitude to physical pain.[49] The Indians do not
react visibly to physical abuse: they do not flinch at inflicted pain and they
certainly do not complain vocally. This attitude is hardly understood by the
non-Indian onlookers. Various textual examples manifest this particular
relationship with the body, which is common to all Indians in the novel:
the nameless mass of workers, the varayok's, and the hero Rendón Willka.
Adrian K'oto, the elected leader (*cabecilla*) of Bruno's serfs, demonstrates
this attitude toward pain as he speaks to his lord: "if you spill my blood
here, master, with these red flowers that cover the ground it would not
even be noticed."[50] The narrative voice of the novel becomes obsessed by
the motif of the Indians' apparent insensibility, repeated in the opinions of
the characters of every strata of society, from the San Pedro townspeople,
to the workers, to the narrative voice itself.[51] The mine workers first call the
Indians "beasts" for performing the hardest work for free. The narrative
voice describes the "Indian mass" when they listen to the orders of their
master, "as if for real they had dry clay instead of soul."[52] When adolescent Rendón silently walks away after being flagellated at school, blood
dripping from his head and back, one of his persecutors comments: "It is
like we have not done anything to him. . . . It is like blood is not blood for
them."[53] Never does the narrative voice say, "it looked like it did not hurt,
but really it hurt badly, and he had to bear it." The text suggests, though,
that the capacity to bear this suffering is contingent upon the functionality
of the community: the varayok's can bear physical pain and survive a near-
death experience on the torture instrument called "the rack" (*la barra*)
because they have a clear relationship with the community.

Rendón Willka and the Dialectics of Finitude and Self-Sacrifice

Rendón's death exemplifies the finitude-attitude as it is born from the Andean categories of individuality and community, which do not conceptualize death as work of building a community. At the same time, we must acknowledge that Rendón does make his own personal death experience into a political action.[54]

First and foremost, Rendón's death is an exercise in the consciousness of finitude that stages the inextricable link that connects Rendón to his ayllu. This is the key moment where we read the novel's theoretical contribution to rethinking the metaphysics of the subject from the point of view of the Andean conceptual universe and which is in tune with Nancy's proposal. Second, Rendón's death is staged as martyrdom, a sacrifice, which promises unification through debts to be canceled, as in García Linera's theorization, the position exactly opposite to Nancy's option. Third, Rendón's death evokes the deaths of the Indians in the colonial holocaust and reactivates the myth of the leader Willka, placed in the "dynasty" from Túpac Amaru to Túpac Kathari.

It could be said that this death is a cleavage between the past and the future: while reactivating the colonial myth of resistance, it also consolidates the unity of the Indian community, from which they might place demands on the emerging state. Besides, in the declaration before his death, that the "Indians have come to know fatherland," Rendón expresses that the Indians, to a certain degree, recognize the state. This is real news in the novel because throughout the novel the Indians manifest a frank ignorance of and indifference to the state and its authorities—the attitude most intolerable for a discourse on national unity. Our next question must be the following: if the Indians, in Rendón's words, "have come to know fatherland," has the fatherland Peru come to know the Indians? To rephrase this question in terms of Gayatri Chakravorty Spivak's seminal question, if the subaltern even begins to speak, will the state be able to listen and hear? The firing squad seems to suggest otherwise. In terms of our conceptual discussion, the essential community of the nation continues to be deadly, as it wants to eliminate any alternative form of political subjectivity and sovereignty on its territory. The Indians' proposition, a pendulum between the essential small community of reduced sovereignty and a larger kind of being-in-common hinged on a nonessential alliance, remains misunderstood by the state that pretends to absolute hegemony. The concept "fatherland" is, in fact, modified by the Indians' nonessential, contingent experience shared with Fermín and the workers. The state cannot understand the scenario where the Indians meet the fatherland—as they see it—through the work of the mine because it is a nonessential, different kind of fatherland. The only "mediator" between these two conflicting propositions and two understandings of the elusive "fatherland" are bullets, which eliminate one of the contending parts of the equation.

In Rendón Willka's discourse, the possibility of imagining this layered model of being-in-common stems from his double conceptual system, which combines the precepts of the Western tradition of thought and the Andean conception of community. As we saw above, for the Indians the vision of afterlife is a direct transposition of earthly life onto the mountain K'oropata, where the dead Indians work and sleep as they did in their earthly existence. The only difference is that there are no lords in the afterlife, with the exception of Saint Francis as their overseer, and there are no profits to be gained, and therefore all the work is done in the ritualized mode of faena. On the surface, we might say that this is one of the sides of Rendón Willka's attitude toward death, of his double logic. His tranquil attitude is due to the indigenous concept of the afterlife that sees life as a continuation of earthly existence, as opposed to the Christian vision of an opportunity for punishment or reward, or a senseless void offered by a strictly secular discourse. Nonetheless, a careful reader will observe that Rendón has distanced himself from the indigenous belief in the afterlife. This becomes evident in his reply to Anto at the very beginning of the novel: "The dead guy is the dead guy, dear old Anto. The sparrow sings for those who are alive."[55]

But although Rendón does not see himself working on K'oropata after his own death, his belief in the role of the community in giving the individual his birth and his death does not dwindle because of this. His belief in this power of community becomes evident in his solemn participation in the ritual of Doña Rosario's burial, side by side with Don Bruno, as they both act as leaders of the Indian community, performing the ritual for Bruno's dead mother.[56] Rendón might not believe in life after death for himself, but he acutely senses the social implications of his fellow Indians' profound belief in it. Rendón's ability to say to Don Fermín, "death exists" ("¡Está bien, patrón! Muerte existe"),[57] meaning "I will die shortly, but I am not afraid of death or of what awaits me after it," stems from the realization of the role of the community in the rite of passage from the "neighborhood" of the living to that of the dead.

The other Indians' attitude toward death is best captured in the words of Adrian K'oto, the leader of the serfs in Bruno's hacienda:

> Nothing matters. . . . We do not come to know His will [of the Christian God]; but death is sadder for His children than for us. Sadder. That is why, when higher up in the mountains, or in the fire of the valleys where they send us by turns to work[58] for other masters, our vein extinguishes in silence. They die, it seems, without solace. They do not know, neither their fathers, nor their sons, neither the big priest, nor the little priest, where they go after their breath ceases. The Father Pukasira is going to be at the big council. He takes in every one of his sons, either dead or alive.[59]

K'oto distinguishes between the death experience of the non-Indians, who die "without solace," and an Indian's death, "in silence," in peace. The fact that the mountain Pukasira takes in any one of his sons, whether they are dead or alive, good or bad, shows that death is countered by the belief in continuity of the community. The certain knowledge of the Indians about their posthumous destiny is contrasted with the non-Indians' existentialist void. This is important since the contrary topic of Indians' not-knowledge often surfaces in this novel and in Arguedas's other writings.[60] For example, Don Bruno's serfs cry at Doña Rosario's and Gregorio's burial as the narrative voice comments that they "do not know why they cry." At these two burials, it seems that the non-Indians' orphanlike metaphysical emptiness that surfaces in the face of death reminds the Indian serfs of their own miserable situation in *this* life. In an oblique explanation, one of the serfs says that he cries because he has not even a dog of his own, since everything belongs to Don Bruno.[61] The serfs do not cry about their metaphysics, as Fermín's wife Matilde does at Gregorio's burial, but about the very physical misery of their existence. They do not worry about the afterlife, and therefore can concentrate on their finite, here and now existence.

It is difficult to distill Rendón's position on metaphysics, because his discourse is ambiguous and changing, and his declarations enter into a sort of dialectical opposition to one another. On the one hand, he mocks the indigenous holistic view of this world where the birds, the animals, and the trees send out signs to men so as to reveal their destiny. Although he sees that the sun shines on a feather of a flying falcon, he only seems to appreciate it aesthetically. Saying to Anto, "we see the same thing, but we understand it differently,"[62] Rendón distances himself from this worldview. But he is not blind to the worldly implications of those rituals and signs, and also knows how to linguistically and behaviorally operate within their semantic universe.

Metaphysics have to do with the unchanging and the eternal, which often spells out the question of divinity. Rendón evokes God ("Dios," with a capital letter, as Arguedas spells the Christian deity) when he talks to Cabrejos. Let us hear Rendón's response when Cabrejos, smartly enough, doubts Demetrio's sincerity as the hero mentions "Dios." Rendón replies, speaking about his own self in the third person, "Just an Indian from an ayllu, Rendón does not need money-poison, money that is not from work, that is not from God. . . . When clean is the money of persons, that is when (*ahistá*), I reckon, is God; there and then (*ahí*) the heart rejoices. When it is not clean, the dark beats the breast on its inside, the breast where God is nurtured."[63] Even written with the capital *D,* it is definitely not Don Bruno's punishing Christian God, the transcendental signifier that gives meaning to the entire system of values. In the first part of the sentence, the Spanish deictic of place and time, *ahistá,* points out that the God is "where there is clean money of persons." In this part of his declaration, Rendón locates the existence of God in "clean money," in other words, in communal work that does not yield personal profits and does not harm others. In the second part of his statement, God is "nurtured" (*se cría*) in Rendón's chest and seems to be a concept that refers to Rendón's personal consciousness. It is not an all-powerful deity; either in its exterior manifestation as the good that comes out of immanent work, or as a consciousness of Demetrio's finite person, it is a god of finitude. This deity teaches Rendón to remain true to his own self as he negotiates between the different subjectivities and sovereignties. Demetrio's god revealed to Cabrejos and the reader in this statement opens a window for the concept of personal finitude, which brings about a personal responsibility and sacrifice. If K'oto, when talking of death, speaks not about himself but about Indians in general—"the mountain Pukasira takes in all of us, the Indians"—Demetrio here refers to his own option and destiny. The conceptual place of Demetrio's personal position is in the dialectic between communal and individual subjectivity, and because of that Rendón Willka is the only character able to switch from one sovereign framework to the other and remain operative in both. Understanding his finitude, but profoundly aware of the community-oriented meaning of rituals, Rendón goes from one political space to the other and stays true to himself. This provides the key to his elusive political positioning through the novel, one of the sites where the Andean theory of nonessential community is born.

Rendón does not fear the experience of death itself, "the passage," so to speak, or the pain that the moment of death implies. As mentioned in reference to his school-going experience, he does not fear pain, just like the other Indians in the novel. This valor has nothing to do with his relation to any deity but with certain rules of conduct; that is, you do not show that you suffer to those who are incapable of feeling anything for you. Demetrio's attitude toward the afterlife is the other facet of the same problem. As we have seen from his comment to Anto, Rendón does not believe in life after death, unlike the Indians who never left the sierra (Adrian K'oto or Anto). For him there is no mountain K'oropata, nor "salvation" as there is for Bruno, but "just the good earth" ("tierrita no mas").[64] And, as for god, we just saw that Rendón's deity is finite and its home is, ambiguously, in the value of the "clean money" that comes from communal work in its relationship to the community, and in Rendón's chest when dealing with Rendón's individualized subjectivity.

His valor in the face of death is complemented by his capacity to self-sacrifice. But "sacrifice" returns us to a rigid conceptualization of community of death. Maybe we should say, much less compactly, "his ability to die bravely when the state gets him, and when his organizational labor is complete"? Rendón says that he can die (it almost sounds like "he can allow himself the luxury to be executed") because he sees that the Indian serfs of the hacienda, embodied in one woman, have learned, either from him or from experience, to construct a type of united front in opposition to the oppressive state and to self-govern in the absence of outside authorities. Rendón, literally, thinks, "Now they can execute me. It does not matter!" ("Ya pueden fusilarme. ¡No importa!").[65] This statement matters very much indeed. Rendón does not look for recognition as a hero or for immortality in a guaranteed life after death. He is simply satisfied with the fruits of the labor of his earthly, finite existence.

The already mentioned other occasion when Rendón demonstrates this attitude is when Fermín threatens Demetrio with a gun and he calmly comments, "All good, master. Death exists."[66] Death does not promise anything "on the other side," and yet, it is "all right"—it can almost be celebrated. What is it, then, on "this side"? Let us try to read the answer in Rendón's last words, directed to the captain who will execute him momentarily:

> Captain! Captain sir! . . . Here, now, in these villages and haciendas, only the big trees cry. The rifles will neither extinguish the sun, nor dry the rivers, and even less take the life of all the Indians. Keep on shooting. We do not have factory weapons, which do not count. Our heart is of fire. Here, and everywhere! We have finally come to know fatherland. And you, sir, will not kill fatherland. There it is; it looks dead. No! The pisonay-tree is crying, and will spill its flowers for eternity of eternities, growing. Now from pain, tomorrow from happiness. The factory rifle is deaf, it is like a log; it does not

understand. We are men who will live forever. If you want, if it suits you, give me the tiny death, the little death, captain![67]

Rendón establishes a complex chain of associations between nature (sun, rivers), the Indians, and the fatherland. The Indians, representing the origins of the nation, are not relegated to their Incan past; they are alive "here and now," and will "live eternally." Demetrio's "little death" does not matter, because the "we"—Indians? Peruvians?—will live after his death. This interpretation is clearly full of tropes of romantic discourse that lie at the foundation of Latin American nationalism: landscape, territory, and homeland, and ultimately, transcendence. However, Rendón's references are not only rooted in this tradition but also in the indigenous Andean philosophy. This world view is characterized by what the Bolivian philosopher Jorge Miranda-Luizaga calls the "holistic vision" that sees humanity as part of a spatial-temporal unity that includes the human, mineral, animal, and astronomical phenomena, always tied to an experience of a specific geographical region.[68] While speaking of his own death and of survival of community, Rendón explicitly evokes the connection between the "we" of the Indians who will live forever, just as the "sun" will shine forever, unreachable by the abusive power wielded by the soldiers. In terms of time, Miranda-Luizaga also points to what he calls the "a-chronical cyclicity" of the Andean conception of time, which sees every event, including the material death of a person, as a part of a cycle of death and rebirth.[69] The temporality of this cycle is "a-chronical" because it is impossible to measure it with precision. In Rendón's speech, the cyclical vision is expressed when he says, "it looks dead" (I imagine him pointing at the executed woman's body when he says that) and then immediately denies the definitiveness of the woman's (and fatherland's) death with a forceful "no!" The pisonay tree also embodies the cyclical nature of death and rebirth as reflected in the hyperbolic image of infinite blooming and shedding of red flowers. The tree is indifferent to "pain" or "happiness," which come cyclically between "today and tomorrow." This mirrors one of the main arguments of this charged speech, namely, the unimportance of Rendón's "little death" in the face of the persistence of the indigenous community.

But now we must read closely the lineal temporality of Rendón's final manifesto, which works alongside the Andean motif of cyclical time. What is the meaning of "here, now," "finally," and "already"? The "here" is the Peruvian sierra and the "now" is contemporary Peru. But what is so fundamentally different at the moment presented in *Todas las sangres*? The key is the moment when Rendón decides to die: "Demetrio was listening to the woman's responses with a tranquil joy. Now they can execute me. It does not matter already!—he thought."[70] Here, the "already" again appears in the hero's thoughts. In this fragment it seems to refer to the successful conclusion of his organizational activity. What is there in the replies of the woman that move Rendón to make this decision? First, she replies fearlessly to the soldier: like Rendón before, she is not afraid of pain, or death, or of plain power represented by a soldier with his gun. Second, she negates any political affiliation on the part of the Indians and sends the soldier "to look for Communists elsewhere."[71] Third and most importantly, she negates Rendón Willka's central authority or responsibility for organization of the Indians: "Rendón Willka? His people? He has no people of his own. We are the community Indians; we are all over the hacienda, anywhere."[72] The woman circumvents the concept of a political representation, which would demand that the power be deposited in a leader.[73] Instead, she brings about a notion that we might call a collective subjective agency, which diffuses the responsibility and makes it impossible to disarticulate the indigenous community by killing one or even many of its members. From the pronoun "his" the woman moves straight to a "we" ("we, the Indians of the community"). At the same time, she does refer to the individual Rendón as a legitimate administrator who follows Bruno's orders. Therefore, the responses of the Indian woman suggest that Rendón Willka exists between the two notions of subjectivity, the Western and the indigenous. This straddling position has direct consequences for his ability to negotiate between the two modes of sovereignty at play. By occupying the equivocal position, Rendón personally embodies the prescriptive ideal he proposes. Consequently, in his speech, the "already" can be read as referring to the historical moment when the two kinds of subjectivities can coexist without one eliminating the other. "Finally" refers to the particular historical conjunction when it is possible to be citizens of Peru without ceasing to be Indians. His emphatic "now" of the present refers to the moment when the layered alliances, like Rendón's, become possible, when the ayllu with its agency and singularity can come to know the fatherland Peru, in Rendón's words. This would mean that one might find a place for the indigenous community between the two concepts of subjectivity: an ideal Andean singularity, an Indian, and a citizen at the same time. This proposal would supersede Spivak's verdict about the impossibility for the subaltern to speak. In Rendón's proposition, the subalterns speak while still occupying the culturally distinctive position that marks them as subalterns. More than that, they speak on their own terms.

But it seems that the moment of speech arrives on the verge of, or after, the execution of physical violence against the Indians, who must constantly cope with the arbitrary nature of this violence that falls on them as individuals and as communities. The rage of the old-time lords was arbitrary, but so is the violence executed by the officials of the Peruvian state. The mestizo Bellido, the adolescent Pablo Pumayauri, the Indian woman, and Rendón himself—all are victims of this arbitrariness, falling into the silence of the unanswered question, phrased by the Indian woman executed just minutes after voicing it: "¿Para qué fusilar?": "To execute, for what purpose?"[74] Rendón does not look to give some transcendental meaning to the sacrifices of the dead, which hang in the void like tragic, heroic gestures. This would actually go against his project. Instead, Rendón maximizes the accomplishments of his own earthly existence by the fact that he is not afraid of death and is prepared to meet it when the time comes. Fearless of the consequences for his own, finite, and mortal person, he can complete the organizational task of creating political awareness among the Indians as community.[75] Before the execution, Demetrio understands that it won't matter if he physically dies because the fruits of his elusive work can exist without his finite presence. At this point in the narrative, the Indians' capacity to organize should not be conceptualized as a residue of Rendón's life. It is a product that becomes independent and can persist by itself. Rendón is finished; but, in his own words, it does not matter anymore.

According to Nancy's proposal, a *nonproject* must be based on moving away from the concept of individual subjectivity. With this proposal, Nancy in the France of the 1980s criticizes nationalisms at the moment of decline of the nation-states. In *Todas las sangres,* written at a time when the nation-state was, in effect, an undeniable and desired horizon, Rendón's proclamation deduces a type of national being-in-common that does not annihilate the indigenous community. He, in fact, declares that Indians had come to know the fatherland, that is, Indians wanted to continue existing within the structure of the ayllu, but they also saw national alliances as necessary. The equation between the indigenous people and fatherland would imply the necessity of recognition of their rights as citizens. But let us reiterate the key question we posited above: has the fatherland come to know the Indians? During the entire novel the state tries to either close its eyes or destroy by force the Indians' cultural difference and relative autonomy. The essential fatherland, as represented by its agents the soldiers, wants to know only the de-Indianized Indians, the homogeneous product to be subsumed into a national unity.

When the soldiers kill Rendón Willka, the Peruvian state is shown as a serpent that bites its own tail. The state short-circuits and eliminates the people who place their demands within its own, the state's, logic and rhetoric. In the last section of this chapter we will review the discourses against which Demetrio Rendón Willka constructs his multifaceted vision of layered and unessential community.

The Deadly Communities

The gravest accusation at the roundtable labeled *Todas las sangres* as reactionary, and therefore harmful for Peru. In 1965, the contradiction between "reactionary" and "progressive" positions appeared as a question: Have all the poor been made culturally homogeneous and proletarized yet? The progressive Marxist intellectuals aspired to use what were considered the modern tools of analysis, moving away from the caste system, founding their reflection on strictly economic categories. They desired to show that the Peruvian poor as a culturally homogeneous social group were ready to enter as a working class into the industrialized reality of the modern nation. In *Todas las sangres,* we clearly see this proletarization tendency illustrated: the Quechua-speaking people leave their towns to work in the mine; the impoverished white villagers aspire to do the same and immigrate to Lima to work in factories. The narrative voice of the novel does not present this as something necessarily positive, but it does not present it as negative either. The differential representation of the workers' housing near the mine gives us a picture where the narrative voice confronts developmentalist ideas. It starts by drawing the map of two types of housing, the "corrugated iron houses" ("casas de calamina"), provided by the mine, all squeezed into the actual lot of the town, and the shacks built on the slope of the mountain. While the more de-Indianized, mestizo Spanish-speaking professionals live on the only town street, more recent arrivals, freshly torn from their communities and who all work as unskilled workers, live in the shacks. The narrative voice comments in the following manner on this distribution of the workers in the mining town: "Those in the shacks felt more at ease than the skilled workers of the mining town. Each one had their tree or a bush; those few who took a wife in San Pedro or arrived with their women, built a fence to create a corral where the pasture grew. . . . The skilled workers considered these customs as typical of the Indian, who *is not a worker yet,* and who hardly, if ever, will become a skilled worker. They were blocking their way to promotion by treating them with compassion."[76]

We see heterogeneity even in the mining town, supposedly a "melting pot" where everyone becomes a worker, a proletarian. There is a clear difference between "more indigenous" and "less indigenous" workers, the categories measured by seniority at the workplace and living habits. This manner of distinction suggests that the classification is not rigid and can change with time, as the unskilled workers acquire experience. Nonetheless, we see them discriminated against on the basis of the developmentalist ideas that rule among the maestros of the mining town (and not only among the social scientists of the 1960s). The unskilled workers are despised because their more mestisized colleagues consider that their cultural baggage, like their living habits, will prevent them from being good professionals. But the narrative voice tells us that the more indigenous workers feel more comfortable than their socially superior comrades: they each have a "tree of their own." In other words, however feeble it may be, these unskilled workers construct a sort of feeling of belonging to the land. What is more, to strengthen this image, the narrator mentions that some of them have taken a wife, while the maestros tend to go to prostitutes. In the Quechua and Aymara worldview, this is a very important moment because only in marriage does a person become fully a person and, in the traditional community, can begin to exercise a position of responsibility.[77] It seems that the more indigenous workers make their life more bearable, less "sad," by reenacting in a new, atomized situation the rituals and habits of the communities of which they still have vivid memories. As we see in the quote above, the narrative voice marks these practices positively, but I must emphasize that this does not make the unskilled workers less exploited. In the novel we see many poor people who find themselves between a rock and a hard place, between the old structures of domination that are still operative and the new, impersonal, seductive, and consequently more dangerous structures.

The novel represents rather accurately the historical reality. Theoretically, industrialization should have had a capacity to liberate the Indians from the control of landowners by proletarizing them, guaranteeing a fair salary, and recognizing their rights to citizenship. And yet, historical studies show that, on the contrary, the transnational capital entered into alliances with the local elite on the national and provincial levels.[78] The cooperation between those from above always harmed the indigenous masses and other underprivileged sectors of the population. As we saw above, the novel presents a sort of possibility of a "popular front" of local powerful people and the bases against the transnational capital, but it also speaks up against the sad historical facts of transnational companies' abuse in the sierra, backed up by both local political powers and national government.

The liberating and progressive potential of the mine surfaces in the fear expressed by the cruel landowner Don Lucas as he comments that some of his serfs escape to the mine, and categorizes the mine and the Indians uniformly as his enemies: "For the Indians and the consortiums nothing but ashes!"⁷⁹ Nonetheless, the text reveals that the mine's politically democratizing capacity is phantasmal because there is no relation of representation between the poor masses and the state, and, as we have seen above, the state can hardly move beyond the logic of representation while dealing with its heterogeneous population. In other words, the novel shows that economic advancement by itself will not bring about a healthy democratization of society. Rather, what is needed in order to activate the liberating potential of the salaried labor is a deep restructuring of the political relationship between the state and the persons who populate its territory, both Indians and non-Indians.

The discussion between two of the vilest characters of the novel—a Lima-grown young landowner Aquíles and a nouveau-riche Cisneros—reveals the hard truths about the logic of transnational capital and its effects for a nation like Peru. In their dialogue, we see the prospects for the Indians of the region in the process of modernization and a precise description of the mechanics of globalization. The young Aquíles explains to Cisneros how the modern world works: "The consortiums do not have fatherland . . . but only business; business in Africa, destroying the Negroes; in Asia, killing the yellow people.⁸⁰ . . . Although they bring civilization, they prefer to come to agreement with people like you, who are intent on keeping the old customs. They do not want people to have eyes. It is better if they only obey and pray."⁸¹

And Cisneros summarizes, then: "As you say, they are. . . . An endless chain of heads, of demons that we cannot see, that do not show their face; of the suckers of riches, who, like a spider damned by God, has the world under its belly and craps on the same bread that it eats."⁸² This view of the industrialization and the collectivities it creates definitely does not respond to the great promise of modernization. In Peru, modernization does not produce the dissolution of the old structures but reactualizes them in the new context. The pessimistic, if not apocalyptical, perception of modernization becomes evident in the eschatological and death imagery that dominates the description of the society created by the combined system of domination. The subjects this system needs are "people who do not have eyes," that is to say, the easily exploitable, politically unaware, and uninformed persons. The system itself is an invisible, phantasmal chain with millions of heads that do not show their faces. We see in this description a motif of lack of knowledge, and also of decay and void that marks the individuals and collectivities created in the situation of rapid industrialization. Feces are the only products of this modernization, brought from the outside. The collectivities of the impoverished residents of San Pedro and of the workers of the mine are symbolically defecated upon and trashed by the process of their forced transformation into a commodity, a labor force. This transformation is made possible by the destruction and loss of the communal bonds, which shape complex singularities, like those of Rendón Willka and Don Bruno.

Transnational capital does not want a politically charged singularity connected to the community but a desubjectivized individual,[83] an engineer Cabrejos who obeys any order for money, or a soldier who obeys because "he must" and is held unaccountable for the violence he exercises. In this sense, the transnational capital does not want a community of any sort, and especially it is afraid of the essentialized communities: the nation and the ayllu. This is the reason why the engineer Cabrejos's most articulated rivalry is with Fermín Aragón, the visionary of an essential nationhood, and Rendón Willka, one of whose alliances lies with the essentially constructed ayllu. The models of unaccountable, destitute subjectivity make it impossible to resist the encroachments of the transnational capital. In fact, the novel obsessively portrays different instances of this impossibility, as if working through all the options in order to arrive ad absurdum at one functional construction of the common front of resistance. Following the novel's deductive method, let me consider here the two failed responses to modernization that the novel portrays: the case of the *mistis* of San Pedro and the attempts of resistance through the parties devoted to progressive politics (the Alianza Popular Revolucionaria Americana [APRA] and the Communist Party).

The town of San Pedro is in ruins and has become increasingly dismal due to two factors: the capital of the province has moved to another town and the Aragón family has concentrated all the political and economic power in their hands. The industrialist Fermín plans to make the same use of the indigenous peasants and the old-time small aristocracy by transforming all of them into wage laborers. But it does not quite work this way. The non-Indian townspeople sell out, spying on and provoking the other townsfolk for the benefit of Fermín and the mine and against the interests of the town's community as a whole, but they fail to transform into wage-laborers. The poor white ex-landowners refuse to enter the logic of capital and alienated labor and immigrate to the coast. The last scene of San Pedro as a colonial aristocratic town ("villa de vecinos") is of its burning church, marking its disappearance as a community. They carry this church in their hearts, according to one of the townsmen, but this memory brings only the paralysis of melancholy. The misti San Pedro does not attempt to create anything: it is a ruin buried under the weight of resignation. In this landscape of ruin the readers witness the scene that marks the failure of the Peruvian state.

The judge and the subprefect of the district arrive in San Pedro to announce the law passed by the government concerning the expropriation of land for the benefit of the mine. The townspeople decide to resist the decree, but there is no organization among them, no decisions made, and their actions are random and confused. When the truck with soldiers enters the town, an old mestizo insults the soldiers, and they respond with machine-gun fire that breaks the old man's legs. In the presence of the old man bleeding to death, the townspeople, soldiers, and district officials begin to negotiate. This absurd "negotiation" includes the tocsin played on the church bells; the Indians' testimony in Quechua not being understood by the Spanish-monolingual official; the lieutenant's declaration that he does not think but only obeys orders; and machine-gun fire against the church tower, which silences the bells. The government officials leave the town; the townspeople burn their church and decide to immigrate to Lima so as not to work for the "monster," the mining company. The Peruvian state apparatus proves disjointed and arbitrary; the executive and judicial branch is in absolute disharmony; and the armed forces obey the corrupt, ignorant official who does not know the language of the people he faces. We see a self-devouring nation, impoverishing its own population for the sake of industrialization that extracts natural resources without building the economy. The tocsin that the verger plays on the San Pedro bells tolls not only for San Pedro but also for Peru as a modern nation.

The mining town is another communal formation that resists the theoretical chain of equivalences "industrialization = homogenization = nation-building"—a theory at which Fermín is adept. Although the narrator of *Todas las sangres* in a way sympathizes with this theory, he also has an empiricist imperative to show all the aspects that frustrate its completion. The newly formed community of the mining town is represented in a complex dialectic of loss and transformation. It is a mini-slum of the kind that appeared especially around Lima but also around other industrial centers, where the newly arrived from rural areas settled. The neighborhood around the mine houses many kinds of people. All the regions of Peru are represented here; there are workers who speak Spanish, or Quechua, or both; they listen to traditional Indian music and rock-and-roll; some of them just arrived from their indigenous communities freshly destroyed by famine; some of them are Lima-born mestizos and professional miners.[84] Their work in the mine brings them together. What kind of being-together do these people create and practice in this social situation?

This communality is full of fissures. Ambition and contempt separate the professional workers from their more indigenous comrades. The conversations of the workers show that the strategy that Fermín entertains in his living room—to fire up workers' ambition and weaken their capacity to unite—is working well. The workers try out the leftist party alliances, but instead of uniting them these alliances only produce more dissent. The Communists confront the APRA affiliates; members of both parties a priori despise the Indians as incapable of organization or political action. Camargo, the overseer of the mine, explains to the engineer Cabrejos, "An APRA affiliate prefers his master against a Commie, and vice versa. Let them do politics, it's better for us!"[85] Here, progressive politics is explained from the point of view of corporate interests and ends up being an effective tool for dissipating the organizing potential of the fragmented and weakly articulated Left. The association with the parties of the Left is, in fact, dangerous for any alternative program of resistance, since any action not in line with the modernizing politics of the government is labeled as Communist to justify the persecution of its promoters. The only effective leader of the novel, Rendón Willka, interrogated by Fermín on the meaning of "Communism," comments on the dangerous use of this political term by the repressive forces:

> Communism? There it is, master: you Communist if Rendón kills engineer; Rendón also a Communist; the Misters Orrantías, San Isidros[86] no way Communists; men eating with pigs at the Montón or other slums when they come out to ask for a little bit of food, screaming, there you have Communist! When make hut on nobody's sand slope to find a little shade, there you have Communist! . . . Master, I am no orphan and I know clearly about Communism. Engineer knows, too. With his mouth, with his finger he says: Communist! And right then and there they come to either beat you or to shoot you, accordingly.[87]

Communism, in Rendón's interpretation, only serves as a label to consolidate all resistance to the advancement of capital backed by the state, a term perversely used to create the category of enemy. It is a common pit into which a noncollaborator landowner or his rebellious employee falls if they try to oppose the plans of the engineer, who represents the state-sponsored transnational capital.

There are obvious dangers in alliances with the parties of the Left, but progressive politics do serve one purpose: they raise the workers' consciousness about their condition of exploitation. As a result, they know that alienated work aborts the possibility of creating an effective community. We can see that Palacios, a Communist worker, admires the Indians' approach to work: "If all of us only could work like this. . . . Work would not be a curse. Try to understand that one day we will be like them, one day when we will not be working to make those who exploit us only stronger!"[88] The fascinated "like this" refers to the fact that the Indians' work is not mediated by money and therefore its value is not an exchange value. In fact, its value resides in the work as a communal experience, which cannot be substituted for money. In this revelation glimpsed by Palacios, the reader sees a possibility of resistance to the alienation brought about by industrialization and the logic of capitalist production where everything is exchangeable—both people and things. The textual suggestion here is truly ground-breaking, building on Marxist theory and going beyond it: there is a way to escape alienation, even without having a direct possession of the means of production, but it works by altering the organization of work in the capitalist system, as the Indians do.

This important transformation of the meaning of labor happens by engaging memory as a tool of resistance to exploitation. Memory in *Todas las sangres* manifests itself as mourning for the dead or for dying traditions. It can also be read as a profound historical memory, which positively evokes structures like the ayllu and its modality of ritualized work, in order to oppose the logic of complete substitution without a remainder, which is a characteristic of the capitalist concept of labor. In this sense, memory contributes to developing a vision of community and subjectivities, capable of consolidating a common front against the invasion of transnational capital. Concern with memory, one might say, caused Arguedas the gravest trouble in his discussions with fellow-intellectuals, since *Todas las sangres* has been read as a "social novel," and social novels have nothing to do with remembering. They have to represent the social reality of the present and propose a project for the future of the country. In readings of Arguedas's early novels, many critics concentrate on the aspect of loss and memory, but from *Yawar fiesta* on it seems as if he has abandoned this theme. I would insist that memory work still dominates Arguedas's later narratives, both in *Todas las sangres* and *The Foxes,* and fulfills a theoretical and practical function. Through memory, the Indians remain connected to the communitarian experience, which practically makes the hardships of an Indian worker's life more bearable.

To get insight into how memory works positively in *Todas las sangres,* we should consider the role of memory in the world of commodities. Memory must be disposed of since the market requires new commodities to replace the previous ones. The suppression of memory also aims at forgetting the barbaric origins of the global market. According to Sigmund Freud, a mourner does not want to conclude his task: he resists the substitution proper to the logic of the market because mourning is a process of unproductive work. Either mourning or its counterpart melancholy is, in fact, an equally unproductive process, outside the category of "useful," arguably the chief concept in the logic of production. This consideration inspired my reflection on memory in *Todas las sangres,* despite the fact that the novel does not represent a society ruled by the logic of the market. In the sierra we see a mostly agrarian society with the mining company beginning to introduce industrialization and wage labor into the work relations—the moment when the barbaric origins of the market reveal themselves. As we pointed out at the beginning of this chapter, all of the Arguedean corpus can be read as a lament for the millions of indigenous lives lost in centuries of domination, and *Todas las sangres* is not an exception. We can call it a mourning of "long duration,"[89] so to speak, of historic profundity, because Arguedas mourns victims of centuries-long oppression.

Here we arrive at the postcolonial kernel of Arguedean thought. As José Rabasa points out, postcolonial studies is concerned with the continuities of the colonial pasts in the postcolonial presents.[90] *Todas las sangres* shows that in the mid-twentieth century, colonial structures still persist and still have their victims. Then we must ask: Is it possible to mourn Indians who perished in the rebellions and were forced to work in the mines when thousands of them are still exploited in the mines and shot by Peruvian troops in the suppression of the La Convención rebellion, a year before the publication of *Todas las sangres?* Conversely, if the Indians work as a community and have an attitude toward death such as we discussed above, can we say that the logic of substitution does not work in the Indian community? In other words, how is the Indian community a solution to the problem of the interchangeable unskilled workers who are treated as cheap labor, of less value than machines? In addition, on one hand, we have continuous victimization of Indians. On the other hand, Arguedas seems to reflect on the supposedly disappearing ayllu, which, nonetheless, is still documented there. How can one mourn something that has not disappeared? Where is the loss?

Arguedas's ethnographic data show that ayllu as structure was alive and well; but the most advanced theories of the time insisted that it must disappear sooner or later, for the better future of the Peruvian nation. Besides, many individual communities were, in fact, annihilated with the advance of industrialization. Also, while indigenous resistance as a phenomenon has been a strong tradition since the conquest, the individual combatants of this resistance, victims of colonial and postcolonial violence were dead. We saw the dialectic between the humanistic concept of the individual and a communal subjectivity in our discussion of Rendón Willka's complex subjectivity, the conceptual construct in which Arguedas explores the relation between individuality and community. Arguedas's mourning is also subject to this dialectic and is dedicated to both real and already dead individual Indians and to the supposedly inevitable structural death of the ayllu.[91]

This anticipated lament is for the ayllu's death sentence dictated by developmentalist sociology. But Arguedas was also writing against another kind of ideological opposition: the neoliberal discourse on modernization. From the point of view of this discourse, Arguedas's unwillingness to move on and forget the dead Indians and vanished communities was simply unproductive. The remembrance in *Todas las sangres* becomes a tool of resistance, if only because it signals that there will always be a remainder, a leftover of the old, which cannot be cleanly substituted by the new. As we have seen, for Arguedas the modern Peruvian nation could not be constructed without turning to its historically profound structures like the ayllu. Remembrance, thus, questions the logic of clean substitution of workers (persons), and the ayllu (structures) and counters it with a model where the communality does not dissolve the importance of the individual, which is exemplified by an ayllu working in the ritual modality of faena. The *nonproject* for the wider Peruvian being-in-common envisioned in *Todas las sangres* incorporates this kind of ayllu as part of the Andean singularities that constitute its makeup.

Failure of the Essential Peruvian Nation

What have we learned so far? Cultural and class differences in Peru will not be surpassed by means of forced industrialization. Industrialization will not transform the class-caste of cholos or Indians into a category of a pure class because the cultural residue will not be erased. The logic of representation, on which the workings of the modern state depend, does not function while the indigenous non-representational communality persists. And if this communality disappears, the project of any unity will short-circuit due to its incapacity to create any alternative communalities—neither a nation, nor a working class able to resist international capital, nor an Indian, lost alongside his ayllu.

Todas las sangres does not present a vision of Peru as a modern nation because the reality of Peru in the 1960s was not corresponding with this vision. The novel reveals the positive and negative sides of modernizing and traditionalist standpoints. Progressive politics informs the workers and raises their consciousness but does not forge a unified front against exploiters. Fermín's actions promoting order and progress forges a sort of national popular front, or at least a momentary alliance, against the transnational company, but his actions also contribute to migrations from poor provinces of Peru and thus to the alienation of ex-Indians. On the opposite end, the old-timer Bruno's colonial Christian value system permits him to abuse his serfs—he is repeatedly called an "Indian-eater"—but ultimately drives him to change his position and to contribute to the Indians' prosperity and liberation. We could say that the "choral" construction of the novel[92] helps to find the salvageable parts of various discourses that dialogue in *Todas las sangres*—salvageable for Arguedas's proposition for the future of Peru. The narrative voice of the novel privileges the discourses of characters that guarantee the least damage to the ayllu as structure. But, besides the defense of the ayllu, the narrative voice constructs its alliances around other axes, for example, the negotiation of the ayllu's and individual Indians' place in the nation and the place of the dead Indians and disappeared communities in the national memory. Finally, and of utmost importance, the novel defends Peru's sovereignty in the face of the transnational capital but without canceling out the preoccupation for other communalities and singularities.

Just as Anibal Quijano points out, instead of converting into a working class, people who recently left their indigenous communities developed into a category he calls a "class-caste" of cholos.[93] In Quijano's vision of 1965, those people of emerging identity were on their way to shed the "caste" part of the category. Yet, as Arguedas shows in *Todas las sangres,* the exploited miners are far from escaping from the classification of "caste" because the relations of domination are embedded in their new social position. Thus, the people newly incorporated into the mine proletariat suffer from a double system of marginalization. As proletarians, they experience alienation from the means of production, which do not belong to them; as Indians they are still dominated and discriminated against on the basis of an insufficient domination of the Spanish language or a lack of education, which limits them professionally. Their condition is still marked by racist categories, which is nonerasable, and makes it impossible to bring them into the fold of the modern nation. Above we saw that this situation of double marginalization works as an imperative for Arguedas to think about a possibility to turn it around and consider a modality of nonalienated labor despite the fact that these workers do not have direct possession of the modes of production.[94]

Modernization in the Peruvian sierra, we learn from *Todas las sangres,* contributes to a marginalization of the previously existing options of communality, especially the ayllu, while failing to offer any alternatives. Neither the Peruvian nation, nor the Communist Party, nor an indigenous community on its own is a feasible possibility, and none of these essential communalities can reproduce itself successfully. We must look for other concepts and negotiate new subject positions to create a kind of being-together, an unessential nonproject of a national front, which would also accommodate the essential ayllu as part of its atomized elements.

While having this nonproject as our (and Arguedas's) positive horizon, I must underline the kernel of the imperative to consider such an alternative community. The call for this new concept has been illustrated here ad absurdum: we must think of how to avoid the situation where the state kills people arbitrarily, moved only by its own impotence to consolidate hegemony in the postcolonial situation labeled by Ranajit Guha as dominance without hegemony.

CHAPTER 3

"WHY HAVE YOU KILLED ME?"

Violence, Law, and Justice in *Todas las sangres*

> When the public powers violate the rights and fundamental liberties guaranteed by the Constitution, resistance to oppression is a right and a duty of the citizen.
> —An article proposed to be included in the Italian Constitution

The pages of *Todas las sangres* repeatedly depict moments of violence, when the blood of common people is spilled in their clashes with the state. Let us consider this telling example. The soldiers enter the town of San Pedro, accompanying the judge of the district and the *subprefecto*—representatives of the judicial and executive powers of the Peruvian state. Everybody in town knows that the soldiers and the judges are coming to impose the illegal expropriation of the town's lands in favor of the transnational mining company. The townspeople confront the delegation, and one of them, an old mestizo artisan named Bellido, runs behind the soldiers shouting insults. The soldiers machine-gun the old man and break his legs. When the authorities set about to read a government resolution, the other townspeople bring dying Bellido and put him on the table in front of the authorities. As he bleeds to death he asks the subprefecto, "Why have you killed me?" ("¿Por qué me has matado?"), and then he dies. The official responds to the corpse and the witnesses of this unnecessary death: "government orders" ("Orden del gobierno").[1] In this chapter, I will not look for the answer to this painful "why?" of many deaths that bloody the pages of *Todas las sangres,* but I will, rather, analyze the structures that make them possible. Why do all the police operations appear as arbitrary and bloody? How is this arbitrary loss of lives permitted? What is the relation between the state and the law, the judicial and the executive powers in the novel? Is there a place for justice in the Peruvian sierra?

In *Todas las sangres,* we see a society where the state is looming on the horizon and only appears vaguely to the Indians and Don Bruno in the form of the Peruvian flag colors on the insignia of indigenous authority, the *vara.*[2] This state sends out, from Lima, its center, a kind of reconnaissance mission into the sierra, the territory that is largely beyond its reach. The absence of hegemony of the state, due to the postcolonial heterogeneous framework, makes impossible the functioning of the prescriptive liberal theory of relation between law, state, and subjects. In such a fragmented social space, the law ends up showing only its violent side.

In order to conceptualize the legal situation in the Peruvian sierra, I turn to Walter Benjamin's classical essay on violence, Jacques Derrida's reflection of the "force of law," and Giorgio Agamben's theory on the "state of exception."[3] These theoretical texts have one aspect in common. The philosophers (as well as Arguedas) explore the problematic relationship among the concepts of violence, justice, and law and question their function in modern democracies. Arguedas, by bringing to the forefront the foundational moment of what should be a democratic Peruvian nation, unearths the violent origins of democracy, origins the democracy wants to hide.[4]

Derrida, in his commentary on Benjamin, elaborates upon the concept of the "spirit of police," which both critics consider as the "degraded" face of democracy.[5] In *Todas las sangres,* we see a modern state in the process of consolidation, whose only heralds turn out to be exactly the military police and the "spirit of police." This foundational moment is marked by the situation that Giorgio Agamben calls the "state of exception." Toward the end of the novel, martial law and a "state of siege" are proclaimed in the province of San Pedro, but as will become evident from my analysis, the state of exception seems to be permanent in Arguedean Peru. The state of exception, according to Agamben, is declared when the sovereignty of the state is threatened, and the legislative and the executive powers converge and create an amorphous and hardly controllable type of power. The term "state of exception" has a connotation of a temporary condition and exceptionality from the "normal." But, if there is no solid state, nor settled legality, then the condition of exception, which should be transitory, acquires a characteristic of imprecise and uncontrolled extension, a legal void that extends indefinitely. In the face of such a reality, *Todas las sangres* could be read as an argument for the legitimate use of violence on the part of the indigenous communities for the sake of their inclusion as citizens (but, inclusion into what kind of state?). This legitimized violence offers resistance to the modern state and to its pretensions to monopolize violence.

The indigenous people find themselves in a place that structurally allows for this resistance due to the juridical heterogeneity, inherited from colonial times, which contests the monopoly on violence that should constitute, theoretically, one of the attributes of the modern state. Let us enumerate the judicial systems of the Peruvian sierra in order to discuss them in detail. In *Todas las sangres,* "communitarian justice" (*justicia comunitaria*) works in the indigenous community.[6] In Don Bruno's hacienda, the sovereign lord is the "living law," to use Agamben's term. But the Peruvian state, because it claims hegemony on the entire territory, acts as if the state law ("positive law")[7] also envelops the hacienda and the ayllus. This situation is further complicated by a conceptual distinction between law and custom. While the state theoretically operates on the basis of the written laws, the hacienda and the ayllu obey customs and oral traditions established through centuries of practice.[8]

As we will see from textual examples, in the sierra much depends on the personal (beneficent or vile) will of the officials (sergeants, judges, subprefectos, etc.) and not on the institutionality of their position. Not everything depends on the law but on the factual decisions that have the "force of law," in Agamben's interpretation of Derrida's concept.[9] This situation does not follow the Roman principle "law is harsh, but it's the law," but its inverse: "no one knows the law, but I act as if my actions were following the law." This state of affairs, not surprisingly, leaves a huge margin for arbitrary use of power, which is not a new phenomenon in the sierra, but one inscribed within its colonial legacy and deepened due to the uncertain legality of the modern state. The modernizing industrialist Don Fermín Aragón, occupies center stage in an episode that illustrates clearly the dialectic between continuity and rupture.

Fermín proposes a symbolic substitution of the "old" order of normativity based on colonial customs for the new "modern" law. He rebukes the *mistis* of San Pedro for using the colonial torture instrument, the rack (*barra*), on those Indians who appeal to national law demanding a salary. Fermín calls the rack "*infamante*": shameful, infamous. Why is it shameful? The text refers here not to the shame of those subjected to the torture, but to the shame of the society that "still" (in quotation marks, because this "still" never becomes a "not anymore") permits such a means of unmediated execution of justice. We remember from the previous chapter that Fermín dreams of "order and progress" for Peru, wants to transform the Indians from serfs into salaried workers, and cannot permit that the rack, a symbol of premodern social relations, continues to exist in his native town. So, he throws the rack into the river. At first glance, it seems this is the moment of transition to modern law, where the exercise of violence is monopolized by the state and must be mediated by judicial process. It seems that with this gesture Fermín wants to indicate that a new era has begun in the sierra. But has it really? Beyond the magnificent gesture, the nature of this change does not coincide with the image of transition to modernity that Fermín desires.

Fermín, inspired by his deceased father's practice of paternalistic protection of the ayllu and the new rhetoric of modernization and emancipation, proclaims that the Indians' requests for a salary are "in accordance with the [positive] law (derecho)."[10] Here, Fermín appeals to the idea of the "right," employing the vocabulary that brings the Indians of the Lahuaymarca community closer to the idea of citizenship. It looks as if the old law is dead: it sank in the river, together with the rack. But, in a dialectic movement so characteristic of *Todas las sangres,* the narrative voice informs the reader that the Indians continued treating the *vecinos* with the same respect as before, although they refused to work for them for free. Why do the same social rituals survive if the social relations supposedly changed? The source of the power that can declare the abolition of a symbol of colonial domination (namely, Fermín Aragón) is in itself colonial, thus manifesting the contradictory nature of the power of the highland industrializing bourgeoisie, emerging from the centuries-old land-based power structures. The old law is resuscitated, pale and worn out, but still active, in the same moment of its supposed abolition. The events we witness during the rest of the novel suggest that the substitution of the old legal order by the new one was far from clean but left a substantial remainder. And yet, after all, the rack-destroying episode was important: it opened a possibility for the Indian community to gain some ground and to make its demands for salary, and at the same time, contradictorily, renewed the authority of Fermín Aragón. It marked an incomplete and problematic transition, not toward a state of greater modernity but toward an increased judicial heterogeneity.

The Layers of the Postcolonial Judicial System

In the situation of increased judicial heterogeneity, we can analyze the ayllu and the hacienda as formations that function within a judicial system formed by different layers. Within Bruno's hacienda, his will has the force of law, but the hacienda as a whole also has to interact with other haciendas and with the judicial system of the state. The Paraybamba community is ruled on the inside by its authorities (the *varayok's* and the communal assembly) but also has to face the state law. Historically, the complex interaction of these layers was practiced de facto. For instance, in the 1960s the indigenous communities already had an idea of national law and its usefulness. They appealed to it to protect their rights on land or to make demands for salary, which resulted in approbation of land reform and abolition of unpaid labor in the reforms of 1964. In *Todas las sangres,* the Indians and Don Bruno confront the subprefecto of the province capital after they punish Adalberto Cisneros, and then leave upon having defended themselves successfully, showing that at times they manage to negotiate with the state officials.

The internal regulations of the haciendas and indigenous communities are based on custom, the traditional practices that are not written down, but which the community follows by consensus over an extended period of time. Recent anthropological and legal studies focus on the effect of what Jeremy Adelman calls the weak, "unfinished states" in the Andes,[11] where the liberal democratic legal framework does not erase the remainder of the functioning structures that bear the seal of both pre-Hispanic and colonial traditions, even in the wake of the twenty-first century. For instance, Carlos Vilas and Richard Stoller study the cases of lynchings in Peru and Bolivia as paradigmatic of the clash between state legality and the communal justice that claims its authority, appealing to the importance and functionality of customs. They conclude that the lynchings are caused primarily by the weak, ineffective presence of the state, which makes the community members take justice into their own hands—only after the repetitive recourse to the state institutions fails. Moreover, while the structures of the community justice that drive the lynchings can be considered as the exercise of traditional Andean structures, the fact that they often have a fatal effect separates them dramatically from the customary exercise of community justice, "in which physical punishment may have its place in the extremes, but never to the point of death." Thus, Vilas and Stoller show that the customs and the state legal framework do not exist in a cleanly delineated domain in the Andes but, rather, the absence of the state contributes to a certain "perversion" of the old judicial structures of the ayllus and radicalizes them to the point of brutality.[12] The two sources of authority both clash and modify each other in their constant interaction.

The weak presence of the state in the Peruvian sierra and the consequent importance of custom become evident in one scene from *Todas las sangres.* The important landowners of the province, Cisneros, Don Lucas, and young Aquíles, come to Don Bruno's hacienda to accuse him of "transgressing the custom" by letting his serfs trade with the Paraybamba community. The discussion that results from this meeting shows how each character negotiates his space of power between tradition and modernity.

Only one source of normativity dominates the discussion: customs and traditions. But in the mutual threats emerge two sources of the punitive power: the sovereign power of the landowners and the repressive apparatus of the state. Don Bruno, Don Lucas, and Cisneros threaten one another with, literally, waging war (*guerra*), that is to say, invading the other landowner's property with the private army of the serfs, thereby reasserting their power as local sovereigns who can declare war on one another. At the same time, young Aquíles accuses Bruno of being a Communist and threatens him with ending up in Frontón jail.[13] Here is the contradictory kernel of the problem: Aquíles attacks Bruno for reforming an old custom; Bruno justifies his right to do so also by reference to the same old custom; and the threat with Frontón jail to which Aquíles appeals is the only image through which the Peruvian state incites itself in this negotiation.

There is no consensus among the characters about the relation between normativity and reality, between law and life. The only point of agreement among all the hacendados is about the rights of serfs, thus phrased by Bruno: "The rights of the serfs . . . depend on the will of the lord,"[14] the statement that again affirms their sovereign power. But then the question of the right (*derecho*) of Bruno himself to implement administrative reforms on his hacienda is raised, as Aquíles tells him: "You . . . as a landowner have no right to stir up the Indians. Everyone else will want to do the same as your serfs. And not only will we be ruined, but also our authority would be put at risk."[15] The other landowners recognize the self-subverting nature of Bruno's reforms and attempt to limit his sovereign rights by appealing to the same custom that gives Bruno the liberty to act as he does. The other landowners' accusations make it clear that Bruno's project, in fact, requires the "perverse" use of the custom. By affirming his sovereign rights based on custom, Bruno acts in the way he considers legal and just, declares himself responsible for the doings of his serfs, and in this manner works as a shield for the actions of the Indians. As we will see further on, this act unites him spiritually and programmatically with the subversive block that emerges toward the end of the novel, as the text compels the reader to side, definitively, with Bruno, Rendón Willka, and the narrative voice.

As we have already seen in the previous chapter, the antipode of Don Bruno is the nouveau-riche Cisneros, a product of social mobility based on accumulation of capital, who introduces yet another interesting facet into the discussion of norms (laws) and their execution: "What caste are you talking about?! Those times are gone. The one who has money, who has more of it, that one is in charge; that one is the lord. I will prove it to you . . . I have influence. I made the deputy and even the senator with my dough."[16] In this vision, the law as normativity is basically irrelevant. Cisneros is a sovereign like Bruno, but he is not bound by the key aspect that determines Bruno's decisions: the metaphysics of sovereignty, the idea that God made him lord, and that consequently he is responsible in the face of divinity for the way he treats his serfs. In Cisneros's view, money, and his own personal astuteness and ruthlessness, made him who he is. Because of this, he does not answer to any god. This fact takes away from Cisneros's legitimacy in the normative frame of the old custom as interpreted by Don Bruno: "They fear and obey me; I am lord from my most ancient forefathers; but they only hate you. *You are not sanctified* in your possessions by the law of seniorial heredity."[17] The word "*consagrado*" (sanctified) is essential here to underline that Bruno's legitimacy derives directly from God. Cisneros also does not answer to the state law because it appears here only in the figures of the deputy and the senator, whom Cisneros made with his money. At the same time, Cisneros straddles between the dying normativity of premodern sovereignty and modern social mobility as he successfully appropriates parts of both systems to augment his possessions and power. In order to understand the power that emanates from the figure of Cisneros, it is useful to remember Flores Galindo's observation about the power of the landholding elite at the beginning of the twentieth century. They combined land ownership with local political power and economics with politics, which made it almost impossible to keep them in check.[18] Cisneros emerges as a morally and aesthetically repugnant figure, which condenses the impunity implied by the legal void. It seems that this man who possesses vast lands, a puppeteer of local authorities and free of Christian scruples that could circumscribe his decisions, is out of reach of any justice, either human or divine. But Cisneros is not as invulnerable as he seems. In the argument of the novel, only one type of justice can get him: the indigenous communitarian justice that punishes him without mediation and without giving him the opportunity to look for the help of the judges and the soldiers. In what follows, we will study how this just punishment becomes possible and how it dialogues with state normativity.

Punishments without Crimes

At the very end of the novel, Arguedas leaves the reader with this image: "Don Adalberto was crying at the mountaintop, accompanied by twenty soldiers. 'Am I naked?' he asked. 'These Indians, trained by Rendón, froze me to death. I think they froze me forever.'"[19] In the very last moment we are not left with the majestic figures of Rendón, Bruno, or at least cruel but patriotic Fermín. We are left with the repulsive image of the naked man whose descriptions in the novel border on the grotesque: "half of his face was covered by a sparse and black beard . . . he was short, and his buttocks were almost swollen"; "the man of fat, without soul"; "ugly macho."[20] Considering Arguedas's obsession with the majestic and the beautiful, there must be a good reason for this final image. It is a didactic illustration of the efficient functioning of communitarian justice, executed by the Indian community of Cisneros's hacienda, Parquiña. The effectiveness is underlined by the fact that the punishment, finally, has profoundly affected Cisneros's decaying humanity, as he says that he will stay "frozen forever." The presence of the police, post factum, does not help Cisneros in any way. The repressive power of the state is on his side, but it is useless when faced with justice finally fulfilled. This final scene is a replay of a previous scene in the novel, where the Paraybamba community punishes Cisneros for his land usurpations, physical abuses of men, and rapes of women.[21] This first example of communitarian justice is described in detail, and therefore the reader can complete the elliptic and summary description of the Parquiña event at the end of the novel, and understand the implications of both of Cisneros's punishments.

In Paraybamba, Cisneros's first punishment is both physical and ritual-symbolic, and obviously obeys principles other than those of modern laws. While punishment in the modern state is always private, behind the walls of the prison, punishment in an ayllu must be "public," that is to say, has to take place in the presence of the entire community, a fact that derives from the lack of separation of the public and the private spheres. In the recent studies that compare Inca punishments and the contemporary exercise of communitarian justice, exile emerges as the preferred modus operandi.[22] Exile, the act of "throwing out" a corrupt element from the body of the community, symbolically restores the disrupted order. In *Todas las sangres,* we see that instead of killing Cisneros, the Indians opt for a ritual punishment that effectively cleanses the community from the "pus" that his abuses left in the bodies of Paraybamba as a community and in the bodies of the Indians of the village as individuals.[23] Symbolically, after the punishment is executed, a Paraybamban girl who was raped by Cisneros promises to keep alive her child, the result of the rape, because the ritual punishment had cleansed the community and the victim; "now she has been reborn," in the words of an old varayok.[24]

Having established the effectiveness of communitarian justice in the novel, we must now see how the state reacts to this exercise of local law. The reader witnesses the repressive response in three sites: the indigenous community of Paraybamba, the capital of the province San Pedro, and in Lima. This segment of the novel deserves the title "Punishments without Crimes" because, even if the indigenous justice applied to Cisneros is conceptualized as a "crime" because it stands outside of the legal proceeding of the state, the multiple reactions by the police do not have a direct correspondence to this single event. The military police, in fact, punish preemptively, only using the Cisneros incident as an excuse for unfolding the repressive apparatus and reading in it the Indians' readiness for possible further resistance.

First, soldiers arrive in Paraybamba. Second, in the capital of the province, Don Bruno and the authorities of Paraybamba are officially judged for what is considered an offense against the "honorable person" of Cisneros. Third, the soldiers beat up the immigrants from San Pedro at the gathering of their club in Lima. The three events are connected, although their connection is not obvious at first. When Indians of the province appear ready for resistance, the state deploys the police force against the determined group; this time, it is a geographically determined group, coming from San Pedro and its vicinity.[25]

Punishment, in order to be conceptualized as such, needs to presuppose a crime. Crime is a prerequisite that gives the state the legitimacy to deploy its repressive apparatus, making use of its monopoly on violence. With this logic, the indigenous insurrection would be a way of negatively creating the absent state; if there is a revolt against the state, there must be a state, after all. Nonetheless, the multiple sovereignties and heterogeneity of judicial systems, which we have been observing here, do not produce revolt. Instead, this situation produces a wall between persons that exist within different sovereignties and an unaggressive ignorance on the part of the Indians about the state. In this situation, the punishment that the soldiers bring to Paraybamba imagines the crime in order to create the punishment, and thereby to call into existence state hegemony. However, the triple repression after the Cisneros incident betrays the state's permanent vigilance and fear of rebellion, in its constant readiness to repress at a minimal sign of unrest, and also to strip the contesting forces of all their rights. The state's attitude to the Indians' possible resistance thus straddles between the fear of the rebellion and the desire for it, and the hesitant behavior of the individual soldiers betrays this contradictory stand. The police do not treat the Indians of Paraybamba or the vecinos-immigrants at the club in Lima as citizens. If not citizens, who are these people?

The soldiers arrive in Paraybamba with the following order: "To kill anyone who resists. Take the five varayok's prisoners. Then . . . look for David K'oto. Kill him at the first sign of resistance or flight."[26] This injunction does not sound like an order to treat the Indians as citizens who transgress the law, but as enemies in an armed conflict. But the Indians, in fact, are unarmed. Nor do they show any sign of resistance when the soldiers arrive at Tokoswayk'o, where the Indians are working the land, and start shooting above the Indians' heads. Why this treatment of persons who do not display any signs of violent behavior? The reason is fear of the generalized rebellion of the Indians, and the result is a deployment of police force by the judicial branch of the state, since it sees itself in a sort of competition with the justice of the ayllu. Far from being democratic and consolidating its imagery on the basis of its popular majorities—the Indians—the state identifies itself with the centuries-long tradition of oppression. As an oppressor, it fears the oppressed.

Conversely, the ambiguous, painful position of the soldiers, who see themselves obliged to point guns at persons who sing a song that reminds them of their childhood,[27] exasperates the situation. The young soldiers start shooting to avoid speaking and to avoid recognizing themselves in the persons whom they must shoot "at the slightest sign of resistance." The ambiguous status of the Indians allows the soldiers this "luxury" because they are not citizens, not even prisoners of war. They are "just Indians," which implies that a soldier does not have to bear responsibility for their deaths, does not even have to count the bodies of these persons, whose legal status is uncertain because they inhabit what Agamben would characterize as the undetermined situation of the "state of exception." This is so because they live at the intersection of multiple systems of normativity: the modern state, the structures inherited from the colonial times, and pre-Hispanic indigenous traditions of communitarian justice.

The novel makes it evident that this state of things is tragic both for the Indians, the targets of the bullets, and for the soldiers, their executors. The sergeant puts the bullets between the Indians, with whom he identifies through his own "bare life" Indian childhood, and his present self (perhaps as a Peruvian citizen). But the only demand the old varayok' presents to the soldier is for words instead of bullets. The sergeant asks, surprised, "you wanted me to talk to you?" and the varayok' patiently explains, "Yes, sir

Government authority. A man speaks; Government authority speak. Thugs kill without talking, in the night."[28] He demands to be recognized as a speaking being, no more, no less.[29] The varayok's first claim for recognition is his demand for speech; but then he also claims his right to give the last orders to the community before he is taken to prison. In the words of a witness to the scene, "every prisoner is given a little time to settle his things." But the sergeant replies, "But not the Indians. They do not need it. They do not have anything."[30] The Indians are not "any prisoner" because they do not possess private property since, as we have seen, the separation into public and private spheres does not exist in the ayllu. Because the protection of private property is the basis of positive law, the fact of not sharing in this preoccupation makes the varayok' a prisoner of an ambiguous status, a "bare life," in Agamben's sense.

This scene suggests, disturbingly, that any Indian at any moment can be reduced to the status of absolute vulnerability, and the "punishment without crime" can be applied to any indigenous person simply for being one, and thereby for threatening the state's foundations in positive law. While this situation resembles the colonial division of power, which separated the world into señores (who speak) and indios (those who don't speak), we must observe that the vulnerability of the varayok's is practically doubled because in this scene they are subject to remnants of colonial prejudices and to the state of exception declared by the modern Peruvian state. During the colonial times, the "two republics" functioned because the Indians had juridical status when facing the republic of Spaniards. The erosion of this legal division and consequently imprecise legality of the (very long) moment of transition from the postindependence republic to a supposedly liberal democracy that *Todas las sangres* narrates puts the Indians in a situation of double vulnerability: the colonial legacy aggravated by the gaping legal lacunae left by the weak, ineffective state.

"Order of the Government,"
or the Tragedy of Subjective Destitution

In the words of Derrida,

> The police that thus capitalize on violence are not simply the police. They do
> not simply consist of policemen in uniform, occasionally helmeted, armed
> and organized in a civil structure on a military model to whom the right
> to strike is refused, and so forth. By definition, the police are present or

represented everywhere there is a force of law. They are present, sometimes invisible but always effective, wherever there is a preservation of social order. The police are not only the police (today more or less than ever), they are there, the figure without a face or figure of a *Dasein* coextensive with the *Dasein* of the *polis*.[31]

The vulnerability of the varayok' finds its reflection, its other face, in the equally tragic dilemma of the soldiers who have to shoot at the Indians. By presenting this painful contradiction, *Todas las sangres* proposes, on a theoretical level, that Derrida's "spirit of the police" erodes not only the Indians' capacity to become citizens of Peru but also destroys this pos-sibility for the military police recruits. The novel completely contradicts the theory that proposes a more or less automatic shift from soldier to citizen.[32] In my study of what occurs with the political subjectivity of the soldiers, I want to suggest the term "subjective destitution" for the persons on both sides of the fence: the vulnerable Indians on one hand, and the soldiers, unaccountable for their actions, on the other hand.

Let us observe, again, the chain of events around the "Cisneros inci-dent": (1) Cisneros abuses the Paraybamba community; (2) Paraybamba punishes Cisneros, without killing him; (3) the Peruvian state punishes the indigenous persons from Paraybamba and any other person from the same region that happens to be in the way, killing a number of people. Our analysis has shown that the category of justice is inapplicable to the repres-sions carried out by the state. Now we must ask, are these repressions at least legal? And if they are not, how can they be carried out? Or what we see on the pages of *Todas las sangres* is something akin to the Hobbsean state of nature, of a war of everyone against everyone, where the soldiers shoot only because they are the ones who happen to be armed?

Derrida elaborates Benjamin's idea that the "police spirit," or police-as-spirit, does more damage in a democracy than in a monarchy.[33] The quote from Derrida that opens this section explains the idea of the police-as-spirit, an omnipresent entity, spectral and ineludible at the same time. In *Todas las sangres,* we can see this nature of the police force clearly, as the police are present in the text even when they are absent. For instance, Fermín comments that it is not time yet to call the police, but "I will call on them when the time comes";[34] and Aquíles threatens Don Bruno with being raped in the Frontón jail. The varayok' of Paraybamba says that the Indians will be "waiting for the uniformed ones in the company of our Lord (God). They will kill us calmly"[35] because they know that the forces of order will appear soon after the community punishes Cisneros. The police extend a dark blanket of its presence-in-absence over all the characters of the novel, conditioning their behavior, either in fear or in defiance of the repressive forces.

This presence-in-absence is the "ignoble" part of the police in democracy, according to Benjamin and Derrida. Although in monarchy the police openly combine executive and judicial powers before the separation of powers, in democracy the police become more vile as they fail to recognize their capacity to make law as they go along.[36] That is to say, the police are supposed to be only a force that preserves the existing order, while "forgetting" the fact that they must act as a maker of law in each concrete situation. This attribute of the police becomes especially problematic in *Todas las sangres,* where we do not see any manifestation of law as institutional normativity, but only in the form of police repression.

It is useful to conceptualize the figure of a military policeman as an inverse image of the figure of a "good judge" that Derrida calls forth. This philosopher observes that a just action demands a conscious, responsible decision, which simultaneously engages the preestablished law and also rewrites the law for each particular case. Thus, a judge should not be a mere automaton that applies law.[37] He or she must be the point of encounter between the universality of the law and the singularity of each tragedy, each crime. For instance, in *Todas las sangres,* the character closest to this model is Don Bruno, whose sovereign responsibility we discussed above. Conversely, a military policeman in the novel, as shown in the scene that opened this chapter, is an inverse image of this good judge because he invents the law for each particular situation, but he is not moved by the ideals of legality or justice. And, most importantly, a soldier will always negate the moment of decision, which implies personal responsibility. With the words "government orders," the sergeant justifies his arbitrary killing of Bellido. In the scene of repression at Paraybamba, the sergeant points his gun at the Indians and, according to the narrative voice, suppresses his "ganas de matar" (desire to kill). This desire comes from his personal consciousness and not from the order he had received from his superiors. In this situation, convinced not to shoot, he desists. But the narrative voice makes it clear that in that very moment he could have decided otherwise and contributed more victims to the bloody pages of the novel.

In the novel, a police official will not admit that he is responsible for ordering a violent suppression of a revolt (either real or imaginary, as we have seen above). He will say that he "is fulfilling his duty" as a representative of the state. It is a moment of depersonalization of power, and of deferment of responsibility to the sphere of the state. It is an amorphous notion, especially in the situation reflected in *Todas las sangres,* where this state appears ghostly to the Indians and to the soldiers alike. This deferment of responsibility results in practically infinite freedom for the official who must consider various means to control social manifestations. But the word "freedom" is inappropriate here, as the infinite freedom of the official seems to coincide with his infinite subjection to the law of the state. The orders of the state are never clear, and consequently a soldier never knows if he really is "fulfilling" his "duty," although he uses this phrase to escape personal responsibility. Unaccountability of a soldier is not a feature of freedom but of subjective destitution and implies incomplete existence as a citizen, akin to that of a minor or a madman.

We must underline that the cause of the subjective destitution is not deferment of responsibility in itself. The varayok's use a similar tactic very differently. They defer the violence of the vecinos from the community to their own bodies: they suffer the torture on the rack but declare that they cannot alter the community's decision on demanding higher salaries. The varayok's deny their authority to make decisions personally, that is, to act as a private person when carrying the vara, the sign of their authority within the community. But they do assume the responsibility of representing the community to the outside world, constituted by the miserable remains of old aristocracy and the officials of the Peruvian state. In direct opposition to this tactic, the police assume the power to discipline and punish but deflect personal responsibility for their actions. We can speak of two patterns of deferment of responsibility in *Todas las sangres*. The first one, protective of the physical integrity of other persons, is represented by indigenous authorities. The other pattern, destructive to bodies and lives, is represented by the police. This difference is aggravated by the fact that the indigenous authorities respond to their community, with whom they have a clear and immediate relationship, while the soldiers respond to the phantasmal and remote state. In other words, the community and the state foster different types of political subjectivity. In the case of the police, we see a relationship where the subject disappears in favor of institutional incarnation, and this destitute subject does not even know what power expects from him. These anxieties are absent from the gravity of the varayok's, who are absolutely certain about the nexus that links them to the community and the authority they carry. The novel proposes that a just decision can only be born from a solid subjectivity like the one displayed by the varayok's, since the subjective void of the policemen and their superiors remains outside of the conceptual sphere of justice.

Our discussion up to this point helps us respond to a perhaps naïve question about *Todas las sangres* and about the logic of police repressions in general: Why does a person, in the moment he or she puts on a uniform, cease to act as the compassionate private individual that he or she probably is when wearing civilian clothing? The novel suggests that this becomes possible by a double movement of positioning of the soldiers in relation to the state and in relation to their victims. In their rapport with the state, the soldiers position themselves as minors or crazy people who cannot be responsible for their actions. In a complementary movement, they construct their victim as an absolute other, a nonspeaking being, a bare life incapable of being subject to the law and having rights.

These subjective formations, which can hardly be called political subjectivities in a classic sense, make problematic yet another precept about the relation of the state, law, and violence. The state should have a monopoly on violence and the police should be the instrument that executes this monopoly. This legitimate violence must be directed toward avoiding greater violence and preserving the preexisting law. But in *Todas las sangres,* we never see the law the police must preserve. If the police are not preserving the law, then they must be doing something else. Are they actually founding a new order, the order of the modern nation-state?

If we conceptualize the violence of the police as Benjaminean founding violence,[38] we can explain the absence of justice in the police actions in *Todas las sangres.* These actions are before-the-law. If we define justice, rephrasing Derrida, as an actualization of a preexisting order by an urgent and responsible decision, then the police in *Todas las sangres* cannot produce justice in any way. There is no preexisting order to actualize, and there is no subjectivity from which to make a responsible decision. From the point of view of the state, these actions are neither legal nor illegal, as they exist in a legal vacuum, namely, in the province of San Pedro, marked by the state of exception. This is also the place in the sierra where custom, which is not recognized as law by the state, governs the behavior of Don Bruno and the Indians. From the point of view of these subjects of custom-based normativity, the actions of the police appear as criminal, excessive, incomprehensible, unjust. This injustice permeates every corner of the Peruvian state apparatus, as we will see in what follows.

The Silence of the Positive Law

Agamben would call the "state of exception" the situation we witness in *Todas las sangres,* where the judicial and executive powers confuse their attributions, and the frontier between politics and law erodes.[39] Far from being independent, the judges appear as subaltern to the subprefectos, the representatives of the executive power in the province, who enjoy practically unlimited powers. Let us return once again to the scene of the soldiers' arrival in San Pedro.[40] Subprefecto Llerena forces the judge of the province to accompany him on the mission to San Pedro to read the decree of expropriation of land. The judge resists because he knows that the decree is not only "unjust" (it takes away the last means of subsistence from about three hundred persons) but also illegal and unconstitutional. But the judge obeys, threatened by the subprefecto and his soldiers. When the situation turns violent, he has no choice but to assist Llerena. In another scene, an eloquent description of the judges' offices illustrates this subservient position of judicial power: "The office of the judge was more disheveled and miserable than that of the subprefecto. . . . Besides, it smelled of mold."[41] This description of the judge's office reflects the nature of the judges' performance of their duties. As an example of this rotten, "moldy" condition, the old local judge, despite his personal integrity, ends up involved in a proceeding that is illegal, corrupt, and costs the life of an innocent citizen, the mestizo Bellido.

The situation of dependence of judicial power is aggravated by the fact that subprefectos and judges receive miserable salaries and therefore are very easily corrupted. Besides, their appointments are not based on merit. The men least adequate for the job are in positions that determine the resolutions of conflicts in the province. For example, "the subprefecto . . . was a starving vecino from a far away province; as an activist for an already-elected senator, he stayed up many nights during the two months of the election campaign."[42] The unprofessional officials are constantly at a loss about what to do and are afraid to lose face in front of their subalterns and other authorities. This anxiety aggravates their unpredictable and cruel decisions, and this is the case when subprefecto Llerena orders Bellido to be shot, and also, more absurdly, that the church tower of San Pedro be shot to silence its bells. The official, just as "unaccountable" and subjectively destitute as his soldiers, has another source of anxiety: uncertainty of his relation to the power of the state that he serves. The repulsive figure of Llerena ends up acquiring a tragic dimension when he is taken to be imprisoned in the Sexto jail as punishment for his precipitated actions in San Pedro. In this sense, silence rules both the relation between the state and the government official, as well as the relationship between the government official and his subalterns and the people. Just like the soldiers in the scene of repression in Paraybamba, Llerena prefers to use bullets instead of words to avoid a moment of identification or negotiation with the people he faces. His behavior is conditioned by his position in front of the state. He, like his victims, in a blink of an eye passes from citizen to detainee with an ambiguous legal status because the state is also silent for him about his rights and duties. This silence and subjective destitution might be the psychological effects of the permanent state of exception these persons experience.

Silence extends to all instances of state power. Instead of public announcements of decrees, which would perhaps open a possibility to a dialogue and to discursive constructions of hegemony, we see only immediate enforcement of the laws, before they are made known to the public. In fact, the decree of the expropriation of the land of La Esmeralda from the villagers of San Pedro, which subprefecto Llerena must read to them, is "hidden" from the public.[43] Besides, the decree is "illegal" because, according to the constitution, the expropriation can be only in favor of the state, and never of the private persons or entities.[44] Nonetheless, it does not stop the execution of the decree: "The one who governs with no law, like this government, how will it respect the law?," Don Anatolio, a defender of San Pedro in Lima, tells Don Fermín.[45] As it mixes economic interests with political ones, another feature that Agamben discusses as typical of the modern state of exception,[46] the Peruvian state dictates the laws that Zar, the representative of the transnational capital in the novel, dictates to it.[47] Therefore, the law as such, incarnate in the constitution, ends up subordinate to the decree dictated by the government following the interests of transnational capital. This decree, in Agamben's take on Derrida's idea, has the "force of law" without being the law, yet another feature of the state of exception.[48] The application of the norm makes it law, as it also betrays the gap between the normativity and its application. At the same time Llerena carries out anxious, brutal, and useless repression, the situation in the capital of the province parallels the violence suffered by the San Pedro villagers. There, the soldiers kill and wound the women of the town who spontaneously organize in defense of the Paraybamban varayok's.

The plot, which with each page moves further not only from justice but from legality and into deeper official silence, opens the stage for one more actor: the Lima press, which reports "truthfully" the tragic events in the province (quotation marks of the narrative voice).[49] "The daily papers in Lima informed almost with the same words about the burning down of the San Pedro church and death of Cabrejos. The death of the mestiza woman and the silver-master Bellido were ignored."[50] After blaming the deaths and the destruction of the church of San Pedro on the villagers and townspeople of the provincial capital, the newspaper article concludes: "Onto those responsible for these disturbances that we are reporting will fall all the weight of the law *in defense of democracy*."[51] In one of the definitions of the state of exception, Agamben states that it marks the "threshold of indeterminacy between democracy and absolutism."[52] This definition dialogues well with the situation portrayed in *Todas las sangres,* where we must contrast the image of the president who orders to kill women in the marginal neighborhoods of Lima with the assertion of the press that all the forces of law will be directed to the defense of democracy. Agamben shows in his genealogical study that the "state of exception" is an institution born *not* out of an absolutist tradition but out of a liberal democratic one. This theoretical conclusion elicits a legitimate doubt about the liberal representational democracy as a social order that guarantees the best legality and justness in the treatment of its citizens. Instead, Agamben suggests that the institution of the state of exception becomes increasingly a paradigm of government in the modern democracies, and *Todas las sangres* depicts vividly how such a "threshold" democracy creates legal situations, which easily reduce persons to a condition of noncitizens. What talk of justice or even legality can there be in this situation?

Above, we have discussed the cases of execution of communitarian justice that question the monopoly of the state on violence and signal that in the absence of effective positive law, another normativity must appear that will fulfill the work of justice. Now we will read into two individual intents to bring about this kind of justice, incommensurable with the positive law, through revenge. These acts are agonic, tragic, and powerless. How do they fit into our mapping of subjectivities capable of bringing about legality and justice?

Justice Outside the Law

Let us return for a moment to the aftermath of Cisneros's punishment. After the fact, Don Bruno meets his brother Fermín and tells him about the feat of Paraybamba: "I saw the old Indian mayor administer justice as in a drama of Calderon de la Barca."[53] This comparison with Spanish Golden Age drama reflects Bruno's admiration for the varayok's acts and his respect for the ceremonious, theatrical mode of execution of justice so proper to the representative public sphere. We have seen that Fermín accused Bruno of being "theatrical" because for Fermín the principle of performativity of the representative public sphere has lost its meaning. Fermín again angrily replies: "Which drama? What similarity can there be between an Indian and a Spaniard?,"[54] thereby reinstating the absolute colonial division between the Indians and the Spaniards, and downplaying the degree of admirability of the Indians' spectacular act. In his turn, Bruno underlines the similarity between the judicial modus operandi employed

by an indigenous authority of the twentieth century and the Spanish justice of the seventeenth.[55] From the brothers' exchange we learn that Don
Bruno's definition of justice and his vision of *administrar justicia* (administer justice) coincides largely with the Indians' definition. Since the state
does not share this definition, Bruno must take justice into his own hands,
which materializes in the form of his father's old gun.

Bruno commits an act that, for the police powers of the state, falls into
the same category as communitarian justice: infringements on the law that
must be punished, a crime. Bruno kills the cruel landowner Don Lucas and
tries to shoot his own brother Fermín but only wounds him, not having the
heart to finish him off. Then, he turns himself over to the police. Within
the logic of modern state processual conventions, Bruno is taken prisoner,
and at the end of the novel we do not know his fate, but we can guess it
from the repeated allusions to rapes in the Frontón and Sexto jails.[56] In
a parallel action, a young lady from San Pedro, Asunta, shoots the chief
engineer of the mine and also turns herself over to the state powers with
these stumbling, chaotic words: "Beloved village, I have avenged thee! . . .
He sold my village, without it being his; gentlemen, take me prisoner.
And look at this traitor of God and of the poor people: that is how we kill
them."[57] Asunta speaks of Caberjos's "betrayal of God" and vengeance. But
what is God in this sentence? We could say that it is a category close to one
used by Bruno when he conceptualizes his power as coming from God and
therefore considers himself responsible to God for his actions. "God" here
coincides with the concept of the old order of normativity, which demands
that both of these characters, Bruno and Asunta alike, turn to homicide in
a situation where they see no sign of justice coming from the new order,
that of the emerging modern state.

Asunta's and Bruno's actions should be understood under the caption
of vengeance. Nietzsche's etymological exploration of concepts of German
law leads him to conceptualize punishment and justice as a payback action,
where over time equivalents are established between damages done and
the retribution to be paid by the criminal.[58] In the novel, Bruno makes
Lucas pay with his life for the lives of the tortured and starved Indians.
Asunta makes Cabrejos pay with his life for the definite decay of her town,
since she sees him as personally responsible for this disaster. Nonetheless,
Rendón Willka describes thus the balance of Asunta's actions: "Cabrejos
is not Wisther. A servant replaces the other servant. Our girl, like Bellido,
sacrificed her life for nothing. For the fury (*rabia*)."[59] Impotence: this is
Rendón Willka's evaluation of Asunta'a act. This example falls neatly within
Jacques Derrida's theoretical reflection, inspired by Pascal: "La justice sans
la force est impuissante. Justice without force is powerless—in other words,

justice is not justice, it is not achieved if it does not have the force to be 'enforced'; a powerless justice is not justice, in the sense of law."[60]

A similar evaluation can be applied to Bruno's killing of Don Lucas: by killing one cruel landowner, Bruno does not eliminate the dominant class as such. Nevertheless, these two homicides must be punished from the point of view of the state, as they clash with the state judiciary system. Don Bruno's vengeance, although an act of a private person, threatens the state in a similar manner as communitarian justice because he questions the monopoly of the state on violence. His logic could be threaded into this sequence: the modern state power allows Don Lucas to torment a thousand Indians who are in his power. This is unjust. I must therefore be the instrument of justice and change this situation. I will kill the tormentor. Bruno sees himself as a hand of God, a servant to the concept of justice that overflows the law, almost a passive tool, as he meditates about his role in the events that unfold in the province: "I cannot oppose the will of the Supreme One."[61] With his belief in himself as a God-sent lord, he represents a tiny personal sovereignty inside the state that pretends hegemony and thereby constitutes a threat since he is fundamentally questioning the legitimacy of the state power.

Let us understand Bruno's actions through Derrida's "philosophical figure" of a good judge. A good judge must base his or her decision on a preexisting law and there must be a moment of urgent decision that reinvents this law. The fact of assuming personal responsibility for such a decision makes it just, as opposed to another type of situation where an authority figure must only follow the rules mechanically to arrive at a verdict. When taking on responsibility for such an urgent decision, one can never be absolutely sure that the decision is correct. This moment of taking a risk and the responsibility of producing a judgment from one's own subjectivity is an absolute prerequisite for a decision to be evaluated as just or unjust. Otherwise, it simply stays outside this ontological category. But the distinction between law and justice does not function in Don Bruno's vision of normativity exactly as it functions in the secular law Derrida discusses. He "cannot know God's will," and so the preexisting law for Bruno is a more vague notion than the written positive law for Derrida's good judge. Although acting within a supposedly preexisting normativity, Bruno must reinvent it even more actively than Derrida's ideal judge in a court. While for this ideal judge to be a law-applying automaton is, theoretically, an option, for a Catholic like Bruno (a "mystic" or "fanatic," as he is repeatedly called in the novel), it is not. The supposedly preexisting law is deposited in a person's consciousness, the same consciousness that must give birth to a responsible decision. As we discuss this point, the God of

Don Bruno and the God of Rendón Willka—which we discussed previously—begin to look more similar than they seemed to on the surface. In reality, both of these gods are personal divinities that condition the characters' actions. Thus, we are left with a problematic question: Where does their normativity, their preexisting law, come from, and against what do they measure their actions?

Fermín, whose measure of normativity coincides with the modern state law, evaluates Bruno's actions with these words: "Mad, mad, son of my father and of my mother, and of that God of his."[62] Precisely, Bruno is the son of "that God of his," who is, in other words, the old order and his own consciousness, the subjectivity produced within this old order. His principles are so different from the principles of "civilization" and modern state law with which Fermín sides that his only evaluation of his brother is a conceptual short-circuit: "he is mad." But even so, Fermín has to admit and respect Bruno's dedication and incorruptibility: "every man that I know has a price, except Bruno."[63]

In the cases of both assassins, Bruno and Asunta, their purity and firm Catholic beliefs[64] are of utmost importance. The narrative voice and the other characters underline repeatedly that Asunta is a señorita, a virgin. Bruno can decide to execute his revenge only at the very end of the novel, when he is "cleansed" from his dual guilt: polygamous lust and abuse of power. At the beginning of the novel, the adolescent Bruno rapes the madwoman Gertrudis and subsequently seduces many women, makes them pregnant, and produces a flock of illegitimate children all over the province. He also exercises his raw power against his Indians, resorting to physical punishments. But after Bruno undergoes his transformation, seemingly under the influence of Rendón Willka, he moves away from these abusive habits. He marries a mestizo woman whom he got pregnant (and also declares that he has some profound feelings for her), and gives away land to his serfs. These two actions liberate Bruno, in his own worldview, from his sins and only after these two symbolic acts can he assume the role of a "hand of God" and can carry out his revenge plan. The private virtues become, in fact, a prerequisite for just public action in this worldview, which does not separate the public and private spheres. Bruno's actions are represented as just by the narrative voice, but they are powerless because they have no force of law to back them up. They are dangerous in the eyes of the state, not because of the killing but because they contest the sovereignty of the state and its monopoly on violence. Therefore, they seal Bruno's fate and pave his road to jail. But Fermín's last comment on his brother's fate suggests that the more appropriate place for him would be a madhouse, where people with ideas that cause conceptual short circuits should be isolated from society.

Although there are parallels between Don Bruno's and Rendón Willka's self-sacrifices, ideologically, Rendón Willka's death serves a purpose, while Don Bruno's vengeance does not. Rendón's actions positively contribute to the future of the Indian community and resistance; Bruno's action is only a gesture. Rendón's organizational activity pretends to change the law in the long run. Bruno's action only symbolically marks Lucas's and Fermín's behavior as morally reprehensible. But this moralist condemnation is useless, as the system that shapes the condemnation, the system of Christian values, stays on the outside of the political debate. The lesson of this analysis can be the following. Arguedas desires that in Peru law and justice meet. But he portrays all the instances when they do not interact: it's one or the other. But, from the comparison between Rendón's and Bruno's sacrifices, we learn that in order to change anything, we must not just kill individuals, products of social structures, but must change the structure itself and the ways of thinking in this society. This is what Rendón does as he organizes the Indians in their resistance.

Yawar mayu, Justified Violence

The description of Bruno's state of mind that motivates him to execute Don Lucas is described through the metaphor of *yawar mayu* (river of blood),[65] the same metaphor that is used later in the narrative to represent Rendón Willka's heroic and fatal confrontation with the police. The narrator states, after Bruno's killings, that "the river of blood . . . already had crushed those it had to crush."[66] The narrative voice is expressing here an explicit approval of Don Bruno's unmediated violence. In clear opposition to the logic of the state, the text consolidates a subversive block that questions the validity, legality, and justice of the positive law and its application. This subversive block is composed by Bruno, Rendón Willka, and the narrative voice. The difficult, but effective, alliance between Bruno and Rendón Willka culminates in a beautiful passage toward the end of the novel: "Rendón Willka was contemplating his lord as if he had handed over to him the world, sad and with blood on the outside, powerfully crying, and with salvation, and glory, under the dirty shell. Don Bruno was feeling almost exactly Demetrio's consciousness."[67] The narrator penetrates the thoughts of the two characters and connects their understanding and their destinies inextricably. Then, consolidating the subversive block, the narrator welcomes the "river of blood" awakened by Bruno and Rendón.

As a result of our discussion of judicial heterogeneity and the situations of violence it brings about, we must conclude that in *Todas las sangres* violence is not evaluated as an absolutely negative phenomenon. The narrative voice rejoices at the punishment of Cisneros; it describes with epic overtones the heroic figure of Don Bruno, the killer of Lucas; it welcomes Rendón Willka's self-sacrifice because—in a very important cause/effect relation—*it promises more effective resistance*.

The text expresses a necessity for organized resistance, not because of colonial resentment or vengeance but in the name of justice and in the name of a new law that will effectively offer guarantees to the Indians. Establishment of a new law requires violence because violence lies at the heart of any law, as Benjamin theorizes in his "Critique of Violence." Yawar mayu, the Indian rebellion that the narrative formulates as the object of the reader's desire, can be interpreted as pure violence in a Benjaminean sense, as it fundamentally questions the existence of the state on the basis of domination. As Flores Galindo observes, the rebellions in the Andes were aiming at a substantial overturning of the tables.[68] These revolts were pursuing "something more" than just the material revindication of land but rather, abolition of the (post)colonial order as such, a pachakuti. Flores Galindo illustrates his point with a forceful quote from Arguedas: "The social classes in Andean Peru, when they fight, they do so barbarically, [and] the fight does not only take its impulse from an economic interest; other spiritual, profound and violent forces fire up the enemies, shake them up with an implacable force, with incessant and inescapable violence."[69] The Indians' violence in *Todas las sangres* is a revolutionary violence which is, nonetheless, never explicitly portrayed in the novel. The pachakuti is signaled only obliquely with the metaphor of the "river of blood." Just as Derrida shows that it is impossible to speak directly of justice,[70] so it seems that revolutionary violence is inexpressable in direct words. As a result, the armed resistance remains beyond the narrative.

Our reading of *Todas las sangres* indicates that the presupposition about the existence of normative judicial relationships in the Andes in the first half of the twentieth century is false. Instead of consolidated judicial subjects, such as "Indians" or "peasants," the heterogeneous and unstable nature of legality in the highlands forms a set of problematic relations and subjectivities. The failure of the Peruvian state to construct a shared notion of normativity among its supposed subjects creates a situation where the shared public sphere is absent, and the state does not exist, either as a receptor of demands or as the object of rebellion. In this situation, the state is facing an imperative to construct its hegemony, at least as an object against which to rebel. And so it does, re-creating the Indian resistance, as if it were an armed rebellion, by sending out punishing expeditions and declarations of "martial law." Thereby, the state emerges, negatively, as the entity against which the constructed, imaginary crime is perpetrated.[71] In a complementary manner, Rendón Willka's final declaration that the Indians "finally have come to know fatherland" does a big favor to the Peruvian state: it constitutes the possibility of the state as such, as an entity whose existence is recognized, with which some kind of relation is to be had, against which a subject can, at least, rebel. Within this horizon, the yawar mayu rebellion is conceptualized as a necessary exercise in foundational violence because it promises activation of a principle of justice that can be exercised only from a solid and responsible subjectivity, such as the one displayed by Don Bruno, the hero Rendón Willka, and the other indigenous authorities.

CHAPTER 4

MOMENTS OF REVOLUTIONARY TRANSFORMATION IN ARGUEDEAN NOVELS

"It was reading Mariátegui and later, Lenin, that I found a permanent order of things; socialist theory not only offered a road to follow for all my future, but also to all that there was of energy in me, it gave it a destiny and charged it even more with force, by the same fact of channeling it. How well have I understood Socialism? I do not quite know. But it did not kill in me the magic," José María Arguedas revealed in his discourse, "No soy un aculturado."[1] It is one of the few instances when he self-identifies as a Socialist. Picking up on this thought, William Rowe locates Arguedas in the Peruvian Socialist tradition of thought and action, referring to it as "the tradition of Mariátegui, of Vallejo, of Arguedas, of Flores Galindo."[2]

It is useful to reconsider the writing of Arguedas within the Latin American Marxist tradition. First, it is necessary to introduce our reflections with a disclaimer, and at the same time with a revisionist claim. As the critic Bruno Bosteels sharply indicates, "Today, the least we can say about Marxism is that, if it were not for the use of attenuating prefixes such as 'post' or 'neo,' its mere mention has become an unmistakable sign of obsolescence . . . almost nobody really seems to be referring to Marxism anymore as a vital doctrine of political or historical intervention."[3] The mention of Marxist theories, for many, becomes either a swear word or a naïve theory whose failure is made evident by the dissolution of the Soviet Union and its history of human rights abuse. Bosteels, nonetheless, explains that this perception is largely due to a lack of intergenerational dialogue, as the newer generations do not know anything about the movements of the 1960s and 1970s. "The reasons for amnesia in Latin America are complex," Bosteels tells us: the neoliberal catastrophe and the violence of the dictatorships are two dominant reasons for this forgetfulness.[4] What is more, although the concept of class struggle, for instance, seems worn out, and other concepts such as hegemony or antagonism are more current in a present theoretical dialogue, it is important to see the continuity and genealogy between these concepts that seem new, and the Marxian concept of antagonism that still informs them. To speak of Arguedas as a Marxist thinker is to counter this forgetfulness.

Significantly, as Estelle Tarica acutely shows, the figure of Arguedas has acquired a renewed dimension in Peru after the decades of Shining Path violence. The intellectuals of the Peruvian left of 2000s have mined Arguedas's thought for readings that would "save" Socialism from the contamination by violence and the deaths of 80,000 people that occurred, at least partially, under the banner of Socialist and Marxist struggle. In Tarica's words, "Arguedas represents [in 2011] a possibility to find a vision of a nation that is not that of the officialism, nor that of Senderism, that is to say, a position that looks for revolution but without dogmas."[5] Borrowing the term from the theorization of the revolutionary process presented by the Bolivian sociologist Álvaro García Linera, we can say that Arguedas represents, positively, the possibility of "moments of revolutionary transformation."[6] Linera's use of this term emerges from his analysis of the Bolivian process of revision of its juridical, institutional, and economic dimensions and capacities in the last decades. The term does not only emphasize the violent struggle, but also different methods and spheres used in the process of "measuring the forces" of the contestatory indigenous movements against the Bolivian neoliberal state machine in the first two decades of the twenty-first century. In the Bolivian historical situation, it is a fact that the revolutionary bloc did not hide or escape from confrontations; nor can the efforts of the Morales government and the Constituent Assembly be univocally evaluated. But it is also true that transformations did take place, and *did not turn into a bloodbath,* as was the case in Peru with the Shining Path movement. The phrase "moments of revolutionary transformations" appropriates the classical Marxist theorizations on struggle and puts them into a contemporary context for the thinkers of the second decade of the twenty-first century. Despite all the criticism that has been waged on the Morales-Linera government, from both the indigenous and the syndicalist camps between 2006, the year of Morales's election, and

2014 when he is getting ready to run for a new term, Arguedas would be very happy to see Bolivia because its revolution-in-progress accomplishes two tasks that the Arguedean project struggled to further. It produces new theoretical proposals and effectively implements the ideas explored by Arguedas himself, half a century earlier. However problematically and incompletely, the Bolivian process breaks the old postcolonial structures, renews the elites,[7] and has an internationalist and strong anti-imperialist dimension to its struggle—all this without numerous losses of life. In order to understand the reason for the immense "moral and documentary force"[8] that is ascribed today to Arguedean thought by Peruvian intellectuals who ask how Peru can move forward (beyond the tragedy of terrorist-military violence), we need to study the Arguedean call for multiple "moments of revolutionary transformation" that emerge on the pages of his novels.

First, placing the Arguedean texts in a genealogical context of other socialist documents, I will discuss aspects of revolutionary action and its program as it emerges in his last three novels. Second, I will discuss the limits of political negotiations within the realm of party politics, which calls for a different type of popular action, but not necessarily for revolution, as these actions still function within the logic of placing demands on the established state. Third, and as an affective and ethical counterpart to our reflection on the institutional limits of party politics, I will discuss the "limits of tolerance" in Arguedean prose so as to show what triggers the call to a radical overturning of the tables, the call to revolutionary action. Last, I will discuss how the invention of a new language, in the fruitful language gap among Spanish, Quechua, and English, enables Arguedas to articulate a new revolutionary call to action, inspired in classical Socialist discourses and also adapted to the reality of Chimbote, represented in *The Foxes*.

Mariátegui and Arguedas against the Stalinist Orthodoxy

Let us look at the constants that determine the Arguedean thought about radical social change in all of his novelistic productions, link it to the concept of social upheaval elaborated by José Carlos Mariátegui, and then inquire how the concept of this struggle is modified and refined in Arguedas's three last novels, *El Sexto, Todas las sangres,* and *The Foxes*. As I will show shortly, these novels are characterized by the increasing internationalist focus of the emancipatory struggle, and by the increasing ambiguity in the definition of the revolutionary subject, an ambiguity that becomes resolved partially in the "Last Diary" of *The Foxes* and in the final speeches of Father Cardozo.

Let me start by drawing out with bold strokes the constants that define the concept of the revolutionary struggle in the proclamations of the Third and Fourth International (1921–23),[9] Mariátegui's theorizations and Arguedas's thought. The proclamations attribute a trifold simultaneous task to the revolutionary struggle in the Americas: the resolution of the agrarian problem, the anti-imperialist struggle, and anticapitalist struggle. These proclamations negate the necessity of the stage of national and democratic capitalism and emphasize the complicity of the local bourgeoisie with imperialist abuses. They also avoid conceptualizing the socioeconomic situations in the rural areas as "feudalism" and describe the peasant struggle as directed against "agrarian capitalism."

Mariátegui, in turn, elaborates on the triple task proposed by the Third International and also works to negate, in the polemic against the Stalinist orthodoxy that marked the decade of the 1930s, the naturalist vision of the "stagism" of the revolutionary struggle, which saw the succession from feudalism to early capitalism to late capitalism to socialism "as immutable as the sequence of seasons in a year."[10] In a famous phrase, Mariátegui proclaims that the revolution in Latin America "will be socialist or will not be" (será socialista o no será), implying the vision of an uninterrupted struggle, which would fulfill democratic and Socialist tasks at the same time.[11] The national bourgeoisie, for Mariátegui, could not be a subject of revolution and the anti-imperialist struggle. This role corresponded to the proletariat, allied with the indigenous peasants, according to his document "Programmatic Principles of the Socialist Party."

As Alberto Flores Galindo demonstrates in his seminal study, Mariátigui received profound critiques from the Komintern at the moment of formation of the Peruvian Socialist Party.[12] These critiques reveal the importance of the heterodoxy professed by the Peruvian thinker faced with the "Stalinization" of Marxist thought in Latin America in the decade of the 1930s. Against the "stagist" Stalinist theorizations, and quite contrary to the Argentine Communist Party and its leader, Vittorio Codovilla, Mariátegui seems to sympathize with the defeated branch of the Trotskyist current in Marxist thought called the Left Opposition. For instance, Trotsky's text "Where Is England Going?," upon revealing the "transitional stabilization of capitalism,"[13] served to back up Mariátegui's revolt against the Stalinist stagism, a theorization that negated the possibility of the Socialist struggle in Latin America in the historical present of Mariátegui's and Arguedas's lifetimes.

José María Arguedas declared his debt, however problematic, to Mariátegui's legacy on numerous occasions. Just to mention a few instances, we can turn to the discourse that opened this chapter or the novel *Yawar fiesta,* where the *chalos* (recent indigenous immigrants who live in Lima) pray to Mariátegui's portrait before planning what they imagine as an emancipatory action for the Indians of Puquio. The dialectic movement that realizes the synthesis between universal theory (such as Marxism) and the careful study of the reality of the country and continent is strongly present in Arguedean ethnography and novels, just as it is in Mariátegui's texts. The imperative to transform the latifundio as the only solution to the agrarian problem (and, for Arguedas, the cultural problem) is present since the very first short stories. Since the very beginning the struggle against the *principales* (landholding elite and authorities) is in the context of what, according to the Third International, was denominated "agrarian capitalism."[14]

Since his first publication, the antagonism presented on the pages of Arguedean fiction defines the oppressive pole in a largely constant and precise manner, while the political subjectivity of the protagonist of the social struggle tends to change. Ernesto exclaims at the end of the short story "Warma kuyay," "I wish death on all the principales." Another example is the short story "La agonia de Rasu Ñiti," when the *dansak',* in the hour of his death, prophesizes metonymically the death of the *patrón* (lord) saying that the light of the Condor-spirit will destroy his stallion, and without his horse he is nothing. But the subjectivity of the struggle's protagonist vacillates between the "I" of Ernesto, the narrator of the first short stories, and the communal subject of "*indios,*" "mestizos" or "cholos."[15] This ambiguity of the subject of action is a constant in Arguedean narrative until the end, but this same ambiguity inspires an ever more complex and creative elaboration on antagonism and on political subjectivity.

Three aspects are latent in the Arguedean narrative corpus, but they acquire an explicit manifestation beginning with *El Sexto* and culminating with *The Foxes:* (1) anti-imperialism, (2) the struggle for land, and (3) the struggle against capitalism. The last three novels assume these tasks as definitive axes of a possible program of struggle.

The Subject of Revolution in Arguedean Novels

El Sexto is Arguedas's autobiographical novel that narrates his experience of imprisonment in the Lima jail of the same name. Gabriel, the main character, is a university student unaffiliated with any party who finds himself imprisoned on the same floor as the political prisoners of Communist and Aprista persuasion. The affiliates of these leftist parties fight among themselves throughout the narrative, and their dialogues become fertile space for the elaboration of political concepts. On the floors below, the common prisoners are held. Their inhumane living conditions inspire further reflections of the main characters on the nature of oppression, inequality, and the postcolonial ills of Peru. The reader has access to all this material through the vision of Gabriel, the protagonist-narrator of the novel and Arguedas's alter ego.

El Sexto stages the moment of consolidation of class-consciousness as the articulation of anti-imperialist struggle.[16] This text also tries to define, oscillating between the prescriptive theory and a search for realist representation that surpasses any theory, the agent of the socialist revolution, which is articulated as the only action that offers some hope, although not exempt from certain doubts of the protagonist-narrator Gabriel.

The character Alejandro Camac is capable of reflecting social reality in his speech.[17] As Gabriel says, "his words named the facts directly, and the ideas were born from the facts."[18] This discourse has a direct relation to "facts," that is to say, historical reality. It is creative, theoretic, and realist at the same time, and also promises transparent communication, close to incarnating the idea of the "decir limpio" (clean speech) that Arguedas pursued in all of his literary work.[19] Nonetheless, because Camac's words are pronounced on his deathbed and in prison, their impact is only debilitating and even deadly for their enunciator.

Camac, a leader of the miners and a communist who rejects the class alliances or the possibility of a popular front proposed by the Aprista political prisoners, represents the political subject that calls forth the radical change in Peruvian society. He also defines the other side of political antagonism, which emerges here, for the first time in the Arguedean trajectory, with the proper name of North American imperialism. Camac asks Gabriel, who shares his cell and becomes his disciple, "What do you say, what is bigger, the thirst of the gringos and of their Peruvian sidekicks to get rich up to the gates of hell, or this suffering of ours that strengthens our bodies [lit., makes our bodies like steel]? Who will win at the end?"[20] To respond to this question about the future of Peru, Gabriel and the readers see that it is necessary to dedicate one's energy toward the anti-imperialist struggle (against the "gringos"), the struggle against agrarian capitalism and its national representatives ("their Peruvian sidekicks"), and the appropriation of modes of production, concretely, the land.

Let us revisit the detailed analysis of the previous chapters in order to see how this program becomes refined in the pages of *Todas las sangres,* represented by the communal action of the indigenous community, as well as in the final discourse of the indigenous peasant leader, Rendón Willka. The effectiveness of the Andean indigenous community as a collective subject of transformative action is illustrated when Don Bruno sends the serfs to work in the mine. They are not owners of the mine, they do not possess the modes of production, and they serve there by obligation and without pay. But sociologist Silvia Rivera Cusicanqui studies the concept of work and labor in the Andean universe and shows that, contrary to the concept of work as a curse in biblical tradition and in the West, within the Incan order work was connected with ritual and thus escaped the negative connotation and was conceptualized as the basic dimension of dignified human existence.[21] Consequently, upon transforming the work in the mine through the ritual modality of faena, the indigenous serfs escape the process of alienation that affects workers who no longer live in the Indian communities. Thus, we witness the ritual appropriation of work in the mine by the indigenous workers, which signals a possibility of symbolic appropriation of the modes of production, a phenomenon similar to that studied by Michael Taussig in *Devil and Commodity Fetishism*. This ritual and "magic" dimension of Arguedean Socialism emerges as powerful and hope inspiring in *Todas las sangres*. At this moment in the novel, the collective indigenous subject incarnates a political actor capable of taking away, at least symbolically, the means of production from the alienating logic of the capital.

But the subject of emancipatory action becomes more ambiguous in the final discourse of the hero, Rendón Willka: "Captain! Captain sir! . . . Here, now, in these villages and haciendas, only the big trees cry. The rifles will neither extinguish the sun, nor dry the rivers, and even less take the life of all the Indians. Keep on shooting. We do not have factory weapons, which do not count. Our heart is of fire. Here, and everywhere! We have finally come to know fatherland. And you, sir, will not kill fatherland."[22] Rendón constructs here a collectivity that derives, initially, from the third person of "all the Indians," and then slides over into an "us," "who have finally come to know fatherland," which is a category that overflows the ethnic indigenous denomination and includes an alliance of the oppressed, beyond cultural fissures. The definitive trait of this collectivity is that it "finally knows fatherland"; in other words, it opts for the defense of Peru in the face of invasion of the foreign capital in the sierra, incarnated in the mining company. It must be underlined that this "we," at this moment, is articulated in opposition to the soldiers, the representatives of the Peruvian state and at the same time the defenders of the interests of the transnational company. Thus, Arguedas puts his finger in the wound and points out the workings of the internal capitalism that creates the situation when the state betrays the interests of the national population under external economic pressure. This is why the two tasks, the anti-imperialist and the anticapitalist struggles, are inextricably linked in this context.

Finally, how is the revolutionary subject, its tasks and its antagonists, defined in *The Foxes*? This novel, which has received a wealth of critical attention from Martin Lienhardt to Jon Beasley-Murray, portrays the coastal town of Chimbote at a time of rapid industrialization, influx of foreign capital, and massive migration from the Andes to the coast. Chimbote itself could be said to occupy center stage: it is the true main character of the story. The story (*relato*) of the novel is intercalated with the auto-biographical diary entries (*diarios*) by Arguedas the narrator, in which he reflects on the process of writing and on his personal struggle against the impulse to commit suicide. The novel remains unfinished and the "Last Diary" concludes with the author/narrator's suicide, both in real life and in the text, after Arguedas loses his battle against the death impulse. Filled with reflections on Peruvian reality, social inequalities, and political possibilities, the "relato" is teeming with characters who voice different options for the future of Chimbote and Peru.

To summarize and to foreshadow what follows, here the "we," articulated by Rendón, becomes hazy; also, the belief in the emancipating power of the Andean ritual, such as faena in *Todas las sangres,* disappears; and even the face of the oppressors becomes more vast and vague, less definable, because they are located "donde no llega ni sol ni luna" (where neither the sun nor the moon can reach). We could provisionally say that *The Foxes* marks, in what seems to be a threat of dissolution of the political subjectivity, the anguish about the end of the political,[23] while the political action remains within the limits of the local. Let us see now what strategic change the narrative voice proposes, when faced with this new and devastating discovery.

In the "Last Diary" the narrative voice declares:

Perhaps with me one historical cycle draws to a close and another begins in Peru, with all that this represents. It means the closing of the cycle of the consoling calender lark [*sic*],[24] of the whip, of being driven like beasts of burden, of impotent hatred, of mournful funeral "uprisings," of the fear of God and of the predominance of that God and his protégées, his fabricators. It signifies the opening of a cycle of light and of the indomitable, liberating strength of Vietnamese man, of the fiery calender lark, of the Liberator God. That God who is coming back into action. Vallejo was the beginning and the end.[25]

What is the content, then, of this radical change of focus of the social struggle in this new context, or in the face of the new understanding of this context, announced by the entire novel and particularly by this quote from the "Last Diary"? The mad Moncada, one of the characters who offers a synthetic vision of Chimbote, repeatedly and clearly identifies the antagonist of the emancipatory struggle: the transnational capital and its local agents. For instance, he says in his speech, giving the usually positive metaphor of a "star" a new and terrible meaning: "there are drunks-stars, heavenly bodies, the foreigners who drink the liquor of their people-nation of origin and who shit on the people-nation where they amass the incandescence of the sun, the fortune power."[26] This poetic metaphor offers a stark critique of the logic of late capitalism. The "stardom" here does not signify light, but the burning and destructive potential of the system that is supposed, falsely, to self-regulate, while it destroys the dependent economies of postcolonial nations. Moncada's metaphor signals the deathly metaphysics of the capitalist system, where the logic of the capital supposedly acts in the celestial spheres that no human can control. But, upon identifying these "stars" as "drunks" who have a specific national adscription, Moncada reminds the reader that these metaphysics are a falsity and that there are concrete human figures behind the abuses, the "shitting" upon the economically dependent nations such as Peru.

In the first sermon, Moncada identifies concretely his immediate and local antagonist, the capitalist-industrialist Braschi, who "hates him."[27] Nonetheless, he remains at a distance from a concrete articulation of the political subjectivity of the revolutionary agent. In flashes, he offers some partial possibilities for a multiple constitution of a revolutionary agent: the moribund ex-miner Esteban de la Cruz, Moncada himself, the "God's torero," as well as "mixed Indian-Blacks and Chinese of Peru America."[28] Only toward the end of the novel does some degree of a complex articulation of a possible popular pole occur, in the last chapter of the relato ("story") of *The Foxes,* when the leftist-oriented characters of the novel, Maxwell, Ramírez, Bazalár, Father Cardozo, and the Fox from Down Below convene in the priest's office and assay, in their conversation, the complexity of what a revolution might mean in Chimbote and who might incarnate the multiple subjects of such a revolution.

In the quote from the "Last Diary," we find another anchor for this concept, with the central mention of the "man of Vietnam." The narrative voice, when signaling that the "feared uprisings" and "the whip" are in the past, underlines the two sides of the ancient and local struggle of the Indians against the *gamonales.* The passage from this reality to the era of "fiery calender lark" is marked by the implicit parallel between the anti-imperialist and anticapitalist struggle of the "man of Vietnam" and the same struggle on the part of the diffuse political subjectivity of the marginalized and poor of Peru. The change of an era, signaled by the narrative voice, seems to be marked, above all, by an internationalist turn in the struggle for justice and emancipation. This struggle markedly overflows not only the national borders, but also the legalist democratic institutionality of the state and political parties. As in the case of the history of the pan-Andean rebellions, the "politicization of everyday life"[29] accompanies the internationalist turn in the conception of the moments of revolutionary transformation.

Redefinition of the Sphere of the Political beyond Party Politics

José María Arguedas wrote his articles and novels in Peru from the 1930s to the 1960s. The Peruvian arena of these decades was marked by the increasing presence of international investments and companies, movements of the indigenous and poor urban masses claiming their rights to citizenship, and incessant party struggles.[30] As I discussed in previous chapters, a source of special concern (and worry) for Arguedas, whose political sympathies resided with the socialist current of thought, were the party squabbles between the two parties considered to be on the left of the political spectrum: the Peruvian Communist Party (PC) and the APRA. While the programs and rhetoric of both parties announced a possibility of effective opposition to the traditionally powerful pole and parties aligned with it, the historical reality of interaction between the two parties of the left showed that their fights only weakened the oppositional potential. The critique of the disputes between the leftist activists appears in *El Sexto, Todas las sangres,* and *The Foxes.* Particularly, *El Sexto* reads like a treatise on the ills of party politics, and the condemnation of their practices is echoed in the other two novels. In *El Sexto,* the cultural aspect, Arguedas's "way of seeing the world" acquires the power to propose another kind of political sphere. His fiction widens the sphere of the political by separating it from party politics.

In the prison testimony, just as we witnessed in *Todas las sangres,* squabbles between the Communists and the Apristas not only do not further the revolutionary cause but also substantially hinder it. The insults abound among the political prisoners; for instance, the Aprista followers call the Communists "the slaves of Moscow."[31] Conversely, Pedro, the Communist leader, draws a parallel between a necessary hate for APRA and Lenin's thought about the Menshevik party of the October Revolution because "[Lenin] always called them 'those lackeys of the bourgeoisie.'"[32] But Camac, the lucid voice in the novel that always has the last word, contradicts Pedro and all the comrades who radically criticize their fellow political prisoners: "The Aprista miners have betrayed me a lot. . . . But to hate, what is called to hate a worker, maybe it is necessary, but my heart cannot learn to do it. I hate the damned gringos and I will die fighting against them! But as for a cheated workers' leader, I hate him only at the moment of the betrayal; then it goes away. I see them suffer just the same as me; I see them, just like me, being spat on by the gringos and their overseers."[33] Camac critiques the party squabbles that mark relations among the political prisoners in El Sexto, and in the world beyond the walls of the penitentiary. The same motif runs through *Todas las sangres* and appears in *The Foxes,* especially in the portrait of the political leader Teodulo Yauri, a sell-out who fosters party quarrels among the workers of Chimbote.

Therefore, in the Arguedean narrative, the grouping by parties that defines the possibility of a negotiation within a modern democracy appears as a twofold ill, which can be paradigmatically diagnosed referring to the text of *El Sexto.* First, it serves as a weapon for the right to designate its enemy. The political prisoners are in prison because of their belonging to a leftist party, the APRA or the PC. These labels serve the political right or the power bloc to incarcerate anyone who appears to them as a dissident voice. We should remember how Rendón Willka, while not belonging to any party, was shot for being a "subversive communist," and how even the retrograde Don Bruno is persecuted under this label. Second, this division serves the same forces of the right to "divide and conquer," to quote Julius Caesar's principle for a successful imperialist campaign. The squabbles between the workers, caused by their self-adscription to different parties, debilitate the possibility of an effective resistance coming from a popular pole.

But if the political event in Arguedean fiction is removed from the sphere of party politics, then where has it been relocated? The short answer is: the political is relocated to symbolically powerful mass mobilizations that preferably avoid bloodshed. An example of such an action appears already in his earlier novel *Deep Rivers,* Arguedas's first published and widely read novel, an autobiographically based narrative about his school years in Abancay. The schoolboys observe, from a distance imposed on them by the school walls, the life of the town and neighboring haciendas and witness the first mobilization of the indigenous serfs, when the serfs leave the confines of the hacienda and march to town in unison. They demand for mass to be said for them because the whole district is in danger of a "plague" epidemic.[34] Although their demand is phrased within the paternalist logic of the traditional Catholic discourse, the fact itself of leaving the hacienda and placing any demand at all on a representative of the dominant class—in this case, the priest of the district—is a symbolic action that becomes infused with hope for change. Ernesto, when he receives the news of the *colonos*'[35] march, does not believe that they have mobilized to articulate any political action at all, since he is used to seeing them absolutely subdued and passive, held fast by the colonial hierarchies and postcolonial repressive apparatus of the state. He asks the man who saw the march, "Did you say the colonos converged on the *guardias civiles?* The colonos?"[36] And a sergeant who was supposed to stop the avalanche of the colonos speaks of their strengths: "[There exist] better men, you say? Maybe for some things, but not for defying death. Look at them coming, neither the river nor the bullets stopped them. They'll get to Abancay!"[37] This mobilization, which lacks a leader and only demands a mass to ritually scare away the plague, shows the strengths of an Indian mobilization. The first strength lies in the numbers of the Indians, in their being a majority of the population, at least in the sierra, and in their movement in unison. Second, their strength is the mythically inspired, unmovable determinacy. Third, it is the lack of a leader, since this makes the whole movement less vulnerable to bullets: the march will advance even if the first row of Indians is shot down. And, finally, the Indians have nothing to lose and everything to gain, which is why they are not afraid to die for what may appear to outsiders' eyes to be a modest demand—a mass that would absolve and send off in peace the people dying from the epidemic.

A modified version of such a symbolically infused popular action is the transplanting of funeral crosses that Gregorio Bazalár stages in *The Foxes.* When the municipality plans to build a fence around the part of the cemetery that is designated for the rich cadavers, Bazalár orchestrates a march of the slum dwellers. They pull out the wooden funeral crosses from the tombs of their dead in order to transplant them in a separate place, far from the cemetery for the rich, and also far from the actual buried corpses of the poor that the crosses were marking. Bazalár does so, although the authorities did not request or order such a move. What, then, is the purpose of this action? Through organizing the march of the poor people with their crosses on their shoulders Bazalár throws into the face of the Chimbotan society the inequality that these people experience daily. He also identifies these poor, through a strong iconic parallel, with the figure of Christ suffering his Passion. And, finally, his goal is to articulate some sort of unity among these disparate poor who do not have much in common between them, being as they are new immigrants from different parts of Peru. As Horacio Legrás observes regarding this action, Bazalár articulates a community literally founded on nothing, as the crosses are replanted in the places where there are no corpses at all. In Legrás's words, "Given that for four decades the oppositional subject in Arguedas has been thought in terms of ethnic and cultural essentialisms, the most striking feature of Bazalár's discourse lies in its relentless antifoundationalism."[38] In fact, we could postulate that this unfounded popular alliance is articulated discursively through Bazalár's speech, which, surprisingly and strangely, defines both this elusive but collective popular protagonist and its antagonists: the rich cadavers that are, in fact, grounded in the places marked by their tombs. The elusiveness and groundlessness, in this case, seem to make these popular contenders less vulnerable to the tactic of disarticulation that those in power might want to exercise against them. The Chimbotan poor, upon uprooting the crosses that mark the graves of their dead, get nearer to the situation of "nothing to lose and everything to gain," modeled paradoxically on the seemingly vulnerable and abject figure of the fearless colonos from *The Deep Rivers*.

The prophetic dimension of Arguedean thought about popular emancipatory action that overflows the realm of the legalist democratic framework becomes evident when we read accounts of recent struggles in Bolivia, within what has been defined by Bolivian theorists as "the politics of the vital needs." Linera specifically refers to the War of Water in 2000 as the turning point in what he calls the revolutionary transformation of the Bolivian state. The final straw for the Bolivian people, Linera narrates, was when the neoliberal state tried to privatize the "public resources that do not belong to the state," namely, water. This occurred when "almost irrelevant, concrete" protests became effective in the struggle against the "solid, stable neoliberal political system."[39] The popular resistance on the streets of Cochabamba thus illustrated the theoretical dimension of the events: "*The spaces of the political have widened and extended,* at the same time as this movement leaves empty a series of political institutions, such as the party system. The plebeian politics has overflown the liberal spaces, where the people is no more, and only is said to be represented [and/or present]."[40] This limit of the democratic institutions was already present before, but it became evident when the majority reached its limit of tolerance.

Functionality of Intolerance

Arguedas has been described as an advocate for communication and conciliation between "all the bloods" of Peru. Importantly, as Estelle Tarica underlined in her conference talk in Lima,[41] his public persona and his writings have been read in this vein, as today Peru is facing the task of suturing the wound that the violence of the 1980s and 1990s has left in the body of the nation. The Peruvian intellectuals of the nonmilitant Left, as Tarica calls them, thus aim to recover the possibility of leftist politics that would not be infected by discourse and the historical reality of bloodshed, and for this reason they turn to Arguedas's writings, which acquire a great moral and documentary value.

Recognizing the utmost importance of this reading of Arguedas's thought, we must look at the opposite side of his project. His prose was not marked by indifference, which is the affective counterpart of tolerant reason. His prose is passionate; it passes judgments, moralizes, and suggests a way to fix what the narratives define as wrong, rotten, and corrupt. Intolerance to very concrete moral transgressions infuses Arguedas's project with its utopian promise and power. This intolerance is structured according to a hierarchy between virtues and vices, similar to the conceptualization in the drawings of Guaman Poma de Ayala.[42] Because of the cultural syncretism between Quechua and Catholic cosmological and mythical concepts, akin to that of Guaman Poma, Arguedas divides the world into bad and good according to strict rules that are defined simultaneously by these two belief systems.

Silvia Rivera Cusicanqui's study makes Guaman Poma relevant for the decolonizing struggles of the twenty-first century. She discusses how the Andean author of the thousand-page letter to the king of Spain, written in 1612–15, uses the Incan rule as a model for "good government" while denouncing the moral abuses of power on the part of the conquistadors. The main dimensions of these abuses were the exploitation of labor power, the sexual abuse of women, and the dehumanizing discourse that the colonial power constructed about the colonized culture and its peoples.[43] This moment of taking a moral stand is common to Guaman Poma and Arguedas. It is the most "archaic" feature of Arguedean novels, which irritated Mario Vargas Llosa and Julio Cortazar,[44] writers who embrace the attitude of cultural relativism and whose novels are fascinating because, to the contrary, they make a point of not passing judgments on anything or anyone.[45]

Let me proceed to show my point by revisiting the reasons for the image of "Arguedas, the Peaceful." In his autobiographical statements he projects the image of himself as a living link between the Quechua and the creole parts of Peruvian society. He emerges in these declarations, such as in "No soy un aculturado . . ."[46] as translator, mediator, and pardoning voice for the people in power. In his most literary novel *Deep Rivers* the narrative voice locates various characters in the category of *condenado*, an Andean mythical notion of the damned souls of the people who have dirtied themselves morally in their earthly existence and are condemned to wander eternally, without ever finding peaceful rest, in an animalized, pig-like form. But the narrative voice dialectically rescues almost all those condemned toward the end of the novel. Such is the case of the student Añuco, who is condemned at first because he beats up younger and weaker children, but is redeemed at the end because Ernesto the protagonist-narrator sees him as a deeply alienated, suffering individual. The other ambiguous, complex personalities in the novel are the manipulative and influential Father Director of Ernesto's school, or the other students who engage in "impure" practices, such as masturbation or sex with Marcelina, the mad-woman. But all of these characters are either left off-frame or forgiven at the end, thus confirming the interpretation of the novel as seeking recon-ciliation and pardon even for those powerful ones who "live in the situa-tion of the objective sin," in the words of the liberation theology scholar Gustavo Gutiérrez.[47]

But there is one exception to that gallery of redeemed characters: the student Lleras. His condemnation is sealed when he calls the Afro-Peru-vian Brother Miguel a "negro de mierda" (shitty nigger). Ernesto's and the narrator's conciliatory potential cannot counter this outrage. The graphic mythical descriptions of Lleras's body, animalized and rotten in life and death, show the reader his moral rot, literally embodied. Palacitos, an indigenous student whose worldview Ernesto takes very seriously, thus predicts Lleras's future, speaking in Quechua: "This time Lleras will really be turned into a lost soul; growing bristles on his body, he will sweat and frighten the animals of the cordillera. He'll shriek from the mountain-tops in the night, cause rocky crags to tumble down, and rattle his chains. No one, no one, not even his mother will ever forgive him."[48] What is it, exactly, that defines Lleras as the only character in the novel who remains a condenado? It seems that it is the explicitly racist affront directed toward Brother Miguel, who is depicted as an innocent and generous figure. In addition, Lleras is never punished by the school authorities because he is the son of a wealthy and powerful family, while Brother Miguel is of apparently humble origins. Here, racism and its use to insult a socially inferior person, is where Ernesto's (and Arguedas's) tolerance finds its limit.

Tzvetan Todorov studies the question of tolerance and cultural rela-tivism in *The Conquest of America* and *On Human Diversity*. Todorov observes, for the case of the encounter between Cortez and Moctezuma as embodying the encounter between the Spaniards and Aztecs, that the Spaniards could subject the Aztecs as a direct result of the intolerant nature of the Christian religion. When Moctezuma asks Cortez to situate the Mexican gods on one side, and the Christian god on the other side of the temple square, Cortez refuses. This is the reason, Todorov argues, that the Spaniards conquered the Aztecs, as intolerance of the former subdued the tolerant, relativist, and accepting position of the latter. "Intransigence has always defeated tolerance," concludes Todorov.[49] Carl Schmitt also shows the dangers of a tolerant position. He observes that a sovereign state that chooses for itself a tolerant position and refuses to make the ultimate political distinction of friend and enemy when elicited to do so, will be overrun by another power that is willing to make this intolerant stand.[50] Simply, the choice is to either fight or perish.

As for the short-circuit of the idea of tolerance as the ultimate rule of thumb in a society that aspires to be democratic and modern, Todorov comments in his historical study of French philosophical thought on the question of the Other, specifically for the case of Montaigne and his aspirations to offer a model of ultimate cultural relativism in his essay "On Cannibals": "The position of generalized tolerance is untenable . . . it is an internally contradictory position, since it consists in simultaneously declaring that all attitudes are equivalent and preferring one of them, tolerance itself, to all others."[51] Thus, the liberal tolerant position becomes intolerant in the face of a cultural position that precisely does not embrace tolerance as the ultimate value. Slavoj Žižek, in his book *Violence,* studies the "antinomies of tolerant reason."[52] He shows the same short-circuit of the ideology of tolerance in the conflicts of the 2000s, such as the scandal of the Mohammed caricatures in a Danish newspaper. From the point of view of the West, the outrage of the Muslims against the newspaper, Denmark, and the whole Western world was barbaric. But from the Muslim point of view, where writing and paper are traditionally sacred, rage was the only possible reaction to the event. What is more, Žižek documents that Danish Muslims tried at first the European way of solving the conflict and demanded to be heard by Danish authorities, but they were denied this opportunity. Thus, the European country revealed the covert racism in its policy toward immigrants, thereby signaling the limit of its supposed tolerance. All this teaches us a lesson about the supposed absolute tolerance of liberal ideology: it will always have a limit.

Remembering how Arguedas's position has been read as "archaic" by other intellectuals, we may say that Arguedas, in fact, re-covers and uncovers the limits of tolerant reason that a liberal or neoliberal ideology seeks to obfuscate. Horacio Legrás observes that Arguedas's definitive option, up until his writing of *The Foxes,* can be put in terms of a demand for recognition: "Arguedas pushes for an unconditional recognition of indigenous people and their way of inhabiting the world."[53] This focus changes, nonetheless, in the last novel. Where does Arguedas draw the line, and when does the limit of tolerant reason come about? What is the limit of the incantation "que no haya rabia" (let there be no rage), pronounced by many Indian characters in Arguedean fiction? Lleras's racism seals his condemnation in *Deep Rivers*. But this character also displays certain character traits of the "condemned" that echo the abusive practices Guaman Poma de Ayala criticized at the beginning of the seventeenth century. These character traits were a constant in Arguedean fiction until *The Foxes;* one of them is public and it is an abuse of power that publicly humiliates socially inferior or weaker men; its counterpoint is rape, the private abuse of women. As we have seen in previous chapters, the separation into spheres, and the principle of "private vices, public virtues," is foreign to much of the Arguedean universe. When we observe the characters from the point of view of the limits of tolerance, it becomes evident that what could be considered "private" vices elsewhere, in Arguedean fiction bear heavily on the public persona of the abusive characters.

Lleras in *Deep Rivers,* Adalberto Cisneros and the engineer Cabrejos in *Todas las sangres,* Puñalada in *El Sexto,* the most revolting characters of the three novels, display the same pattern of abusive behavior. They physically abuse men and rape women and, in Puñalada's case, an adolescent boy. The narratives punish all three of them. The schoolboys see, prophetically, Lleras's future as a walking, disintegrating corpse. We have seen in previous chapters how Cisneros is effectively punished by indigenous justice and Cabrejos is shot point-blank by the virgin Asunta. Puñalada, the strongest thug in the Sexto prison, abuses all the weaker prisoners but finds his end at the hand of another prisoner who cannot stand looking at these abuses.

As we have seen, the punishments of Cisneros and Cabrejos were not the end of the story. The repression from the Peruvian state came as an immediate response to the exercise of justice on the part of the indigenous community and the private individual, the young Asunta. Similarly, when Puñalada (his name literally meaning "stab wound") is stabbed at the end of *El Sexto,* one of his groupies takes on his job of summoning the prisoners, after being enthroned by the prison guards as the new chief thug of the prison: "[His voice] imitated exactly the melodic line of the old 'Puñalada,' but . . . it did not slither along the dirty walls of the prison like the one emitted by the throat and tongue of the old assassin. . . . Every year, this scream would identify itself more and more with *El Sexto.* The young Negro would be getting the hang of it, if they don't kill him before, or if they don't kill *El Sexto.*"[54]

Gabriel, the character-narrator of *El Sexto* and a political prisoner himself, perceives, in this situation, the truth that by killing one cruel person in a position of power, the abuses are not curtailed. Profound systemic change is needed that would make the existence of *puñaladas* impossible, since the collaboration between the guards and the most merciless of the prisoners exemplifies the systemic ruin that characterizes political and social life in Peru. The prison thus becomes a sort of microcosm, where the social ills existent in the outside world manifest themselves explicitly. According to one of the most lucid voices in the novel, Alejandro Camac, "Here, in El Sexto, the dirt is on the outside; it's worse because of the stench and the hunger. In the palaces of the lords the dirt is from old days, it's more on the inside. I think it comes from laziness, from amassed dough, begotten at the cost of burning up half the world, and at the cost of this stench that we are suffering here."[55]

The reality of the old system of abuse described in this quote is aggravated by the selling out of national resources. The political prisoners, therefore, see themselves as an opposition to an abusive front composed of both traditional national structures of power and the newer imperialist presence of foreign mining companies. According to the visionary Camac, the only possible reaction to the presence of the exploiting foreigners, backed up by the state, is hate: "People from outside that take away the land of one's own; that get fat with that which is one's own; and on top of it, spit at you, order you to be beaten up in prisons, and put up signs in their clubs that say that dogs and Peruvians are forbidden entry. . . . Well, *that is a natural hate, like toward a snake!*"[56] Camac articulates here the ultimate limit of tolerant reason and forgiveness. Its logical consequence is the drawing up of the ultimate political distinction between friend and enemy. In Camac's speech this distinction emerges with a special force as he represents the block of the oppressors as the absolute other, as a natural enemy. According to Carl Schmitt, the language that completely strips the contending party of all humanity betrays that political moment where there is no other solution but the ultimate consequence, namely, war. Camac continues and uses the metaphor of filth, composed of gringos and gamonales, which covers up the strong, shiny metallic body of Peru. Next, his prediction for the near future of this situation stirs up both Gabriel and the reader: "The wind of revolution will blow it all off . . . and Peru will emerge, made of steel, clean and radiant."[57] The strong language of this promise stays with us until the very end of the novel, and lingers with us after the reading is finished. The last sentence of *El Sexto,* quoted above, calls up a vague collectivity of a "they," embedded in the Spanish first-person-plural verb form "*mataban*" (they kill), who are summoned to "kill El Sexto" and all the systemic ills that it condenses within its walls.

But *The Foxes* goes further as it envisions systemic change, and in confused and alluvionic monologues of its characters assembles a puzzle recipe for such a change. First, in the figure of Gregorio Bazalár, *The Foxes* divorces private vices from public virtues. The private "purity" of a subject ceases to be an absolute requisite for Bazalár to perform good acts for his community. Although in *Todas las sangres* Don Bruno had to overcome his polygamous sexual impulses in order to be able to bring about politically positive change for the Indians, this is not the case for the grassroots activist and organizer of the Chimbote slum, Gregorio Bazalár. Second, in the final scene of meeting between Father Cardozo, Maxwell, Bazalár, and Cecilio Ramírez, *The Foxes* offers at least two visions of dealing with the situation of social inequality. On one hand, the text presents the road articulated by Bazalár, one of navigating the existent structures and gaining ground, little by little, for the poorest and most marginalized dwellers of the city. On the other hand, in the words of Father Cardozo, the text calls the other characters and the reader to revolutionary action, the possibility of which depends on drawing the limit of tolerance.

Gregorio Bazalár articulates the new kind of "popular pole," as Legrás shows in his analysis.[58] He is a Quechua speaker who learns how to speak Spanish in order to accomplish concrete actions that benefit the slum community. His goals are to create some solidarity among the shantytown dwellers and to better their living conditions. For instance, he bargains with the municipality to make a private park public so that his fellow neighbors can use it. His other project is to promote cooperation and help from the U.S.-based charity program of "godfathers" that supports with monthly donations the children of poor families. Bazalár does not look to subvert anything or revolutionize the state of things, but only to navigate smartly these political waters. This new articulation of the popular pole is groundless, as Legrás shows with the example of funeral crosses that can be planted anywhere. But the kernel of its resistance resides in the fact that it somehow manages to resist the metropolitan appropriation.

Gregorio Bazalár is a new kind of popular leader, very different from Rendón Willka of *Todas las sangres*. The text emphasizes that Bazalár is effective in two tasks, (1) emerging as a political subject and (2) benefiting his community. This he can do despite his supposed bigamy, which signals a significant shift in Arguedas's thoughts on the characteristics of an effective leader. The text simply does not care that Bazalár might be sleeping with two women. Other things are more important. "At night they [Esmeralda and Juana, two women who live in Bazalár's house] slept well, and it was impossible to ascertain how many times they received Bazalár in their beds, or even if they received him at all. By the glow of their faces it was impossible to know such a thing, either about them or about any of the women more or less like them, who are the majority in the thousands of shantytowns."[59] This description emphasizes that the situation of the women is prevalent, and also draws the reader's attention to the "glow" of the women's faces, which makes us perceive that they are content with the situation. From the perspective of neighbors who wonder about their relationship, they are described as having a serene air of working women, and not that of abused wives. What is most important, "[Juana's children] went around no worse dressed than the neighbors and displayed cheeks plumper and rosier than most, even though their clothing and faces were as dirty as the worst of them. Cheerful. They never spent an hour without being tended by Esmeralda in the morning and Juana in the afternoon."[60] The whole description shows that this family is functional. The Arguedean moralizing voice that polices the private vices is silenced in light of the reality of the situation ("most women of shantytowns are . . . more or less like them"), and in the perceived functionality of the arrangement. If a bourgeois subject was supposed to be nurtured in the cradle of the bourgeois nuclear family, here it seems that the new political dimension of Bazalár's actions is sustained and backed up by his arrangement in an alternative kind of family.

The emergence of this character as a political subject is articulated in terms of "becoming part of," and not in terms of destroying the existing system of oppression. Bazalár thinks about his present and future in these terms: "'Maybe I . . . ,' he thought (no longer able to think in Quechua). 'It could be, maybe, in its lifetime of mine, that I won't be any longer a stranger in this country land where we've been born. First time and first person that ever finalizes that difficult deed in his lifetime existence.'"[61] Thinking in broken and Quechua-influenced Spanish, and not in Quechua anymore, this new kind of political subject envisions the possibility for himself to no longer be "a stranger in this country land where we've been born." The slip from "I" to "we" is very important here, as Bazalár's internal monologue extrapolates his experience to a possible replication in other active and urbanized Quechua migrants who share his challenges in the shantytowns of Peruvian cities.

Father Cardozo, the North American priest, articulates a very different vision of action for a more egalitarian future of Chimbote. Apparently adhering to liberation theology precepts, he articulates his limit of tolerance along the lines articulated by Father Gustavo Gutiérrez: "To love all men does not mean to avoid confrontation, it does not mean to maintain a fictitious harmony. The universal love is the one that is solidarity with the oppressed, and it strives to liberate also the oppressors from their own power, from their ambition and their egotism. Love toward those who live in the condition of objective sin demands of us to fight so as to liberate them from it. The liberation of the poor and that of the rich is realized simultaneously."[62] It is out of love for both the poor and the rich that the social condition of inequality must be avoided. Theologically, it is even more necessary for the benefit of the rich because it is they who find themselves in the condition of the "objective sin." Cardozo finds the limit of tolerance in the face of inequality, and it seems at times that his reflections amount to a call to arms. For instance, he tells Don Cecilio Ramírez that the differences in material possessions and social status can be effectively contested: "That can be fixed if you, Don Cecilio, get angry strongly and sincerely, like you do in front of me, in front of the bosses!"[63] He interpolates Ramírez, urging him to "get angry," and oppose himself strongly to the abuses of Braschi and other capitalists who manage Chimbote. But beyond this "anger" that needs to be born and expressed from the solid political subjectivity of men like Ramírez, Cardozo also articulates the concept of revolution; for instance, "'The revolution,' Cardozo's firm voice was heard to say, 'will not be deeds but instead will be the work of these two examples, one divine and other human, who was born of that divine one: Jesus and Ché.'"[64] But what does it mean that "revolution will not be deeds, but . . . the work of these two examples"? Spoken in a Spanish that is influenced both by English and Quechua interferences, it becomes difficult to unpack the concepts articulated in this speech, and for this reason it is necessary here to turn to the question of language.

On the Revolutionary Potential of Language Gaps

At the end of *The Foxes*, Father Cardozo describes the poorest suburbs of Chimbote: "shantytowns, silent by night, labyrinth uprising noise by day."[65] This sentence condenses Cardozo's idea of the unpredictable but emancipatory potential of the precarious marginal neighborhoods and their dwellers. The description represents plastically the material appearance of such a shantytown, and also the air (or the aura, we may say) that Cardozo feels the dwellers of these neighborhoods exude. The place is "silent by night"; the slums have no movement by night because they have no electric light or running water, and many of them are also sunk in a "night" of marginalization, crime, and drunkenness. But the description of its appearance by day is an energetic string of three forceful nouns: labyrinth, uprising, noise. "Labyrinth" connotes confusing streets, constructed without any urban planning, but also the labyrinth of wills and different subjectivities and experiences that the heterogeneous immigrant settlers bring to such a place. "Uprising" refers to the most abject misery in which many of these persons live and the social discontent that this misery inspires in them. This concept noun means that although a concrete slum may seem subdued and peaceful for the moment, it is, in fact, always a potential uprising, as long as the blazing inequalities persist in places like Chimbote. "Noise" completes the picture, evoking children crying, dogs barking, and all the sounds that fill a tightly populated, busy neighborhood. It also refers to the noise that accompanies any massive mobilization, complementing the idea of "uprising."

This description sentence, constructed in Spanish without prepositions, adjectival suffixes, or clarifying verbs, makes the description dense and laden with conceptual meaning. We saw a similar effect of language use in *Todas las sangres,* when the Indians of the Paraybamba community were designated not as "Paraybambans," but simply, avoiding the adjectival suffix, "Paraybambas." This linguistic move, reflecting the Quechua grammar rules that invade the Spanish text, denotes a more direct, unmediated relation between the Paraybamban Indians and their community, which contrasts with the uncertain relation that many Peruvians have with their community, the nation.

To illustrate the political dimension of such a use of language, let us compare Arguedean writing style with the phrase that designates a collective political subject in the new Bolivian constitution: *campesino indígena originario,* indigenous original peasants.[66] Xavier Albó calls this bulky term a "salomonic" decision, as it signals recognition of different historical experiences of different indigenous groups in Bolivia who participated in drafting the constitution. Here, as Albó explains, the term "indigenous" locates the demands of these persons and communities in the context of recent international recognition of indigenous rights, such as the 1989 Convention 169 of Indigenous and Tribal People in Geneva.[67] The term "original" (*originario*) is the most recent one, which alludes to the fact that the indigenous nations existed prior to Spanish colonization and thus recognizes their special rights as the original population of the national territory. Finally, the term "peasant" (campesino) dates back to the reforms after the Bolivian revolution of 1952, when ethnic terms were considered racist and reformers sought to abolish them, much like Arguedas's interlocutors-sociologists in Peru during the 1960s. The result is a term that may present some difficulties to a jurist, but which becomes more accessible and usable, for the purpose of placing demands both on the state and on the international community, by the beneficiaries of the constitution, the Bolivians of different ethnic affiliations. Albó emphasizes in his analysis of this term that it must be understood as a unity, and the terms should not be handled separately, thus creating a new concept.[68] We can observe that this new juridical and constitutional concept is born by piling up nouns, each one with its own strong conceptual and historically laden charge.

These examples, literary and juridical, teach us how to construct a factory for new concepts. In Arguedas's writing, and in the Bolivian case when the descriptive and the prescriptive documents for a multilingual society are at stake, new concepts are born in the language gap. It is often considered that an imperfect knowledge of a language is a limiting experience for a person who manages more than one language at a time, and both (or more) imperfectly. It is also considered bothersome for the receptor of the message, the audience. Arguedean writing, both fictional and essayistic, teaches us that, in fact, the gaps that such an experience opens are so many invitations to think between the languages, to translate from one language to the other, and from one conceptual universe to the other. What we called the "Andean universe" in our introduction is forcefully present in the gaps opened by this bilingual situation, through the irruption of Quechua syntax and direct translation of certain key Quechua words into Spanish, in surprising contexts. For instance, a complex Quechua expression denoting, among other things, a revolutionary change is "yawar mayu," translated usually and understandably as "río de sangre," "river of blood." In Quechua syntax, however, the two words that construct this very important concept, both in Quechua oral tradition and in Arguedas, are two nouns: "blood water." The elimination of the preposition "of" between the two words makes the expression more forceful. By using this resource, many characters speak between the languages and "infect" one another with their way of speaking. Therefore, an elaboration of concepts starts at the level of form, where form, in fact, becomes inseparable from content. This discovery of the language gap as a womb for new production of thought suggests that Arguedas's position was a privileged one. It is because of living in a language gap, which he was constantly trying to bridge, that he could aspire to be the "living bond" between Spanish-speaking and Quechua-speaking Peru and to connect the two conceptually. Remembering Walter Benjamin's reflection of Kafka as a great author who "is a foreigner in his own tongue," we must say that Arguedas made the most of his own situation of being a foreigner, although differently so, in both of the tongues in which he spoke and wrote.

The creation of innovative concepts of community, subjectivity, and the revolutionary change in the characters' speech is at work in all of Arguedas's narratives, but it reaches its culmination toward the end of his trajectory in *Todas las sangres* and especially in *The Foxes.* In the last scene of the story (relato) in *The Foxes,* the "Yankee priest" Father Cardozo projects a possibility of revolution in Chimbote and elaborates on how revolutionary change should be brought about. He does so in the presence of his guests, another U.S. priest, Hutchinson, and the "mysterious visitor," the mythical Fox from Down Below, Diego, the moving force behind the narrative. As Father Cardozo tries to express his ideas, the other priest is at a loss because of the language used by his colleague: "he [Hutchinson] was making a great effort to understand the muddy torrent of unexpectedly intricate Yankee-Cecilio-Bazalártic language in which the priest spoke, or else in which that messenger was inducing him to express himself."[69] The text suggests that Cardozo is producing this "muddy torrent" of language because the mythical Fox, who steps from *The Huarochiri Manuscrip*t and into the narrative of *The Foxes,* is inspiring him to do so. Cardozo's speech is an accumulation of language gaps that make his nonnative Spanish function in a new way and acquire unexpected new meanings. Cardozo speaks a nonstandard Spanish with a "Yankee" accent. Bricklayer Don Cecilio and pig raiser Bazalár, Cardozo's guests who earlier in this scene expressed their vision of Chimbote, are Quechua speakers who learned to speak Spanish later in life and whose Spanish is full of grammatical mistakes or, better said, new turns and expressions. Cardozo's speech becomes "infected" both with his own imperfections and with the imperfections of his interlocutors. These language gaps give rise to the definition of revolution in this key conversation, which wraps up the tale of *The Foxes.*

Before I turn to a careful reading of this definition, I would like to make two observations. First, this final scene of the novel is almost triumphant: over the most abject human suffering emerges the possibility to organize and to resist the forces that cause inequalities and suffering. Horacio Legrás interprets this vitality as a sign of some recovery from the pure negativism he reads in Arguedas's poem published before *The Foxes,* "Appeal to Some Intellectuals."[70] Second, remembering Nelson Osorio's testimony on Arguedas's statement that he "has finished *The Foxes,*"[71] the story reads as complete, with the evaluation of the present state of things and a program for future action. Arguedas's suicide by gunshot narrated in the "Last Diary" does not take away the articulation of the revolutionary hope in the last chapter of the story.

Another kind of "gunshot" takes center stage in Cardozo's version of the revolution. The conversation takes place in the presence of two martyrs, in effigy: the crucified Jesus Christ and Ché Guevara.

> "Then what, Father Cardoso? Come right out and say it, plain and clear, the way it oughta be."
>
> "Revolution, Don Cecilio! Like the Lord Jesus Christ in his preaching and death, like Ché in his *heroic modern courage preaching . . .*"
>
> "Gunshot?"
>
> "Yes, Don Cecilio. A bullet in the head and heart of each one, not to blow their brains out nor break the *nobility muscle* and empty out its blood. A shot of *understanding light* to give the human being clarity and energy so all human beings can see that Negroes, Chinese Indians, and Indians are just like Our Lord, the way Ché saw them, with real strength and determination *to make themselves respected;* to see that one man is the same as another one."[72]

No doubt, the priest's speech calls for action, but what kind of action? Don Cecilio asks for a straightforward answer, "plain and clear." The priest's response is a committed declaration, for which he could have easily landed in prison in 1970s Peru, but how plain or clear is this declaration? "What is to be done," in other words?

To understand the programmatic dimension of this statement, first we must make a note on the translation. The official English translation sounds much less torn than the Spanish original because of certain syntactic parallels between English and Quechua that differentiate them from the Romance language. For instance, the expression "nobility muscle" referring to the heart is not a travesty in English because in this language, as in Quechua, a noun ("nobility") can be used as an adjective. This is not the case in Spanish.[73] In order to render the syntactic and conceptual novelty of this writing, the Spanish word order should be respected. Heart, "musculo generosidad," should be translated as "muscle generosity." The understandable English demands a preposition here connecting the two words (muscle of generosity?), which is lacking. This way the reader can appreciate the semantic gap that opens up when these nouns are strung together without the support of other parts of speech.

Now, we can try to understand what kind of "gunshot" Father Cardozo, in a language that reminds us of Gustavo Gutiérrez's formulation of the principles of liberation theology, proposes as the answer to the Peruvian inequalities. "Balazo de luz entendimiento," states the Spanish original, meaning, literally, "shot of light understanding." What is missing here is the preposition "of" in English, or "de" in Spanish: light of understanding, in other words, illumination. The call here is not to take up arms, but to antagonize differently and with the purpose to make the oppressors see the truth articulated in liberation theology, that the rich and the oppressors have to seek their own liberation from the situation of "objective sin."

In a characteristically Arguedean dialectical move, Cardozo's inter-locutor Ramírez reminds him that "they, you know, the bosses, make the machine-gun speak."[74] How can one "illuminate" them, the bosses, if they resort to the nonmediating, machine-gun "speech"? But Cardozo, again, contests: "The machine gun, friend compañero Cecilio, is shot by a poor human being's hand, right? The boss doesn't pull the trigger. Wait! The millionaire boss's delicate hand doesn't manufacture the trigger either."[75] Cardozo then tries to remind Don Cecilio that there is hope in those "poor human beings": "Don't you believe, at all, at all, in the man who handles the trigger and the factory?"[76] What is the content of this "belief" that Cardozo elicits from Ramírez? It seems that it is the programmatic call to speak to the poor, desubjectified persons used by the oppressive pole, such as the soldiers we analyzed in *Todas las sangres*. This call, within this fictional universe, precedes the real-life call that the archbishop of Salvador Oscar Romero, one of the thinkers of liberation theology, would make to the soldiers serving in Salvadorean armed forces: "Stop the repression! . . . Before an order to kill that a man may give, the law of God must prevail that says: Thou shalt not kill! No soldier is obliged to obey an order against the law of God."[77]

But Romero's words are extracted from his last Sunday sermon, before he was assassinated by the Salvadorean military. The history speaks not mediation, but martyrdom. The note of justified hate is also the final, con-cluding note in Father Cardozo's speech, on the last page of the story of *The Foxes,* and one of the few instances in Arguedean prose when hatred is presented as a valid option. As Cardozo sits in his study, again in the presence of the images of Christ and El Ché, he reads the excerpt from the Apocalypse of Saint John: "So now faith, hope and love endure forever, but the greatest of these is love." But the priest immediately contradicts the biblical quote, in what is his final reflection:

"And what about hatred?" Cardozo asked in English. "Don Cecilio Ramírez's tearful hatred—that's what's got me unhinged, and has unhinged everybody in the office. Here in Chimbote I've seen visions part apocalyptic and part tender. Lord! Every night and every day I see visions that inflame me and trouble me. This Don Cecilio says more, much more than the body of the young girl who died at childbirth, the one who was lying on the reed mat in the midst of hundreds of flies, out there in the shantytown of Coishco, while her relatives were drinking. Now I know that the flies might have been sucking hatred from that dismal corpse."[78]

The language of reflection here is transparent, uncontaminated by the language gap, since what we are reading is a translation of Cardozo's thoughts in his native English. But it seems that the absence of strange turns of phrase has to be supplemented with the elliptic and enigmatic connections that Cardozo's flow of consciousness presents. Cardozo is "unhinged," in other words, moved, inspired by the attitude of Cecilio Ramírez. The priest reads the "tearful hatred" as the key to this attitude, and also its eloquence, as Don Cecilio "says more" than the corpse of the dead girl. Before we turn to the corpse, let us discuss the content of Ramírez's attitude and life option ("the way of inhabiting the world," in Legrás's wonderful words). The striking characteristic of Ramírez's attitude, encoded here in the expression of "tearful hatred" is his refusal to deposit his hope in anything or anyone. "I've never ever had hope!" Ramírez was heard to say. "I've just kept going strong. Nowadays, with Max givin' a hand, work produces. Real hope, where is it?"[79] Jean-Luc Nancy's attitude of finitude, which we observed in Rendón Willka's declarations, marks Ramírez's discourse as he refuses to project his expectations beyond here and now. In line with his rejection of a utopian horizon—be it the kingdom of God or the dictatorship of the proletariat—Ramírez also refuses to adopt any strong political position, denying that he and Maxwell belong to the Communist Party. "We are just builders," he says. His self-defined essence is in the identification with his trade and with his lot, which is to help other new immigrants who are coming to the slums from the sierra, worse off than Ramírez himself. Ramírez has no hope and no program of fighting; he just fights daily for a piece of bread on the table and for his own dignified existence and for that of others that he takes under his wing. So, what is this "surplus" of Ramírez's discourse, that "says much more" than the abject corpse? What does the corpse say that Ramírez's speech is "more," and "more" in what sense? Is it more powerful? More promising?

In fact, in realist novels, the corpses are silent. The vision of this corpse is what speaks to Cardozo, throwing into his face the abjection of the life that the poor of the slums face daily. The corpse, a young girl who died in childbirth, is in fact presented as an innocent victim of the everyday flagrant injustice in a society such as that of Arguedean Chimbote. The banality of this corpse is evident, as Cardozo mentions that her relatives are drinking while the corpse is being eaten by the flies. They are drinking because a corpse like that is one more in a series of other tragedies that are waiting for the shantytown dwellers every day; they drink to forget the precarious condition of their own life. And meanwhile, the flies, the privileged messengers of affect in this novel, are "sucking hatred from this dismal corpse." They will fly elsewhere and on their tiny legs they will carry the hatred, like pollen or bacteria that flies in their biological reality actually transmit. Hatred becomes a sort of illness that might become a "*malestar social*" (social illness) when these flies will carry the message of hate from this disintegrating corpse of a girl who could have lived on, if the conditions of her material existence were different.

Faced with this crude reality, Cardozo says that he sees "apocalyptic and tender visions." The sight of the corpse, for Cardozo, like the other events he witnesses in Chimbote, acquires epic proportions, and this is why he speaks of having "visions," despite the fact that these are real events that he is witnessing. The vision of the fly-ridden corpse is not just the "apocalyptic" vision of that one corpse, but of all the deaths of innocent victims that the situation of injustice produces. The "tender" vision of the firm, generous, hopeless Don Cecilio Ramírez also goes beyond the figure of Ramírez himself and embodies all those workers, in whom Cardozo calls Ramírez to believe. Ramírez might not have "real hope," in his philosophic standpoint of pure immanence, but his attitude, his actions, and his existence make Cardozo believe in people like Ramírez and their capacity for "becoming agents of their own destiny," an incarnation of what Father Gustavo Gutiérrez phrases as the chief goal of the Catholic church's "option for the poor."[80] The vision of the dead girl inspires hate; but in this reflection on hate, the answer to the question "What is to be done?" is *not* bloodbath. This answer is coded in the figure of Don Cecilio Ramírez and his capacity to become an agent of his own destiny through work that his life story recounts.

NOTES

Introduction. Arguedas: Rethinking Community

Epigraphs: Legrás, *Literature and Subjection*, 208; Žižek, *Violence*, 126.

1. Arguedas, "No soy un aculturado . . . ," 257.

2. In this book, I use the expression "Quechua worldview" and "Andean worldview" as a translation of the now widely used term *cosmovisión andina*. Recent works on indigenous philosophy and cosmogony explore this concept, often citing as a reference the already classical study by Frank Salomon in his introductory essay to the critical edition of *The Huarochiri Manuscript*. For instance, in *Decir nosotros*, Josefa Salmón speaks of *cosmovisión andina* as a term that does not reflect the separation into the spheres of the metaphysical and the secular and operates on the basis of such key concepts as *principio de complementariedad*, prevalent in the Aymara language and worldview, or a particular vision of history that conceives of "walking forward while looking back." This worldview is not characterized by purity, and when scholars speak of the "Andean perspective" in the twentieth or twenty-first century, they always refer to a set of concepts that have evolved from the cultural contact and bear traits of colonial evangelization as well as remainders of the pre-Hispanic philosophies and traditions. See also Luizaga, *Filosofía andina*; Urton, *At the Crossroads*; Urton, *Social Life of Numbers*; Zuidema, *Inca Civilization in Cuzco*; Salomon, introductory essay to *The Huarochiri Manuscript*; Rama, *Formación de una cultura*; Murra, *Formaciones económicas*.

3. On history, see Braudel, *La historia*; quotation from Gutiérrez, "Presencia."

4. The novel *Todas las sangres* (All the bloods) is unavailable in English translation. All the translations from this novel are mine. While rendering into English the invented and concept-laden heterogeneous language of Arguedean characters, a translator needs to invent a new modality of English in order to express the conceptual density of the original. This is the reason why, whenever I offer my own translation of Arguedean prose, I provide the Spanish original in the endnotes. The edition used throughout is *Todas las sangres,* 3rd ed. (1965; repr., Lima: Editorial Horizonte, 1987).

5. The quotes and examples from *Los ríos profundos* are taken from the translation by Barraclough, *Deep Rivers*. The novel *El Sexto* (1961) is unavailable in English. All the translations from this novel are mine. I quote the Spanish original in the endnotes for

the reader's convenience. The edition used throughout is Arguedas, *El Sexto*. Most of the quotes from *The Foxes* are from Barraclough's translation, in Ortega and Fernández, *The Fox from Up Above*. In a few cases, it was necessary for the purposes of my analysis to provide my own translation of the text from the Spanish original edition, Arguedas, *El zorro de arriba*. In those cases, I state that the translation is mine and reference the Spanish original in the endnotes.

6. Strong, "Foreword," xxv.

7. One of the serious critiques on the roundtable that points in the direction of this discussion is Manrique's "Una mirada histórica," 58. Pinilla, *Arguedas, conocimiento y vida,* returns to the discussion of the roundtable as vitally (or mortally) important for Arguedas, and as a historically revealing event that explains the process of consolidation of the discourse of social sciences in Peru. Legrás, *Literature and Subjection,* 211–12, discusses this event as a conceptual short-circuit between the discussants that reveals real, important tensions in Arguedas's project. Fernández, "Arguedas y la crítica," critiques the fact that the roundtable has acquired too much importance in the discussion of Arguedean work. I agree with Fernández insofar as I consider it irrelevant if the roundtable was or was not one of the motives for Arguedas's suicide. But I do believe that the contradictions this event revealed are important because they point to some real fissures which the Arguedean prose addresses.

8. Escobar, *¿He vivido en vano?,* 37.

9. The term "*misti*" is a Quechua expression that signifies a non-Indian Peruvian. I do not translate this term, as it is constitutive of the almost always antagonistic dyad in Arguedas's fiction: Indians versus mistis. Importantly, the mistis may be phonotypical mestizos and may be bilingual in Quechua and Spanish. But their way of life outside the community, in urban settings, and often their position of power and oppression in relation to the Indians define them as the oppressive others from the point of view of the indigenous characters that Arguedean fiction often defends. The Peruvian social scientists use the term "misti" to characterize the situation of abuse of the indigenous population of the sierra by the dominant group. See, for example, Manrique, "Gamonalismo, lanas y violencia," 213.

10. Legrás, *Literature and Subjection,* 212.

11. Escobar, *¿He vivido en vano?,* 67.

12. Stefanoni, "Un nuevo mapa," 10.

13. "Bolivia en este momento de su historia, tiene ante sí el reto histórico de sentar las bases para una convivencia intercultural. Esa tarea requiere ante todo, e inicialmente, de una *voluntad colectiva* de convivir con lo ajeno, voluntad que para ser fructífera debiera, en el futuro, asentarse en una verdadera *comprensión* del Otro en toda su extrañeza y peculiaridad" (Mier Cueto, "Las prácticas jurídicas Aymaras," 61).

14. Salmón, "La presencia indígena."

15. Laclau, "Why Do Empty Signifiers Matter to Politics?"

16. García Linera, *El Estado Plurinacional.*

17. In the new constitution, approved on February 7, 2009, Bolivia declared as its official languages Spanish, Quechua, Aymara, and Guaraní. Bolivia's new name is listed in all four languages in the official documents: Bulibya Mamallaqta (Quechua), Wuliwya Suyu (Aymara), Tetã Volívia (Guaraní), and Estado Plurinacional de Bolivia. In fact, the Bolivian state recognizes as official all thirty-seven languages spoken on its territory, but in practice it manages to publish documents in the major four. The text of the constitution can be consulted at "Constitución Política el Estado" (CPE), February 7, 2009,

bolivia.infoleyes.com/shownorm.php?id=469.

18. Albó, "Sentido de 'naciones y pueblos,'" 20–27.

19. Portocarrero, "La seducción del poder"; García Linera, "Marxismo e Indianismo."

20. Huaco P., "Derechos humanos," 68.

21. Ibid., 76; emphasis added.

22. For more information on the Bagua massacre, see the interview by Carlos Noriega, "Hay más muertos," *Diario la primera*, June 22, 2009, www.diariolaprimeraperu.com/online/entrevista/hay-mas-muertos_40840.html.

23. Bosteels, "Marx and Latin America," 5.

24. Vilas and Stoller, "Lynchings," 110.

25. See Stefanoni, "Un nuevo mapa," 11; and García Linera, "Geopolítica de la Amazonía."

26. Landes, *Cocalero*.

27. Žižek, *Violence*, 109–11.

28. There are other deaths in *Todas las sangres*, like the death of mestizo Bellido and that of the women protesting in the departmental capital. Although protesting, these characters fall as accidental victims of repression. Rendón and Anto, however, give their own deaths an obvious symbolic, ideologically charged meaning.

29. Moore, *En la encrucijada*; Rama, *Transculturación narrativa*.

30. Schmitt, *The Concept of the Political*, 26–27.

31. "Nuestro corazón está de fuego. ¡Aquí, en todas partes! Hemos conocido la patria al fin. Y usted no va a matar la patria, señor" (Arguedas, *Todas las sangres*, 455).

32. Escobar, *¿He vivido en vano?*; Pinilla, *Arguedas, conocimiento y vida*, 153–56; Vargas Llosa, *La utopía arcaica*.

33. Quoted in Legrás, *Literature and Subjection*, 234. Vargas Llosa is a brilliant novelist, but he is committed to the ideal of the modern democracy and is seemingly blind to the internal contradictions that mark this model of government.

34. Tarica, "El 'decir limpio.'"

35. Castro-Klarén, "Like a pig, when he's thinkin.'"

36. Escobar, *¿He vivido en vano?*, 36.

37. Arguedas, *Todas las sangres*; see esp. 108, 122, 132.

38. Legrás, *Literature and Subjection*, 259–60.

39. Conversely, Beasley-Murray interprets this disappearance of the narrative voice through its counterpart, namely, the proliferation of author figures. He states that *The Foxes*, unlike the "thinly" written autobiography of the earlier texts, such as *Deep Rivers*, presents the multiplication of Arguedas's "I's" in Moncada, Diego the Fox, Esteban de la Cruz, and Stut, apart from the voice that appears in the "Diaries" (Beasley-Murray, "*Arguedasmachine*," 116).

40. Cornejo Polar, *Los universos narrativos*, 170.

41. Lienhard, "Avatares del yo."

42. Arguedas, *Todas las sangres*, 100–101.

43. Arguedas, *The Foxes*, 56–57, 63–64.

44. Culler, "Derrida and Democracy," 5.

45. See, e.g., Beasley-Murray, "*Arguedasmachine*"; Lybeer, "Arguedas' Zorros"; Tarica, *The Inner Life*; and Moreiras, "Freedom from Transculturation."

46. Tarica, "Arguedas después de la violencia."

47. Gutiérrez, "Presencia."

48. Portocarrero, "Arguedas, sanador del Peru." *Página de Gonzalo Portocarrero* (blog).

http://gonzaloportocarrero.blogsome.com/2013/06/14/arguedas.

49. Bhabha, *The Location of Culture;* Spivak, "Can the Subaltern Speak?"; Guha, *Dominance without Hegemony;* Beverley, *Subalternity and Representation.*

50. Strong, "Foreword," xxv.

51. Portocarrero, "La seducción del poder."

52. Méndez, "República sin indios," 20–21.

53. Klarén, *Peru;* Thurner, *From Two Republics.*

54. Flores Galindo, *Buscando un Inca,* 252; Mallon, "De ciudadano a 'otro,'" 15.

55. Flores Galindo, *Buscando un Inca,* 233–59; Méndez, "República sin indios," 28–39.

56. Flores Galindo, *Buscando un Inca,* 243.

57. Ibid., 263.

58. Ibid., 282.

59. Cornejo Polar, *Los universos narrativos,* 168–69.

60. Degregori, "Jóvenes y campesinos," 401.

61. The suffrage reforms took place in 1856, 1860, and 1867. The first one included men over twenty-one years of age who owned land and who served in the army. But in 1867, theoretically, all male citizens over twenty-one had the right to vote. See Mallon, "De ciudadano a 'otro,'" 11; Manrique, "Comentario a F. Mallon," 67.

62. Klarén, *Society and Nationhood,* 326; Arguedas, *Todas las sangres,* 264.

63. Arguedas, *Todas las sangres,* 263–64.

64. *Subprefecto* is a rank in the Peruvian police hierarchy, which designates the second-in-command to a local sheriff. In *Todas las sangres,* these officers, whose power is significantly limited, appear as especially abusive toward the Indians. It seems that by way of these arbitrary abuses, they are compensating for their curbed power within the police hierarchy.

65. "Herida no vale. . . . Otro cosa vale, subprefecto. Yo, mayor alcalde, tercer año de primaria. Comuneros vamos a ser respeto. Vamos a saber leer. Comuneros somos tantos, tantos. Con bandera piruana vamos a parar firmes" (Arguedas, *Todas las sangres,* 317).

66. "Las contradicciones [represented in the novel] son las que naturalmente existen entre las diferentes gentes de nuestro país, los diferentes modos de ver el mundo. La gran ambición del libro fue, precisamente, mostrar esta multiplicidad de concepciones, según los grados de aproximación a un mundo en furor" (Arguedas in Escobar, *¿He vivido en vano?,* 27; emphasis added in text).

I believe the enigmatic *"mundo en furor,"* "world of fury," refers to the fast-paced modernization and movement toward what we now know as globalization. Arguedas positions the human collectivities he represents on the pages of the novel according to their distance from, or proximity to, this "fury" of rapid modernization.

67. "La estrategia de Arguedas de insistir en la imposibilidad de subsumir la diferencia cultural en el terreno de la política hegemónica no resulta reactiva frente al terreno de la política, sino que más bien ensancha las fronteras de lo político para incluir en el concepto todas las sutiles formas de dominación y de resistencia que han caracterizado la imposición de un modelo postcolonial por más de dos siglos" (Legrás, *"Yawar Fiesta,"* 77).

68. Ibid.

69. "Contra la extensión de los espacios de la explotación capitalista o el desierto de la expropiación, se ha producido la marea alta de una nueva política de las necesidades vitales, en torno a la cual la gente no sólo se ha organizado para disputar las condiciones de la supervivencia, reproducción y la misma producción en el campo, sino también la recomposición de la vida política. La marea alta ha modificado los bordes de lo político.

Los espacios de la política se han ampliado y extendido, a la vez que este movimiento deja un conjunto de instituciones políticas vacías, como el sistema de partidos. La política plebeya ha desbordado los espacios liberales, donde además el pueblo no está, sólo se dice que está representado" (García Linera et al., "La forma multitud," 192; emphasis added in text).

70. Hardt and Negri, *Multitude;* Virno, *A Grammar of the Multitude;* Agamben, *Means without Ends.*

Chapter I. Sovereignty and Authority in *Todas las sangres*

1. Schmitt, *The Concept.*
2. Milstein, "Between Voluntarism"; Hardt and Negri, *Multitude*, 3.
3. Milstein, "Between Voluntarism."
4. Agamben, *State of Exception,* 74. Agamben's argument can be read as suggesting that as a modern structure of the state, democracy in its essence lacks authority. Consequently, it always tends toward the declaration of all kinds of "states of exception." Agamben's suspicion toward democracy dialogues with a similar affirmation by Schmitt (*The Concept*), who suggests that democracies, in fact, tend toward creation of totalitarian states. Arguedas's skepticism in the face of a supposedly victorious Peruvian modern democratic state is laden with similar suspicions.
5. Agamben, *State of Exception,* 81.
6. "Mysterious means of an obscure nature, while mystical means having a divine meaning that transcends human understanding." From *Roget's New Millennium Thesaurus,* Lexico Publishing Group, LLC, Thesaurus.com, s.v. "Mystical," http://thesaurus .reference.com/browse/mystical (accessed July 20, 2012).
7. Suetonius Tranquilus, *Lives of the Caesars.*
8. "Providencia" is a synonym to "Dios" ("God," spelled with the capital *D*). From Real Academia Española, s.v. "Providencia," http://buscon.rae.es/draeI/SrvltConsulta?TIPO_ BUS=3&LEMA=providencia (accessed July 20, 2012).
9. Arguedas, *Todas las sangres,* 38–42.
10. Ibid., 38–40.
11. "Al momento de reunirse la Asamblea comunal no sólo se convoca a las personas físicas de la comunidad para tomar la decisión, sino que a través de ritos (con hojas de coca y con challa) se hacen presentes las deidades del Ayllu y los antepasados (seres con poderes sobrenaturales) . . . ; ambos seres son considerados parte de la comunidad y por tanto tienen derecho al voto que ejercen por medio de signos particulares en los ritos, en consecuencia la elección de una pareja no sólo tiene la avenencia de las personas sino también de las divinidades. . . .

La autoridad comunal, por tanto, tiene un poder enraizado en una compleja legitimidad política y religiosa, su poder le ha sido otorgado por lo humano pero también por lo sobrehumano, estas condiciones hacen de su legitimidad social una condición fuertemente cimentada. Este poder doblemente estructurado por lo religioso y lo político, en realidad sólo se presenta como dual para los ojos foráneos, pues en el contexto cultural aymara ese poder es unitario y su separación en aquel contexto, aunque para fines analíticos, es inexacta" (Mier Cueto, "Prácticas jurídicas," 67).
12. Arguedas, *Todas las sangres,* 37.
13. Ibid., 263.

14. "Los indios sólo tienen su pueblo o su patrón, los señores tenemos patria: el Perú" (ibid., 247).

15. Schmitt, *The Concept*, 27.

16. Schmitt uses the term in French, "*hors la loi,*" because he traces the practice of proclaiming someone "outside the law" to the French Revolution, as the origin of modern democracies. In this sense, he underlines that the idea of being "outside the law" or in a "state of exception" has its origins in democratic tradition, and not in an authoritarian one as could be expected.

17. Schmitt explains the difference in terms of the Latin words *inimicus* and *hostis.* While inimicus was a private enemy, hostis was the enemy of the republic. While one could forgive one's enemies in the private domain, the biblical advice did not apply to the category hostis. The hostis, in fact, was constituted as a sort of "natural" enemy, a radical other (Schmitt, *The Concept*, 28–29).

18. "¿Comunismo? Ahistá, patrón: tú comunista si Rendón mata inginiero; Rendón también comunista; señores Orrantías, San Isidros nada comunistas; hombres comiendo con chanchos en Montón, en todo barriada, cuando sale pedir, gritando, comidita ¡ahistá comunista! Cuando hacer choza en arenal de nadies para encontrar sombrita ¡ahistá comunista! . . . Patrón, yo ningún huerfano, sabiendo claro de comunismo. Inginiero sabe. Con su boca, con su dedo dice: ¡comunista! Y ahí no más le meten golpe u bala, según" (Arguedas, *Todas las sangres,* 161).

19. Schmitt, *The Concept*, 28.

20. Arguedas, *Todas las sangres,* 425–26.

21. "Contará con el poder suficiente para enfrentarlos [a los indígenas que viven cerca de las tierras de la mina] *en lo económico y lo político*" (ibid., 331; emphasis added in text).

22. "El señor ministro ya ha obtenido el decreto de la expropiación de tierras que eran indispensables para la instalación de centrales" (ibid).

23. "Permaneció mudo durante toda la sesión, pero fue el primero en aproximarse al presidente y felicitarlo" (ibid., 332).

24. *Erythrina edulis*, a large tree native to the tropical Andes, whose flowers are big and red, and whose fruits are edible beans. Wikipedia, s.v. "Erythrinia eulis," http://es.wikipedia.org/wiki/Erythrina_edulis (accessed on July 20, 2012).

25. "Llegaba el sol, recreándose sobre las flores del gran pisonay solitario en el patio" (Arguedas, *Todas las sangres,* 40).

26. "El pisonay, entonces, abrió sus flores que se habían opacado mientras él [Bruno] amenazaba" (ibid., 41).

27. Ibid., 42–44.

28. "Don Bruno se detuvo. El puente no sólo parecía firme sino hermoso. La cruz roja presidía al río angosto y salvaje, proyectaba la sombra de su pasión a uno y a otro lado de la corriente" (ibid., 258).

29. Flores Galindo, *Buscando un Inca,* 247.

30. Ibid., 269.

31. Arguedas, *Todas las sangres,* 435.

32. Ibid., 191.

33. At the roundtable, Arguedas said, "la simpatía por don Bruno es completamente explicable, porque don Bruno es un señor feudal completamente indianizado, como él que está lleno de ideas indígenas . . . y cuando los otros personajes hablan de él . . . lo describen como una persona llena de misterios y estos misterios vienen de que se ha indianizado, y hay una actitud y hay una cosa más" (Escobar, *¿He vivido en vano?,* 27–28).

34. For some examples, see Arguedas, *Todas las sangres,* 31, 33, 40, 56.

35. "Desde la República, cada hacendado era un rey español. Ellos dictaban las leyes y la ley se cumplía únicamente en lo que al señor le convenía" (Arguedas, *Todas las sangres,* 38).

36. Ibid., 42–44.

37. Ibid., 40.

38. The fact that I turn to Habermas's analysis of the medieval institution (*The Structural Transformation*) in order to understand a structure operative in twentieth-century Peru is suggestive in itself. That is, the hacienda La Providencia is a pocket of traditional societal structures where the bourgeois public sphere cannot work because Bruno's power does not recognize the Indians as free, educated, rational individuals. This helps to explain the heterogeneous nature of the society in the Peruvian sierra.

39. Habermas, *The Structural Transformation,* 7–8.

40. Ibid.

41. This is why the paradigm of medieval representation is a religious play, a *mysterium,* where the representation supposes two publics, that of the people and that of God. Before the people, the presence of God is represented by the presence of the sovereign. Before God, the devotion of the people is represented. Because of that, the medieval public sphere is strongly paralleled with a religious rite.

42. The fact that this kind of publicity develops more intensely in a festive setting (like knight tournaments) than at a properly political event such as king's council, testifies to the fact that there is no component of political communication in this kind of publicity.

43. "Sus barbas rubias le daban aire como de un ángel indignado, de un aparecido enviado por los cielos" (Arguedas, *Todas las sangres,* 24).

44. "Entre tanta gente mestiza y de chullo, él, tan rubio, de ojos tan azules y apasibles, tenía no la apariencia de un terrateniente devorado por la lujuria, sino de un creyente notable, cuya inocencia resplandecía" (ibid., 24).

45. "Don Bruno se transfiguró ante la concurrencia de los 'pequeños' señores. A pesar de su poncho, todo el aire de su rostro y de su actitud dominaban la sala: se mostró imponente" (ibid., 33).

46. "¡Yo desafié a Dios! Le di mis indios a Fermín. Traje las máquinas que están convirtiendo en polvo la tierra de maíz bendecida por todas las Vírgenes. ¡Yo he hecho desaparecer en el aire el cuerpo de Anto, que fue padre de mi padre, cuando él estaba loco, por causa mía!" (ibid., 433).

47. Braudel, *La historia y las ciencias,* 122–23.

48. One of Arguedas's best-known short stories, "El sueño del pongo" (1965), explores the scandal of a situation when a serf speaks to a lord. The short story suggests that this sole act implies a *pachakuti,* the turning upside-down of the (post)colonial world.

49. Arguedas, *Todas las sangres,* 42.

50. We will discuss in what follows the motif of "men who speak" (the *señores*) and "men who do not speak" (the Indians), as a recurring motif in racist colonial discourse. Alberto Flores Galindo studies this discursive motif in *Buscando un Inca.* We will see the situation that represents the inverse of Bruno's action: the alcalde of Paraybamba asks the Peruvian soldier to speak to him instead of shooting, but the soldier refuses to understand this demand for recognition. This is another glaring example of opposition between Bruno and the Peruvian state.

51. "El patrón dudó. El cabecilla le interrogaba, com una humildad que le enfrió las entrañas" (Arguedas, *Todas las sangres,* 42).

52. Ibid., 456.

53. Tzvetan Todorov's reading of Joseph Conrad's *Heart of Darkness* and his comment on the role of mute enigmatic gestures in a (post)colonial text inspired my reflection on Don Bruno's and Adrian K'oto's pattern of communication. However, Todorov's observations, in the case of Conrad are quite dissimilar to my own for *Todas las sangres* (Todorov, *Los géneros del discurso*, 189–90).

54. Arguedas, *Todas las sangres*, 441.

55. "¡Levántate! No beses mis pies. No soy ya dios" (ibid., 255).

56. "Carhuamayo había oído el diálogo, entre sorprendido y extraviado. El patrón cambiaba; iba 'medio enloqueciéndose.' Suprimía la reverencia y los besos a sus botas, de las mujeres. ¿Por qué?" (ibid., 256).

57. "¡Viejo! Tengo mucha tierra. Te daré Tokoswayk'o, toda la banda de La Providencia, para que tu pueblo pueda sembrar" (ibid., 257). "El viejo se quedó mirando a don Bruno, como si le hubiera caído un golpe en la nuca. Todos los comuneros tenían la misma expresión" (257).

58. "Carhuamayo: me has mirado más de una vez como si yo hubiera perdido el juicio. Así nos presentamos los que tenemos gran responsabilidad entre los hombres que no hacen sino obedecer; así aparecemos cuando se nos oscurece el camino del bien y del mal" (ibid., 277).

59. Ibid., 259, 264.

60. "Que Cisneros no tenía la expresión feroz de todopoderoso, sino otra, quizás la que correspondía a su verdadera naturaleza: un mestizo ladrón que no puede enfrentarse a un verdadero señor" (ibid., 269; emphasis added in text).

61. "No sois vecinos, pues, amigo Cisneros, conforme a las costumbres que usted mismo defendía en mi hacienda" (ibid., 269).

62. Possibly, the nature of the bourgeois as a private person is why a bourgeois is an ideal citizen of liberal democracy, which requires functionality of the mechanism of representation through delegation. The bourgeois, as a private individual, does not care about the risk of losing his or her political power of voice through delegating the responsibility of representation to a political party. For reflections on this side of the liberal concept of representation, see Pierre Bourdieu, "Formas de acción política y modos de existencia de los grupos," and "La representación política," in *El campo político*. For example, Bourdieu refers to "apolitismo popular y pequeño burgués, que es la condición y el producto del monopolio de los políticos" (74). Thus, in representative democracy the professionalization of the political field produces and depends on apathy, real nonparticipation by the majority of the citizens.

63. Habermas, *The Structural Transformation*, 13.

64. "¿Y tú quien eres? ¿Qué representas?" (Arguedas, *Todas las sangres*, 261).

65. "La gente de la villa lo vio [a Bruno] cruzar las calles al paso majestuoso del potro" (ibid., 209).

66. "Al mediodía, con un sol feroz, entró don Bruno a la hacienda de don Lucas" (ibid., 435).

67. Ibid., 436.

68. "Los indios no hacen comedias. Yo no hago comedias. ¡Vivimos y morimos!" (ibid., 214).

69. Ibid., 70.

70. Ibid., 260, 70.

71. "El alcalde entregó la pistola a don Bruno. El caballero la besó y se la guardó en el cinto, bajo el poncho. Luego el indio se echo a andar, y cuando los dos hermanos bajaron

las gradas del atrio, recuperó su lugar, detrás de los señores. Los anillos de cobre y los dibujos polícromos de su vara resaltaban en la luz" (ibid., 30).

72. "Indio falsificado, excremento del diablo, tienes plata porque les has robado a tus hermanos" (ibid., 261).

73. "¡Cholo Cisneros! ¡Já, já já! ¡Ahora gran señor de Parquiña"; "Aunque sea, siempre cholo, pues" (ibid., 262).

74. Ibid., 268.

75. Agamben, *State of Exception*, 76.

Chapter 2. Andean Community

Epigraph: "Nosotros estamos enteros, para el patria; para la Wisther no habrá ánimo. El cuerpo sin ánimo lo come pronto la mina, el tristeza, el borrachera" (Arguedas, *Todas las sangres*, 279).

1. Nancy, "The Unsacrificeable," 33.

2. Nancy, "Preface," xxxvii.

3. Christopher Fynsk, in the foreword to Nancy's essays, ponders on the meaning of the term "inoperative" used by Nancy. For Fynsk, it is not that Nancy proposes an "idle" or "passive" communality as an option; "inoperativity" refers to this stalling of the concept, the inability to think through the options of community. It is inoperativity of the "tired" concept that must be worked through and overcome (Fynsk, "Foreword," xi).

4. Nancy, "Preface," xxxviii.

5. Nancy, "The Inoperative Community," 15.

6. Fynsk, "Foreword," xi.

7. "Los indios de La Providencia temían a la montaña de Apark'ora; sus boca-minas eran consideradas túneles malditos. En no muy lejanos tiempos habían sido aniquilados en la mina centenares de indios. Se guardaba de esa época un recuerdo brumoso, como de las grandes pestes que pasaron como fuego sobre las aldeas de indios. El nombre de Apark'ora por si mismo, en su sonido despertaba una especie de terror vago pero encarnizado" (Arguedas, *Todas las sangres*, 97).

8. "Por lo general, la sangre y los muertos en los mitos populares dejan pendiente una deuda que reclama a las siguientes generaciones un resarcimiento; son *una convocatoria a la búsqueda de unificación* actuante que satisfaga en el imaginario la recompensa, la reposición simbólica del sacrificio de la vida que podía haber sido la propia" (García Linera, "La muerte," 57; emphasis added and translation is mine).

9. Arguedas, "Cambio de cultura," 28–34.

10. Moore, *En la encrucijada*, 124.

11. Escobar, *¿He vivido en vano?*

12. Arguedas, *Todas las sangres*, 103–4.

13. Here there is no space for me to further explore this Arguedean word "triste" (sad). It is another one of those polysemic words that seem to have an incredible conceptual density (as Melisa Moore observed for the case of the word "rabia" [rage] or "alma" [soul]. "Triste," in rough strokes, encompasses in Arguedas the meaning of deculturation, alienation, existential void, lack of communication, abusive relations mediated by money, abandonment. The little trees on the central plaza of dying San Pedro are repeatedly described as "tristes": they stand there, little and abandoned, thirsty for the rain and uncared for, in the middle of an empty square. Drunken decultured workers are "tristes";

to sleep with a prostitute is "triste," in the words of the Indians and the narrator of *Todas las sangres*. It is not a word that engineer Cabrejos uses, who does not find anything wrong in the use of the ladies' professional services. Rather, it is a word that signals a condition of loss of some previous situation that guaranteed some sense of belonging that sheltered the speaker, and which the speaker had lost. Cabrejos, in words of Don Fermín y Rendón is "químicamente puro" (chemically pure)—he either had not lost anything because he never had it, or had overcome completely this loss.

14. "¡Matilde!—exclamó con energía.—¡Crees que todavía tenemos el derecho de poseer siervos? ¿Crees que los siervos constituyen el bien productivo? Son un peso muerto . . . Ahora los necesito. . . . Los explotaré misericordiosamente y a fondo. . . . Pero, luego, cuando esté suficientemente consolidado y fuera de las garras de los que quieren engullirme, liberaré a los siervos. Tengo mi plan hecho. Bruno debe morir" (Arguedas, *Todas las sangres*, 80).

15. "Daremos una planta eléctrica, escuelas, campo de fútbol, negocios" (ibid., 25).

16. Ibid., 45.

17. "Ustedes los químicamente puros . . . han sido definidos por Rendón: arrojaron su alma" (ibid., 163).

18. "Don Fermín, como yo es, aunque del otro lado" (ibid., 36).

19. Salomon, "Introductory Essay," 10.

20. Arguedas, *Todas las sangres,* 279.

21. "El Perú es de enemigos, creo. Todos nacemos enemigos" (Arguedas, *Todas las sangres,* 279).

22. "Aprista," meaning belonging to the Peruvian center-leftist party, the APRA, founded in 1924 by Victor Raul Haya de la Torre. One of the important studies of the APRA history is by Peter F. Klarén, *Formación de las haciendas azucareras y orígenes del APRA.*

23. Arguedas, *Todas las sangres,* 279.

24. Ibid., 42–43, 67.

25. Arguedas, in Rama, *Formación de una cultura,* 28–34.

26. Arguedas, *Todas las sangres,* 60, 69, 96.

27. Fausto Reinaga, a Bolivian indigenist and Arguedas's contemporary, in a 1960 book *El sentimiento mesiánico del pueblo ruso,* writes with admiration about the concept of "socialist competition" that he witnesses in his visit to the Soviet Union in 1957. His admiration sounds much the same as the admiration of the nonindigenous workers for the Indians in Arguedas's novel. In the "socialist competition," the effort of the worker is remunerated not with money or favors, but with the recognition of fellow workers. In the Soviet Union, the workers' photographs were displayed on a "board of recognition." While Reinaga admires sincerely what he sees, the historical truth is that the workers were hardly content with this merely symbolic reward for their efforts.

28. "Work ceases to be martyrdom" because in the Andean experience within the Incan empire work never was conceptualized as torture, or suffering, or punishment, as Silvia Rivera Cusicanqui documents in her study of Guaman Poma de Ayala's work. This perception of work stands in stark contrast to the biblical narrative, where Adam is punished for his transgression with expulsion from paradise and with having to work to get his daily bread (Rivera Cusicanqui, "Sociología de la imagen"). Mercedes López-Baralt makes a similar observation in *Ícono y conquista.*

29. Arguedas, "Puquio, una cultura," 73–74.

30. Kaufman and Morgan, "Anthropology of the Beginnings," 314–41, quote the clas-

sical study by Robert Hertz, *Death and the Right Hand,* which "showed that death does not coincide with the destruction of an individual's life, that death is a social event and the beginning of a ceremonial process by which the dead person becomes an ancestor, and that death is an initiation into an afterlife, a rebirth" (323).

31. Bascopé Caero, "El sentido de la muerte," 271.

32. On the Quechua concept of work as separate from the idea of suffering, see Rivera Cusicanqui, "Sociología de la imagen."

33. "Horizontal destitution" is a term developed in conversation with Sara Castro-Klarén.

34. Arguedas, "El varayok'"; Brandt and Valdivia, *Justicia comunitaria,* 62, 67.

35. Moore, *En la encrucijada,* 155.

36. "¿Mandas a los indios?—Tú sabiendo, pues, patrón. A indios de hacienda manda, en su alma también, don Bruno. A indios de Lahuaymarca manda cabildo" (Arguedas, *Todas las sangres,* 184).

37. "Cosecharemos, cuidaremos. Don Demetrio nos ha enseñado, sus k'ollanas también" (ibid., 439).

38. For example, Arguedas, *Todas las sangres,* 97, 109.

39. Agamben, *State of Exception,* 74, quoting Hannah Arendt.

40. "Acuerdo del cabildo del común" (Arguedas, *Todas las sangres,* 70).

41. "Los indios no hacen comedias. Yo no hago comedia. ¡Vivimos y morimos!" (ibid., 214).

42. Degregori, "Jóvenes y campesinos," 403–4.

43. "De este modo, en el himno de k'achua recordaban a los mozos fallecidos durante el año, les rendían homenaje y les hacían participar de la fiesta" (Arguedas, *Todas las sangres,* 60).

44. Sheehan, "Sacrifice before the Secular," 15.

45. Ibid., 31.

46. Ibid., 32.

47. Other philosophers (see, e.g., Ptacek, "Sacrificing Sacrifice," and Keenan, *The Question of Sacrifice*) challenge Nancy's idea, arguing that sacrifice is such a fundamental concept in European thought, both theological and secular, that it is naïve to posit the possibility of exiling sacrifice altogether, as a practice or as a phantom.

48. Butler, "Violence, Mourning, Politics," 26–27.

49. The earlier indigenist corpus widely used the commonplace of Indian insensibility (e.g., Jorge Izcaza's *Huasipungo*). Arguedas uses this same commonplace curiously, though with a different effect from Icaza. While in Icaza it demonstrated the abyss that separated the insensible Indians from the sentient creoles, in Arguedas the trope of the Indians' insensibility underlines their incredible courage in bearing physical pain. Thus, Arguedas brings the Indian characters closer to the reader, albeit using the same trope that was used in the earlier indigenist writing to opposite effect.

50. Arguedas, *Todas las sangres,* 42.

51. Ibid., 110, 132.

52. Ibid., 42.

53. "Es como no hacer nada . . . Es como sangre no fuera sangre para ellos" (ibid., 66).

54. Rivera, *Dar la palabra,* 50–52, analyzes the meaning of Arguedas's own death as narrated in *El zorro de arriba y el zorro de abajo.* Rivera concludes, following Martin Lienhard, that Arguedas's suicide needs to be read as a sacrifice in the sense that it self-narrates in the *Diarios* sections of the novel and then leaves space for political action. The novel

is unfinished due to Arguedas's suicide, in order to "spill over" into the political sphere; Arguedas self-destroys, within his narrative, in order to leave space for action of the *pueblo peruano,* the Peruvian people. As we will see, the argument of Rendón Willka's speech before the firing squad follows a similar logic.

55. "El muerto es muerto nomás, padrecito Anto. El pichitanka canta para el vivo" (ibid., 36).

56. Ibid., 216.

57. Ibid., 120.

58. In the original, the concept "mitas" (communal work by turns) refers to the obligatory work for free that the serfs had to perform by turns, sent out by their master to other haciendas. In *Todas las sangres,* Bruno sends his serfs to Fermín's mine.

59. "Nada importa. . . . No alcanzamos a conocer su voluntad [del Dios cristiano]; pero la muerte es más triste para los hijos de El que para nosotros. Más triste. Por eso, cuanto más arriba de la montaña, o en el fuego de los valles donde nos envían en mitas a trabajar para otros señores, nuestra vena se apaga en silencio. Ellos mueren, parece, sin consuelo. No saben, ni sus padres, ni sus hijos, ni el cura grande, ni el cura pequeño, adónde van, después que el aliento se corta. El Padre Pukasira va estar en el cabildo grande. El recoge a cada hijo suyo, muerto o vivo" (Arguedas, *Todas las sangres,* 40).

60. There are numerous references to drunk Indians crying "without knowing why" in Arguedas's essays in the collection *Indios, mestizos y señores.* It is an interesting and very literary device to be used in a newspaper article, which gives a novelistic air to Arguedas's supposedly more "objective" (in comparison to a novel) articles. It sounds as if the narrator could penetrate the heads of the Indians he observes. But what meaning does this old indigenist topic acquire in Arguedas's "indigenismo upside down," to use Martin Lienhardt's term?

61. Arguedas, *Todas las sangres,* 226.

62. "Igual vemos, distinto entendemos" (ibid., 36).

63. "Comunero nomás, comunero Rendón no quiere plata veneno, plata que no es de trabajo, que no es del Dios.

"'¿Del Dios? ¿Crees en Dios?'

"'Cuando es claro la plata de la gente, ahistá, pues, Dios; ahí mismo el corazón alegra. Cuando no es clarito, el oscuro golpea el pecho por su adentro, el pecho en donde el Dios se cría'" (ibid., 86).

64. Ibid., 35.

65. Ibid., 454.

66. Ibid., 120.

67. "¡Capitán! ¡Señor capitán! . . . Aquí, ahora, en estos pueblos y haciendas, los grandes árboles nomás lloran. Los fusiles no van a apagar sol, ni secar los ríos, ni menos quitar la vida a todos los indios. Siga fusilando. Nosotros no tenemos armas de fábrica, que no valen. Nuestro corazón está de fuego. ¡Aquí, en todas partes! Hemos conocido patria al fin. Y usted no va a matar la patria, señor. Ahí está; parece muerta. ¡No! El pisonay llora; derramará sus flores por la eternidad de la eternidad, creciendo. Ahora de pena, mañana de alegría. El fusil de fábrica es sordo, es como palo; no entiende. Somos hombres que ya hemos de vivir eternamente. Si quieres, si te provoca, ¡dame la muertecita, la pequeña muerte, capitán!" (ibid., 455).

68. Miranda Luizaga, *Filosofía andina,* 20.

69. Ibid., 21–22.

70. "Demetrio escuchaba con tranquilo regocijo las respuestas de la mujer. 'Ya pueden

fusilarme. ¡No importa!'—pensó" (ibid., 454).

71. We might ask how "deep" is this assertion or if it just floats on the surface. We must remember that Arguedas was a leftist, and that his sympathies were inclining toward the Communists (as opposed to the APRA). *El Sexto* is the text that documents best this inclination, which I will discuss in chapter 4.

72. "¿Su gente? No tiene gente de él. Somos comuneros; estamos en toda la hacienda, en cualquier parte" (Arguedas, *Todas las sangres*, 454).

73. Arguedas's commentary at the roundtable discussion backs up our interpretation: "Él (Rendón) con su muerte, lo que da es la evidencia de que los indios se pueden manejar por sí mismos, que no es necesario un caudillo para manejarse, y por eso muere" (Escobar, *¿He vivido en vano?*, 47).

74. Arguedas, *Todas las sangres*, 454.

75. Don Bruno has this in common with Rendón Willka. Both characters consume themselves in the name of their ideas. Rendón in the name of a self-governing ayllu incorporated into modern Peru; Bruno in the name of Christian values that oblige him to take revenge on the persons who bring physical suffering to the Indians.

76. "Los de la choza se sentían más cómodos que los maestros del caserío. Cada quien tenía su árbol o arbusto; los poquísimos que habían tomado mujer en San Pedro o habían venido acompañados levantaron un cerco y formaron un corral espacioso donde crecía yerba. . . . El maestro consideraba esta costumbre como típica del indio que no es *todavía obrero* y que difícilmente o nunca llegaría a ser *maestro*. Ellos mismos les cerraban el paso, tratándolos con misericordia" (Arguedas, *Todas las sangres*, 103).

77. See, for example, Ortiz Rascaniere, *La pareja y el mito*. There is a wealth of recent scholarship on the concept of "complimentariedad" (complimenting) of the male and female in the Andean cultures, both Quechua and Aymara, and the traditional necessity of marriage to become a mayor or other indigenous authority. Especially interesting because it is both knowledgeable and critical of the Andean structures is the indigenist feminist study by Paredes, *Hilando fino*.

78. Flores Galindo, *Buscando un Inca*.

79. "¡Para los indios y los consorcios nada más que cenizas!" (Arguedas, *Todas las sangres*, 200).

80. Note that the conception of the wretched of the earth that Aquíles puts forward is based on race, which marks the difference between people in distinct parts of the world. This difference is immediately erased by the exploitation machine of transnational capital.

81. In the text, I translate the excerpts of this passage, which I quote in a fuller version here: "Los consorcios no tienen patria. Han superado el concepto. . . . Oiga usted, don Adalberto, ellos no tienen patria fija, sino el negocio; negocio en África, aniquilando negros; en Asia, matando amarillos. . . . Aunque llevan la civilización, prefieren entenderse con hombres como usted que están decididos a mantener los antiguos costumbres. No les conviene que la gente tenga ojos. Es mejor si solo obedezcan y recen . . . ¿No es la máxima aspiración suya que el indio no progrese, que siga trabajando a cambio de consuelo y de rezo y de tierras y ganadito, pocos? . . . Si en cada pueblo no encontraran gentes que, en pequeño, hacen lo mismo que ellos en grande, no podrían dominar tantos pueblos y pertenencias" (Arguedas, *Todas las sangres*, 205–6).

82. "Por lo que usted me dijo son una. . . . ¿Cómo dijo? Una cadena sin fin de cabezas, de diablos que no podemos ver, que no muestran la cara; de chupadores de riquezas que, cual araña maldita por Dios, tiene al mundo debajo de su panza y caga sobre el mismo pan que come" (ibid., 206).

83. "Desubjectified individual": this term was developed upon in a conversation with Horacio Legrás.

84. Arguedas, *Todas las sangres,* 103–4.

85. "Un aprista prefiere al patrón contra el comunista y viceversa. ¡Que hagan política, mejor!" (ibid., 130).

86. Orrantía and San Isidro are the last names of the traditional Lima aristocracy.

87. "¿Comunismo? Ahistá, patrón: tú comunista si Rendón mata inginiero; Rendón también comunista; señores Orrantías, San Isidros nada comunistas; hombres comiendo con chanchos en Montón, en todo barriada, cuando sale pedir, gritando, comidita ¡ahistá comunista! Cuando hacer choza en arenal de nadies para encontrar sombrita ¡ahistá comunista! . . . Patrón, yo ningún huérfano, sabiendo claro de comunismo. Inginiero sabe. Con su boca, con su dedo dice: ¡comunista! Y ahí no más le meten golpe u bala, según" (Arguedas, *Todas las sangres,* 161).

88. "Si pudiéramos trabajar *así* todos . . . El trabajo no sería una maldición. ¡Entiende que algún día seremos como ellos, cuando no trabajemos para fortalecer a los que nos explotan!" (ibid., 108).

89. I borrow this term from Braudel's "history of mentalities," *La historia y las ciencias sociales,* which is quite useful for analysis of Arguedas's work. It is interesting to note that in the recent indigenous and indigenist discourses in the political arena, such as the official discourse of the Bolivian government, scholars have begun to refer extensively to this same terminology introduced by Braudel.

90. Rabasa, "Postcolonialismo," 220.

91. In Arguedas's journalistic writings, he obsessively wants to describe every piece of indigenous weaving, every Indian song. His optimism about the survival and operativity of the structures of the ayllu and communal work in the modern world is one thing; the other is that his heart aches with each Indian killed and every indigenous artistic skill lost.

92. Cornejo Polar, *Los universos,* 171.

93. Quijano, "Carta," 18–20.

94. The body of the Indian worker, not the machine that he operates, becomes the main mode of production and remains as a site where the worker's creativity can be exercised. This idea is hinted at in the conversation of the miners in *Todas las sangres* and becomes further developed in *El zorro (The Foxes)* in the scene where Don Angel visits the factory and sees the Indians work the heavy industrial machinery.

Chapter 3. "Why Have You Killed Me?" Violence, Law, and Justice in *Todas las sangres*

A part of this chapter has been published as "Heterogeneidad jurídica y violencia fundacional en *Todas las sangres,*" *Revista de Crítica Literaria Latinoamericana* 36, no. 72 (2010): 233–52. Epigraph from Agamben, *State of Exception,* 10.

1. Arguedas, *Todas las sangres,* 370–75.

2. Ibid., 263–64.

3. Benjamin, "Critique of Violence"; Derrida, "Force of Law"; Agamben, *State of Exception.*

4. It is not that democracy's beginnings are violent while the other kind of states' are not. But democracy is especially concerned with hiding these beginnings because it claims

to be born from a consensus of all the citizens in its territory.

5. Derrida, "Force of Law," 278, 280–81.

6. I will quote extensively from Xavier Albó's definition of *justicia comunitaria* and *derecho consuetudinario,* although, as the author himself admits, these definitions are not without problems. We will operatively keep these definitions in mind: "adoptamos operativamente el término 'derecho consuetudinario' para referirnos tanto a las normas como a la práctica basada en 'usos y costumbres' propios de cada pueblo y cultura en un lugar y momento dado, como distintas de las normas formalizadas y escritas en la legislación oficial. Especificamos que se trata de la justicia comunitaria, para referirnos a la aplicacióny administración de estas normas en el contexto comunal e incluso intercomunal" (Albó, "¿Cómo manejar?").

7. "Denominamos derecho positivo al que explicita en leyes y otros cuerpos normativos oficiales del estado, claramente tipificados a través de la terminología y conceptualización propia de la ciencia jurídica. A su vez, llamamos justicia ordinaria a la administración de justicia, en base a un cotejo permanente con las normas del mencionado derecho positivo y realizado por autoridades y otros administradores nombrados por el Estado y especializados para desempeñar este rol" (ibid.).

8. The distinction between law and custom is evident in the legal debates that preceeded the approval of the new Bolivian constitution. In these discussions, the *justicia comunitaria* is linked to *derecho consuetudinario* (lit., legal systems based on customs). A definition of the derecho consuetudinario, also called justicia comunitaria in a resolution of the Bolivian Tribunal Constitucional on a case ofcommunal justice exercised in one of the communities in Uyuni (Sucre) on November 3, 2003, reads: "El Derecho Consuetudinario es fundamentalmente oral, transmitido por sucesivas generaciones, y mantenido en el tiempo sin la necesidad de que se plasme en un documento escrito para que sea reconocido como válido por los comunarios" (Chivi Vargas, *Justicia indígena,* 91–94).

9. Agamben, *State of Exception,* 32–41.

10. Arguedas, *Todas las sangres,* 72.

11. Adelman, "Unfinished States," 41.

12. Vilas and Stoller, "Lynchings," 115.

13. Arguedas, *Todas las sangres* 186, 189

14. "Los derechos de los colonos, amigo Cisneros, dependen de la voluntad del patrón" (ibid., 186).

15. "Usted . . . como hacendado no tiene derecho a solviantar a los indios. Todos van a querer hacer lo mismo que los colonos suyos. Y no solo nos arruinariamos, sino que nuestra autoridad correria peligro" (ibid.).

16. "¡Qué casta ni qué casta! Ya pasaron estos tiempos. El que tiene dinero, el que más tiene, ése manda; ése es el señor. Yo se lo voy a probar. . . . Tengo influencia. Yo hice al diputado y aun al senador con mi plata" (ibid., 187).

17. "A mi me temen y obedecen; soy señor desde mis antepasados mas lejanos, a usted solo lo odian. Usted no está consagrado en sus posesiones por la ley de la herencia señorial" (ibid., 186; emphasis added in text).

18. Flores Galindo, *Buscando un Inca,* 263.

19. "Don Adalberto lloraba en una cima, acompañado por otros veinte guardias.—¿Estoy desnudo?-preguntó.—Me han enfriado estos indios amaestrados por Rendón. Creo que me han enfriado para siempre" (Arguedas, *Todas las sangres,* 456). I translate the expression "Enfriado para siempre" as "they froze me to death" because, literally, it means "they have frozen me forever," and also in Peruvian Spanish, "enfriar" may mean "to kill."

I am thankful to Enrique Cortéz for his observation on translation and interpretation of this quote.

20. "Le cubría medio rostro una barba rala y negra . . . era bajo, de glúteos casi hinchados" (ibid., 185); "el hombre de grasa, sin alma" (276); "macho feo" (273).

21. Ibid., 274.

22. Chivi Vargas, *Justicia indígena.*

23. In Arguedas's Spanish, the members of Paraybamba community are *paraybambas,* of Lahuaymarca—*lahuaymarcas.* The absence of a suffix of belonging (that is, not "*paraybambinos,*" for example) suggests, beyond the influence of Quechua on the formation of these words, direct association of individual and community, unmediated even by morphology.

24. Arguedas, *Todas las sangres,* 279.

25. It seems that the state is negatively calling into being a multitude by deploying its force against persons of the same region, but who, nonetheless, would not immediately recognize their "natural" bond—just like the reader of *Todas las sangres* does not immediately see the connection between all the instances of repression. The state, as we will see, throws the poor white folk, the Indians, and even some landowners into the same sack, thus suggesting the possibility of a territory-based common front. This situation is quite similar to the conformation of multitude as conceptualized by Álvaro García Linera (territory plus a common demand). García Linera et al., "La forma multitud," 168.

26. "Matar al que se resista. Apresar a los cinco varayok'. Luego . . . buscar a David K'oto. Matarlo al primer intento de resistencia o fuga" (Arguedas, *Todas las sangres,* 297).

27. Ibid., 299.

28. "Sí, señor 'Gobiernos.' El hombre habla; 'Gobiernos' habla. Bandoleros matan sin hablar, de noche" (ibid., 301).

29. This claim can be read against the racist labels that Flores Galindo studies in his essay on racism in Peru. One of the prejudices against the Indians was that they "could not speak" and were like a "stupid llama," because speaking Quechua did not count as speaking (Flores Galindo, *Buscando un Inca,* 235, 250).

30. "Señor sargento: a todo preso se le da un tiempecito para arreglar sus cosas," intervino Pedraza. "A los indios, no. No necesitan. No tienen nada" (Arguedas, *Todas las sangres,* 301).

31. Derrida, "Force of Law," 278.

32. Historical studies offer testimony to the fact that after the War of Independence in Peru, it was believed that those who fought on the republican side were going to transform into citizens "automatically" (Flores Galindo, "Soldados y montoneros," in *Buscando un inca;* Thurner, *From Two Republics).*

33. Derrida, "Force of Law," 279.

34. Fermín's exact words are: "Si llamo a la policía [ahora] cundirán el temor y la desconfianza entre indios y obreros. La policía vendrá aquí cuando surja la inevitable tensión entre obreros y patrones, que todavía no existe" (Arguedas, *Todas las sangres,* 107). Here, Fermín plans for the future counting on the police presence-in-absence, which can be transformed into a physical repression at the least sign of unrest.

35. "Esperaremos con nuestro Señor a los uniformados. Tranquilos nos matarán" (ibid., 275).

36. Derrida, "Force of Law," 279.

37. Ibid., 251–52.

38. Benjamin, "Critique of Violence," 283.

39. Agamben, *State of Exception*, 1.

40. The novel abounds with examples of the corrupt judicial system. The subprefecto wants to imprison Don Bruno without the mediation of a judge because Cisneros's overseer Pedraza testifies against him (Arguedas, *Todas las sangres*, 284). The same official physically abuses one of the indigenous authorities for refusing to kneel before Cisneros, a request that goes against both positive law and the old custom (314). Fermín and the judge of the province comment frankly that the judge and all the lawyers of the province have sold out to the transnational mining company Wisther and Bozart because of the miserable salaries they receive from the state (289–90).

41. "El despacho del juez era más desmantelado y miserable que el del subprefecto, y tenía el olor característico. . . . Además, olía a moho. Aragón se sentía allí como en la casa de un vecino hambriento y 'despreciable' de San Pedro de Lahuaymarca" (Arguedas, *Todas las sangres*, 289).

42. "El subprefecto . . . era un vecino hambriento de una lejana provincia del mismo departamento; había trasnochado dos meses durante las elecciones como activista del senador ya elegido" (ibid., 284). I have kept the words "subprefecto" and "vecino" in Spanish, because this is the use of these terms I found in other publications of Arguedas in translation in *Deep Rivers* and in scholarly work on Arguedas such as Legrás, *Literature and Subjection*.

43. Arguedas, *Todas las sangres*, 346.

44. Ibid., 365.

45. "El que manda sin ley, como este gobierno, ¡qué va a respetar, don Fermín!" (ibid., 346).

46. "On several occasions [between 1925 and 1929] . . . the [German] government had recourse to Article 48 (proclaiming state of exception) to cope with the fall of the mark, thus confirming the modern tendency to conflate politico-military and economic crises" (Agamben, *State of Exception*, 15). In the United States, "the New Deal was realized by delegating to the president . . . an unlimited power to regulate and control every aspect of the economic life of the country—a fact that is in perfect conformity with the . . . parallelism between military and economic emergencies that characterizes the politics of the twentieth century" (ibid., 22).

47. Arguedas, *Todas las sangres*, 358.

48. Agamben, *State of Exception*, 38.

49. Arguedas, *Todas las sangres*, 426.

50. "Los diarios de Lima informaron casi con las mismas palabras sobre el incendio de la iglesia de San Pedro y el asesinato de Cabrejos. La muerte de la mestiza en la capital de provincia y la del platero Bellido fueron ignoradas" (ibid.).

51. "Sobre los responsables de las perturbaciones de que damos cuenta caerá todo el peso de las leyes *en defensa de la democracia*" (ibid; emphasis added in text).

52. Agamben, *State of Exception*, 2–3.

53. "Vi administrar justicia al viejo alcalde como en el drama de Calderón de la Barca" (Arguedas, *Todas las sangres*, 281).

54. Ibid.

55. Scholars of communitarian justice point out its heterogeneous makeup, which reflects influences of the colonial judicial proceedings, combining both the Spanish legal tradition of the sixteenth and seventeenth centuries and the Incan system of justice. See Chivi Vargas, *Justicia indígena;* Albó, "¿Cómo manejar la interculturalidad jurídica?"; Vidal, "Derecho oficial y derecho campesino"; Vilas and Stoller, "Lynchings"; Orellana

Halkyer, "Prácticas judiciales."

56. Arguedas, *Todas las sangres,* 387, 393, 446.

57. "Vendió a mi pueblo sin que fuera suyo, señores; llévenme presa. Y vean a un traidor a Dios y a los humildes: así los matamos" (ibid., 367).

58. Nietzsche, *La genealogía,* 88–89. Also see discussion of revenge and justice in Derrida's "Passions."

59. "Cabrejos no es la Wisther. Un sirviente al otro sirviente reemplaza. Nuestra niña, como Bellido, ha sacrificado por nada su vida. Por la rabia" (Arguedas, *Todas las sangres,* 374).

60. Derrida "Force of Law," 238.

61. "Yo no he de oponerme a la voluntad del Altísimo" (ibid., 430).

62. "¡Loco! ¡Loco! Hijo de mi padre y de mi madre, y del Dios que tiene" (ibid., 441).

63. "Sin embargo, todo hombre, menos Bruno, de cuantos conozco, tienen su precio" (ibid., 290).

64. Shirova, "La utopía peruana," 97–144, traces parallels between Arguedas's thought and liberation theology. It is useful to think of Arguedas as both a profoundly (and problematically) Catholic thinker and one very much committed to social change. In *Todas las sangres,* Bruno, Asunta, and Jorge Hidalgo, three characters who defend the Indians and deliver justice against all odds, are devout Catholics. Rendón Willka's syncretic, strategic, and changing metaphysics are not strictly Catholic, but definitely carry an imprint of Franciscan preaching. The parallelism between Franciscan rhetoric and a Quechua traditional holistic view of the world would also explain why these characters feel closer to the Quechua worldview than the "atheists" Fermín or Cisneros. Flores Galindo connects the millenarian movements in the Andes with the writings of Joaquin de Fiore, a Franciscan. That is another point of convergence of Catholicism—especially in its Franciscan version—the indigenous movements and the message that we read in *Todas las sangres* as a promise of *pachakuti.* Conversely, the preaching of the Franciscan friars makes the serfs cry in the hacienda of cruel Lucas and serves as a tool of control of the Indians. Arguedas writes about the role of the church in strengthening the control of the gamonales and the state over the indigenous population in *Deep Rivers.*

65. Critics have discussed widely the meaning of the Quechua metaphor of "river of blood." Melisa Moore summarizes these interpretations as a metaphor that promises a pachakuti, a change of order and beginning of the new era—in other words, the Indians' organized resistance (Moore, *En la encrucijada,* 213, 228). In the final passage of *Todas las sangres,* the connection between the sacrificial death of the hero, the metaphor of the river of blood, and the subaltern resistance is clear: "El oficial lo hizo matar. Pero se quedó solo. Y él, como los otros guardias, escuchó un sonido de grandes torrentes que sacudían el subsuelo, como que si las montañas empezaran a caminar. A esa hora, en la cárcel de la capital de la provincia Adrian K'oto abrazaba a don Bruno" (Arguedas, *Todas las sangres,* 455–56).

66. The full quote states: "Y el río de sangre, tantas horas contenido en el pecho de don Bruno, se desbordó. Ya había arrasado a quienes debía arrasar; ahora tenía que salir al mundo, o matarlo, por dentro" (Arguedas, *Todas las sangres,* 441).

67. "Rendón Willka contemplaba a su patrón como si ese le hubiera entregado en las manos el mundo, triste y con sangre por fuera, llorando poderosamente, y con la salvación, la gloria, debajo de la cascara sucia. Don Bruno sentía casi exactamente la conciencia de Demetrio" (ibid., 304).

68. Flores Galindo says that these rebellions were especially bloody and extreme in the poorer regions of Peru, such as Andahuyalas, where Melisa Moore deduces that the narra-

tive of *Todas las sangres* takes place (Moore, *En la encrucijada*, 114–20).

69. "Las clases sociales en el Perú andino, cuando luchan, y lo hacen bárbaramente, la lucha no es sólo impulsada por el interés económico; otras fuerzas espirituales profundas y violentas enardecen a los bandos, los agitan con implacable fuerza, con incesante e ineludible violencia" (Arguedas quoted in Flores Galindo, *Buscando un Inca*, 25).

70. Derrida, "Force of Law," 231–32.

71. This discussion points toward the fact that the process of subalternization of a sector of a population is a constitutive step in a consolidation of hegemony. In relation to subalternity, we also might remember Gayatri Spivak's essay "Can the Subaltern Speak?" a question to which Spivak would answer no. Spivak's question is an interesting backdrop to the scenario presented in *Todas las sangres*. Indians who speak to the soldiers and demand to be heard, and soldiers who refuse to speak to the Indians is a scene that requires rethinking the process of subalternization in the situation we call judicial heterogeneity, when Indians and soldiers do not participate in the same system of normativity.

Chapter 4. Moments of Revolutionary Transformation in Arguedean Novels

Part of this chapter first appeared as "Moments of Revolutionary Transformation in the Novels of José María Arguedas," *Modern Language Notes* 127 (2012): 302–17, Johns Hopkins University Press, copyright 2012. "Momentos de la transformación revolucionaria" is a term used by Álvaro García Linera to discuss the Bolivian process of 2000–2010. The term emphasizes revolution as a process, as opposed to just one punctual event. Linera shows in his work, as Arguedean fiction does, how the disparate, small protests converge and articulate in the Bolivian historical reality into an effective contestatory block.

1. "Fue leyendo a Mariátegui y después a Lenin que encontré un orden permanente en las cosas; la teoría socialista no sólo dio un cauce a todo el porvenir sino a lo que había en mi de energía, le dio un destino y lo cargó aún más de fuerza por el mismo hecho de encauzarlo. ¿Hasta dónde entendí el socialismo? No lo sé bien. Pero no mató en mi lo mágico" (Arguedas, "No soy un aculturado," 258).

2. Rowe, "No hay mensajero," 75.

3. Bosteels, "Marx and Latin America," 3.

4. Ibid., 5.

5. Tarica, "Arguedas después," 7.

6. García Linera, "La construcción del Estado," 1.

7. Ayo, "Entrevista," 6.

8. Tarica, "Arguedas después," 2.

9. The Internationals' formal titles are "Sobre la revolución en América: Un llamado a la clase trabajadora de las dos Américas" (1921) and "A los trabajadores y los campesinos de América del Sur" (1923). Löwy, *El Marxismo*, 8–17.

10. Löwy, "Introduction," xxi.

11. Mariátegui, "Prologue to Tempest," 28–33.

12. Flores Galindo, *La agonía*.

13. Quoted in Löwy, "Introduction," xx.

14. The latifundio and *gamonalismo* are considered capitalist within Marxist logic because they were characterized by the alienation of workers and indigenous peasants

from the mode of production, namely, land. This is why Mariátegui, in *Siete ensayos,* addresses the problem of the Indian alongside the problem of the land.

15. Lienhard, "Avatares del yo."

16. I say that the novel "stages" the action and the problem because *El Sexto* has a very theatrical logic. All the action is situated in an interior, reduced space; the narrative voice is barely present through Gabriel's internal monologues (sort of theatrical asides), and, largely, the action is presented in dialogues among the characters. In fact, the dialogue *is* the main action of this novel.

17. The authority of this character is reinforced by the Quechua meaning of his name (Castro-Klarén, "'Like a pig,'" 315–16), which means creative force, the poetic capacity of the Andean *huacas* capable of transforming nonliving things into living, the creative capacity that acquires an enormous force in *The Foxes.*

18. "Sus palabras nombraban directamente los hechos, e ideas que nacían de los hechos" (Arguedas, *El Sexto,* 38).

19. Tarica, "El 'decir limpio,'" 33, writes, "¿Qué quiere decir 'limpio' en este caso? Quizás una transmisión transparente, clara y completa; una comunicación plena."

20. "¿Qué es más grande, dices, el afán de los gringos y de sus compadres peruanos para enriquecerse hasta los infiernos o el sufrimiento de nosotros que acera nuestro cuerpo? ¿Quién va a ganar al fin?" (Arguedas, *El Sexto,* 54).

21. Rivera Cusicanqui, "Sociología de la imagen," 26.

22. "¡Señor Capitán! Los fusiles no van a apagar el sol, ni secar los ríos, ni menos quitar la vida a todos los indios. Siga fusilando. Nosotros no tenemos armas de fábrica, que no valen. Nuestro corazón está de fuego. ¡Aquí, en todas partes! Hemos conocido patria al fin. Y usted no va a matar la patria, señor" (Arguedas, *Todas las sangres,* 455). Arguedas comments on Rendón's role as a revolutionary leader in these words: "Él (Rendón) con su muerte, lo que da es la evidencia de que los indios se pueden manejar por sí mismos, que no es necesario un caudillo para manejarse, y por eso muere" (Escobar, *¿He vivido en vano?* 47).

23. If Carl Schmitt defines in *The Concept of the Political* the properly political moment as that of division into friends and enemies, then conversely, the moment when it becomes impossible to define against whom one is fighting, and in alliance with whom (even if one knows why one is fighting), the political action becomes impossible.

24. Wikipedia, s.v. "*Mimus saturninus,*" a bird native to South America, which imitates well a human whistle or music (es.wikipedia.org/wiki/Calandria_com%C3%Ban). In Arguedas's fiction, essays, and poetry the calender lark is a recurrent and polysemic metaphor. Barraclough translates *calandria* as "calender lark," and this is why I quote it under this name. When I researched the Latin name of the bird in English sources, the popular name comes up as "chalk-browed mockingbird." See, for example, www.arthurgrosset.com /sabirds/chalk-browedmockingbird.html.

25. Unlike *Todas las sangres, The Foxes* has been translated into English. In some cases I quote from the English translation, *The Fox from Up Above and the Fox from Down Below;* in other cases I opt for translating from the Spanish original. I will indicate which I have used for each quote by listing either the English title or the Spanish title. This quote comes from the English critical edition of *The Foxes* (259). The Spanish version reads: "Quizá conmigo empieza a cerrarse un ciclo y a abrirse otro en el Perú y lo que él representa; se cierra el de la calandria consoladora, del azote, del arriheraje, del odio impotente, de los fúnebres 'alzamientos,' del temor a Dios y del predominio de ese Dios y sus protegidos, sus fabricantes; se abre el de la luz y de la fuerza liberadora invencible del hombre de

Vietnam, el de la calandria de fuego, el del dios liberador, Aquel que se reintegra. Vallejo era el principio y el fin" (Arguedas, *El zorro*, 246).

26. Spanish original reads: "hay borrachos estrellas, astros, extranjeros que toman licor de su pueblo-nación de origen y se zurran en el pueblo-nación donde amasan la incandescencia del sol, la fortuna poder" (Arguedas, *El zorro*, 142; my translation in text).

27. "¡El sol sabe quien soy yo, de mi quedará la memoria! Braschi me odia" (ibid., 55).

28. "Torero de díos"; "zambos y chinos del Perú América."

29. Rivera Cusicanqui, "El otro bicentenario," 10.

30. The antilegalist and antiliberal content of Arguedean political thought establishes a direct link between his critique of party politics and a similar critique elaborated by Carl Schmitt. Schmitt wrote on the concept of the political in 1932 during the Weimar Republic. Having the state, a unified entity, as an ideal horizon, Schmitt was appalled by what he was witnessing: radical parties both of the left and the right, among them Hitler's Nazi party, were tearing apart the unity of the Weimar state. According to Schmitt scholar Georges Schwab, the writing of *The Concept of the Political* was prompted by the urgency to critique the basic legalist and liberal precept that was implemented by Weimar leader Paul von Hindenburg: that any party, however radical, could legally compete within the sphere of domestic politics (Schwab, "Introduction," 13–14).

Schmitt saw this tendency of conceptualizing the political as primarily "party squabbles" as damaging to the sovereignty of the state and destructive of the sphere of the political itself. In the historical situation that was his destiny, Schmitt thought it mandatory to redefine the sphere of the political as separate from the domain of party squabbles and other concerns, such as economic or religious ones. It is important to establish the useful and antiliberal link between Arguedas and Schmitt, but also to observe the differences between the two. Primarily, Schmitt was worried about the sovereignty and monopoly of the state, while Arguedas's concern was about the possibility of consolidation of an oppositional pole.

31. Arguedas, *El Sexto*, 72.

32. "Lenin siempre los llamaba: 'Esos lacayos de la burguesía'" (ibid., 74).

33. "Me han traicionado los mineros apristas mucho.—dijo Camac—. Pero odiar, odiar que se diga a un obrero, será pues necesario, pero mi corazón no aprende. ¡Odio a los gringos malditos y moriré luchando contra ellos! Pero a un cabecilla obrero engañado, sólo en el momento de su traición; después se me pasa. Los veo sufrir igual, igualito que yo; escupidos lo mismo por los gringos y sus capataces" (ibid., 73–74).

34. Arguedas, *Deep Rivers*, 225–26.

35. The English translation of Arguedas's *Los rios profundos* uses, in italics, the words "colono" and "guardia." See, for example, the quoted pages in Arguedas, *Deep Rivers*, 225–26.

36. Ibid., 226.

37. Ibid., 229.

38. Legrás, *Literature and Subjection*, 231.

39. García Linera, "La construcción del estado," 9.

40. "Contra la extensión de los espacios de la explotación capitalista o el desierto de la expropiación, se ha producido la marea alta de una nueva política de las necesidades vitales, en torno a la cual la gente no sólo se ha organizado para disputar las condiciones de la supervivencia, reproducción y la misma producción en el campo, sino también la recomposición de la vida política. La marea alta ha modificado los bordes de lo político. Los espacios de la política se han ampliado y extendido, a la vez que este movimiento

deja un conjunto de instituciones políticas vacías, como el sistema de partidos. La política plebeya ha desbordado los espacios liberales, donde además el pueblo no está, sólo se dice que está representado" (García Linera et al., "La forma multitud," 192).

41. Tarica, "Arguedas después."

42. Lópéz-Baralt, *Ícono y conquista*, 291–99.

43. Rivera Cusicanqui, "Sociología de la imagen," 19–33.

44. Vargas Llosa, *La utopia arcaica;* see Arguedas's polemic with Cortazar in the diaries of *The Foxes* (esp. in Arguedas, *El zorro*, 13–14).

45. Good examples are Cortazar's *Hopscotch* (*Rayuela*) and Vargas Llosa's *The Feast of the Goat* (*La fiesta del chivo*). Particularly revealing in Cortazar's case is the episode that describes, dispassionately, Chinese torture. In *The Feast*, Vargas Llosa's mastery consists in managing not to condemn completely the father who gives his daughter Urania to be raped by the dictator Trujillo, even though the story, incredibly, is told from the daughter's point of view.

46. Arguedas, "No soy un aculturado."

47. Gustavo Gutiérrez, "Teología de la liberación," 739.

48. Arguedas, *Deep Rivers,*154.

49. Todorov, *The Conquest of America,* 106.

50. "It would be a mistake to believe that a nation could eliminate the distinction of friend and enemy by declaring its friendship for the entire world or by voluntarily disarming itself. . . . If a people is afraid of the trials and risks implied by existing in the sphere of politics, then another people will appear which will assume these trials by protecting it against foreign enemies and thereby taking over political rule. The protector then decides who the enemy is by virtue of the eternal relation of protection and obedience" (Schmitt, *The Concept,* 51–52). The "weak" and pacifist people thus lose their right to sovereignty.

51. Todorov, *On Human Diversity,* 42.

52. Žižek, *Violence,* 105–29.

53. Legrás, *Literature and Subjection,* 198.

54. "La voz . . . imitaba exactamente la línea melódica del viejo 'Puñalada,' pero . . . no se arrastraba por los sucios paredes del penal como la emitida por la garganta y la lengua del viejo asesino. . . . Cada año, ese grito se iría identificando más con el El Sexto. El negro joven iría aprendiendo, si no lo mataban antes o mataban 'El Sexto'" (Arguedas, *El Sexto,* 228).

55. "Aquí, en el Sexto, la mugre está afuera; es por la pestilencia y el hambre. En los palacios de los señores la mugre es de antiguo, es más por adentro. Vendrá de la ociosidad, de la plata guardada, conseguida a costa de la quemazón de medio mundo, de esta pestilencia que estamos sufriendo" (ibid., 54).

56. "Gente de afuera que lleva la tierra de uno; que se engorda con lo de uno; y todavía te escupe, te hace moler a patadas en las cárceles, pone letreros en sus clubes diciendo que a perros y peruanos es prohibido entrar . . . ¡Es odio natural, pues, como a una serpiente!" (ibid., 75; emphasis added in text).

57. "El viento de la revolución lo barrerá" y dejará el Perú de acero, limpio y brillante" (ibid., 76).

58. Legrás, *Literature and Subjection*, 231.

59. Arguedas, *The Foxes,* 228.

60. Ibid, 227.

61. Ibid., 227–28.

62. Gustavo Gutierrez, "Teología de la liberación," 739.

63. Arguedas, *The Foxes,* 252.

64. Ibid., 250.

65. This quote in the text of the chapter is taken from the English translation of *The Foxes.* The Spanish original reads: "silencio de noche, bulla laberinto alzamiento en el día" (Arguedas, *El zorro,* 237). The Spanish version has a different sequence of nouns than the English translation. Literally, it is "noise labyrinth uprising."

66. Albó, "Sentido de naciones."

67. International Labour Organization, "Convention concerning the Indigenous and Tribal People in Independent Countries C169," 1989, www.ilo.org/ilolex/cgi-lex/convde .pl?C169.

68. "Quienes han definido este concepto complejo de [NyP]IOC han sido los numerosos constituyentes procedentes de esos pueblos, de modo que, esta vez, a quienes hay que aclarar su alcance es más bien a los juristas que tienden a interpretar cada término por separado" (Albó, "Sentido de naciones," 24).

69. Arguedas, *El zorro,* 251.

70. Legrás, *Literature and Subjection.*

71. Osorio, interview in the film *Hermano compañero.*

72. This quote comes from the English translation in Arguedas, *The Foxes,* 252 (emphasis added in text). The Spanish original reads: "Balazo a la cabeza y corazón de cada uno, no para hacer saltar el seso o romper ese músculo generosidad y vaciarle su sangre. Balazo de luz entendimiento para darle claridad y energía de modo que pueda ver el humano y todos los humanos, negros, injertos, indios, igualito que nuestro Señor, como el '"Che' los veía, con fuerza verdadero, decisión hacerse respetar; ver que un hombre es igual a otro hombre" (Arguedas, *El zorro,* 238).

73. Arguedas, *El zorro,* 238.

74. Ibid.; my translation in the text.

75. Arguedas, *The Foxes,* 252.

76. Arguedas, *El zorro,* 238; my translation in the text.

77. "A la violencia de la Fuerza Armada, debo recordar su deber de estar al servicio del pueblo y no de los privilegios de unos pocos. . . . Quisiéramos ver que reprimen con igual furia la subversión de la derecha, que es peor de criminal que la de la izquierda . . . y que puede ser mejor controlada por las fuerzas de seguridad. . . . A esta violencia intransigente de la derecha, vuelto a repetir la severa admonición de la Iglesia cuando le hace culpable de la cólera y de la desesperación del pueblo. . . . Ellos son el verdadero germen y el verdadero peligro del comunismo que hipócritamente denuncian" (Romero, *Homilia del tercer domingo*).

78. Arguedas, *The Foxes,* 255.

79. Ibid., 253.

80. Gustavo Gutiérrez, *Teología de la liberación,* 323.

BIBLIOGRAPHY

Adelman, Jeremy. "Unfinished States: Historical Perspectives on the Andes." In *State and Society in Conflict: Comparative Perspectives on Andean Crises,* edited by Paul W. Drake and Eric Hershberg, 41–73. Pittsburgh: University of Pittsburgh Press, 2006.

Agamben, Giorgio. *Means without Ends: Notes on Politics.* Minneapolis: University of Minnesota Press, 2000.

———. *State of Exception.* Chicago: University of Chicago Press, 2005.

Albó, Xavier. "¿Cómo manejar la interculturalidad jurídica en un país intercultural?" *Justicia Comunitaria.* Sucre, Bolivia: Poder Judicial, Instituto de la Judiciatura de Bolivia, 2003.

———. "Sentido de 'naciones y pueblos indígena originario campesinos' en la CPE." *Artículo Primero: Revista de debate cultural y jurídico* 13, no. 20 (2011): 20–27.

Aldrich, Earl. "The Quechua World of José María Arguedas." *Hispania* 45, no. 1 (1962): 62–66.

Alemany Bay, Carmen. "Revisión del concepto de neoindigenismo a través de tres narradores contemporáneos: J. M. Arguedas, Roa Bastos y José Donoso." *Anthropos* 128 (1992): 74–76.

Archibald, Priscilla. "Andean Anthropology in the Era of Development Theory: The Work of José María Arguedas." In *José María Arguedas: Reconsiderations for Latin American Cultural Studies,* edited by Ciro Sandoval and Sandra Boschetto-Sandoval, 3–34. Athens: Ohio University Press, 1998.

Arguedas, José María. "Cambio de cultura en las comunidades indígenas económicamente fuertes." In *Formación de una cultura nacional indoamericana,* edited by Ángel Rama, 28–33. Mexico, DF: Siglo Veintiuno Editores, 1975.

———. *Deep Rivers.* Translated by Frances Horning Barraclough. Long Grove, IL: Waveland Press, 2002.

———. "El complejo cultural en el Perú y el primer congreso de peruanistas. (Lo indio, lo occidental y lo mestizo. Los prejuicios culturales, la segregación social y la creación artística)." *Formación de una cultura nacional indoamericana,* edited by Ángel Rama, 1–8. Mexico, DF: Siglo Veintinuno Editores, 1975.

———. "El indigenismo en el Perú." *Indios, mestizos y señores,* 9–20. Lima: Editorial Horizonte, 1989.

———. *El Sexto.* 1964. Reprint, Barcelona: Editorial Laia, 1974.

———. "El valor documental de la fiesta del Señor de la Caña." *Indios, mestizos y señores,* 125–28. Lima: Editorial Horizonte, 1989.

———. "El varayok', eje de la vida civil del ayllu." *Indios, mestizos y señores,* 109–12. Lima: Editorial Horizonte, 1989.

———. *El zorro de arriba y el zorro de abajo.* Madrid: Colección Archivos, 1990.

———. "Entre el kechwa y el castellano, la angustia del mestizo." *Indios, mestizos y señores,* 25–27. Lima: Editorial Horizonte, 1989.

———. *Indios, mestizos y señores.* Lima: Editorial Horizonte, 1989.

———. *Katatay.* Lima: Editorial Horizonte, 1984.

———. "La feria." *Indios, mestizos y señores,* 67–70. Lima: Editorial Horizonte, 1989.

———. "La muerte y los funerales." *Indios, mestizos y señores,* 141–43. Lima: Editorial Horizonte, 1989.

———. "No soy un aculturado . . ." In *El zorro de arriba y el zorro de abajo,* edited by Eve-Marie Fell, 256–58. Madrid: Colección Archivos, 1990.

———. "Puquio, una cultura en proceso de cambio." In *Formación de una cultura nacional Indoamericana,* edited by Ángel Rama, 34–79. Mexico, DF: Siglo Veintinuno Editores, 1975.

———. *Todas las sangres,* 3rd ed. 1965. Reprint, Lima: Editorial Horizonte, 1987.

———. *The Fox from Up Above and the Fox from Down Below.* Translated by Frances Horning Barraclough. Edited by Julio Ortega and Christian Fernández. Pittsburgh: University of Pittsburgh Press, 2000.

———. *Yawar Fiesta.* Buenos Aires: Losada, 1974.

Arguedas, José María, and Hugo Blanco. "Correspondencia entre Hugo Blanco y José María Arguedas." *Amaru* 11 (1969): 13–14.

Asamblea Constituyente and Honorable Congreso Nacional. *Nueva Constitución Política del Estado.* La Paz: Representación Presidencial para la Asamblea Constituyente, 2008.

Avelar, Idelber. *The Untimely Present.* Durham, NC: Duke University Press, 1999.

Ayo, Diego. "Entrevista: La revolución burguesa de raigambre indígena." *Pukara* 7, no. 80 (April 2013): 6–8.

Bajtín, Mijaíl. *Problemas de la poética de Dostoyevski.* Translated by Tatiana Bubnova. Madrid: Fondo de cultura económica, 2004.

Barragan, Rossana. "Entre polleras, ñañacas y lliqllas: Los mestizos y cholos en la conformación de la 'tercera república.'" In *Tradición y modernidad en los Andes,* edited by Henrique Urbano, 43–74. Cusco: Centro de Estudio Regionales Andinos Bartolomé de las Casas, 1994.

Basadre, Jorge. *Historia de la Republica del Perú.* Lima: Editorial Universitaria, 1983.

Bascopé Caero, Víctor. "El sentido de la muerte en la cosmovisión andina; el caso de los valles andinos de Cochabamba." *Chungara, Revista de Antropología Chilena* 33, no. 2 (2001): 271–77.

Beasley-Murray, Jon. "*Arguedasmachine:* Modernity and Affect in the Andes." *Iberoamericana* 8, no. 30 (June 2008): 113–28.

Benjamin, Walter. "Critique of Violence." In *Reflections,* edited by Peter Demetz, 277–300. New York: Schocken Books, 1986.

Beverley, John. *Subalternity and Representation: Arguments in Cultural Theory.* Durham, NC: Duke University Press, 1999.

Bhabha, Homi K. *The Location of Culture.* London: Routledge, 1994.

Borricaud, François. "Sociología de una novela peruana." *El Comercio,* January 1, 1958, 2.

Bosteels, Bruno. "Marx and Latin America Revisited." The New School. Janey Lecture at the New School, New York, Fall 2010. www.ebookbrowse.com/bosteels-janey-fall-10-lecture-pdf-d30173665.

Boschetto-Sandoval, Sandra, and Ciro Sandoval, eds. *José María Arguedas: Reconsiderations for Latin American Cultural Studies.* Athens: Ohio University Press, 1998.

Bourdieu, Pierre. *El campo político.* La Paz: Plural, 2001.

———. *Poder, derecho y clases sociales.* Bilbao: Desclée de Brouwer, 2001.

Brandt, Hans-Jurgen, and Rocio Franco Valdivia, comps. *Justicia comunitaria en los Andes: Perú y Ecuador. Normas, valores y preocedimientos en la justicia comunitaria.* Lima: Instituto de Defensa Legal, 2007.

Braudel, Fernand. *La historia y las ciencias sociales.* Madrid: Alianza Editorial, 1974.

Bravo, Victor Antonio. "Arguedas: La escritura como realidad-realidad." *Plural: Revista Cultural de Excelsior* 11, no. 7 (1982): 16–26.

Bredekamp, Horst, Melissa Thorson Hause, and Jackson Bond. "From Walter Benjamin to Carl Schmitt, via Thomas Hobbes." *Critical Inquiry* 25, no. 2 (1999): 247–66.

Butler, Judith. "Violence, Mourning, Politics." *Precarious Life: The Power of Mourning and Violence,* 19–49. London: Verso, 2004.

Butler, Judith, Ernesto Laclau, and Slavoj Žižek. *Contingencia, hegemonía, universalidad.* Buenos Aires: Fondo de Cultura Económica, 2003.

Carrillo, Francisco. *Literatura quechua clásica.* Lima: Editorial Horizonte, 1986.

Castro-Klarén, Sara. "Crímen y castigo: Sexualidad en J. M. Arguedas." *Revista Iberoamericana* 49 (1985): 55–65.

———. *El mundo mágico de José María Arguedas.* Lima: Instituto de Estudios Peruanos, 1973.

———. "Todos los cuentos de Arguedas." *Amaru* (April–June 1967): 87–89.

———. "'Like a pig, when he's thinkin': Arguedas on Affect and on Becoming an Animal." Translated by Fred Fornoff. In *The Fox from Up Above and the Fox from Down Below,* edited by Julio Ortega and Christian Fernández, 307–23. Pittsburgh: University of Pittsburgh Press, 2000.

Chahín Lupo, Juan Antonio. "Ley de Hermandad Jurídica para fortalecer el Estado de Derecho." In *Justicia Comunitaria en los pueblos originarios de Bolivia,* edited by Instituto de Judicatura de Bolivia, 41–60. Sucre: Instituto de la Judicatura de Bolivia, 2003.

Chivi Vargas, Idón Moisés. *Justicia indígena.* La Paz: Azul Editores, 2006.

Cincotta de Moncero, Susana. "Polivalencia de la sangre en *Todas las sangres* de José María Arguedas." *Celehis: Revista del Centro de Letras Hispanoamericanas* 5, nos. 6–8 (1996): 143–56.

"Constitución Política el Estado" (CPE), February 7, 2009. www.bolivia.infoleyes.com/shownorm.php?id=469. Accessed February 15, 2014.

Cornejo Polar, Antonio. *Escribir en el aire. Ensayo sobre la heterogeneidad sociocultural en las literaturas andinas.* Lima: Editorial Horizonte, 1994.

———. "Indigenist and Heterogeneous Literatures: Their Dual Sociocultural Status." *Latin American Perspectives* 16, no. 2 (1989): 12–28.

———. *Los universos narrativos de José María Arguedas.* Lima: Editorial Horizonte, 1997.

———. "Una heterogeneidad no dialéctica: Sujeto y discurso migrantes en el Perú moderno." *Revista Iberoamericana* 62, nos. 176–77 (1996): 837–44.

Cortázar, Julio. *Rayuela.* Buenos Aires: Editorial Sudamericana, 1963.

Cruz-Leal, Petra. "Arrojo y heroicidad en algunos personajes de José María Arguedas." *Anthropos* 128 (1992): 40–43.

Culler, Jonathan. "Derrida and Democracy." *Diacritics* 38, nos. 1–2 (Spring–Summer 2008): 2–6.

Degregori, Carlos Iván. "Jóvenes y campesinos ante la violencia política: Ayacucho 1980–1983." In *Poder y violencia en los Andes,* edited by Henrique Urbano, 395–416. Cusco: Centro de Estudios Regionales Andinos Bartolomé de las Casas, 1990.

Derrida, Jacques. "Force of Law: The 'Mystical Foundation of Authority." In *Acts of Religion,* edited by Gil Anidjar, 228–98. 1989. Reprint, New York: Routledge, 2002.

———. "Passions: An Oblique Offering." In *Derrida: A Critical Reader,* edited by David Wood, 5–35. Oxford: Blackwell, 1992.

Escajadillo, Tomás. "Entrevista a José María Arguedas." *Cultura y Pueblo* 7–8 (1965): 22–23.

Escobar, Alberto. *Arguedas, o la utopía de la lengua.* Lima: Instituto de Estudios Peruanos, 1984.

———. *El imaginario nacional.* Lima: IEP Ediciones, 1989.

———. "José María Arguedas, el desmitificador del indio y del rito indigenista." *Nova Americana* 3 (1980): 141–96.

———. "La guerra silenciosa en *Todas las sangres.*" *Revista Peruana de Cultura* 5 (1965): 37–49.

Escobar, Alberto, ed. *La narración en el Perú.* Lima: Editorial Letras, 1955.

———. *¿He vivido en vano? Mesa Redonda sobre Todas las Sangres 23 de junio de 1965.* Lima: IEP, 1985.

Executive Committee of the Communist International. "On the Revolution in America." In *Marxism in Latin America from 1909 to the Present: An Anthology,* edited by Michael Löwy, 8–14. New York: Humanity Books, 1992.

Favre, Henri. "José María Arguedas y yo: ¿Un breve encuentro o una cita frustrada?" *Cuadernos Americanos* 56, no. 2 (1996): 23–31.

Fernández, Christian. "J. M. Arguedas y la crítica en la encrucijada: La mesa del poder o el poder de la mesa sobre *Todas las sangres.*" *Revista de Crítica Literaria Latinoamericana* Año 36, no. 72 Lima-Boston (2nd semester of 2010): 299–317.

Flores Galindo, Alberto. *Buscando un Inca.* Vol. 3, *Obras Completas (I).* Lima: Casa de Estudios del Socialismo, 2005.

———. *La agonía de Mariátegui.* Vol. 2, *Obras Completas.* Lima: Casa de Estudios del Socialismo, 2005.

Forgues, Roland. *José María Arguedas: Del pensamiento dialéctico al pensamiento trágico.* Lima: Editorial Horizonte, 1989.

———. "Las estructuras socioeconómicas de la explotación de la tierra en la sierra peruana, según *Todas las sangres,* de José María Arguedas." *Letras de Deusto* 7, no. 13 (1977): 159–80.

———. "*Todas las sangres* (o el relato de un proceso de cambio socioeconómico y sociocultural en la sierra peruana)." *Cuadernos Hispanoamericanos: Revista Mensual de Cultura Hispánica* 300 (1975): 659–74.

Foucault, Michel. *La verdad y las formas jurídicas.* Mexico: Gedisa, 1986.

———. *Vigilar y castigar. Nacimiento de la prisión.* Mexico: Siglo XXI, 1997.

Fourth Congress of the Communist International. "To the Workers and Peasants of South America." In *Marxism in Latin America from 1909 to the Present: An Anthology,* edited by Michael Löwy, 14–17. New York: Humanity Books, 1992.

Franco, Sergio R., ed. *José María Arguedas: Hacia una poética migrante.* Pittsburgh: International Institute of Latin American Literature, 2006.

Fynsk, Christopher. "Foreword: Experiences of Finitude." In *The Inoperative Community*, edited by Christopher Fynsk, vii–xxxv. Minneapolis: University of Minnesota Press, 2001.

García Linera, Álvaro. "Ayuda memoria y algunos criterios (políticos) sobre el balance del primer año de gestión de la presidencia de Juan Evo Morales Ayma." *El Deber*, January 21, 2007.

———. *El Estado Plurinacional*. La Paz: Vice presidencia del Estado Plurinacional, 2009.

———. *Geopolítica de la Amazonía. Poder hacendal-patrimonial y la acumulación capitalista*. La Paz: Vice presidencia del Estado Plurinacional y Presidencia de la Asamblea Legislativa Plurinacional, 2012.

———. "La construcción del estado." Paper presented at Facultad de Derecho de la Universidad de Buenos Aires. Buenos Aires, Argentina, April 8, 2010.

———. "La muerte de la condición obrera del siglo XX: La Marcha Minera por la Vida." In *El retorno de la Bolivia plebeya*, edited by Grupo Comuna, 23–60. La Paz: La Muela del Diablo, 2000.

———. "Marxismo e Indianismo." Paper presented at Cornell University, New York, September 18, 2007.

García Linera, Álvaro, Raquel Gutiérrez, and Luís Tapia. "La forma multitud de la política de las necesidades vitales." In *El retorno de la Bolivia plebeya*, edited by Grupo Comuna, 143–95. La Paz: La Muela del Diablo, 2000.

Glave, Luis Miguel. "Arguedas y la historia." In *José María Arguedas, veinte años después: Huellas y horizonte*, compiled by Rodrigo Montoya, 65–72. Lima: Escuela de Antropología de la Universidad Nacional Mayor de San Marcos, 1991.

Goldmann, Lucien. *Para una sociología de la novela*. Madrid: Ciencia Nueva, 1967.

Gow, Rosalind. "Inkarri and Revolutionary Leadership in the Southern Andes." *Journal of Latin American Lore* 8, no. 2 (1882): 197–221.

Guaman Poma de Ayala, Felipe. *Nueva crónica y buen gobierno*. Ed. J. V. Murra, R. Adorno and J. L. Urioste. Madrid: Historia 16, 1987.

Guha, Ranajit. *Dominance without Hegemony: History and Power in Colonial India*. Cambridge, MA: Harvard University Press, 1997.

Gutiérrez, Gustavo. *Entre las calandrias*. Lima: Centro de Estudios Peruanos, 2011.

———. "Presencia de José María Arguedas." Paper presented at the Congress Arguedas: La dinámica de encuentros culturales, Pontífica Universidad Católica del Perú, June 24, 2011, Lima, Peru.

———. "Teología de la liberación." In *Huellas de las literaturas hispanoamericanas*, edited by John F. Gargangio et al., 732–40. Upper Saddle River, NJ: Prentice Hall, 2002.

———. *Teología de la liberación*. Lima: Centro de Estudios Peruanos, 2008.

Gutiérrez, Miguel. "Estructura e ideología de *Todas las sangres*." *Revista de Crítica Literaria Latinoamericana* 6, no. 12 (1980): 139–76.

Habermas, Jürgen. "Consciousness-Raising or Redemption Criticism: The Contemporaneity of Walter Benjamin." *New German Critique* 17 (1979): 30–59.

———. *The Structural Transformation of the Public Sphere*. Cambridge, MA: MIT Press, 1991.

Hardt, Michael, and Antonio Negri. *Multitude: War and Democracy in the Age of Empire*. New York: Penguin Books, 2004.

Hertz, Robert. *Death and the Right Hand*. Glencoe, IL: Free Press, 1960.

Hobbes, Thomas. *Leviathan*. Indianapolis: Hackett, 1994.

Huaco P., Marco Antonio. "Derechos humanos, Estado y Pueblos Indígenas. Bagua y su trasfondo: La lucha indígena contra Ugkaju." *Artículo primero: Revista de debate cultural y jurídico* 13, no. 20 (2011): 67–77.

Icaza, Jorge. *Huasipungo, novela.* Quito: Tipo-lito "Romero," 1937.

Ilarregui, Gladys. "Una nueva espacialidad poético-discursiva: *Oda al jet / Jetman haylli* de José María Arguedas." In *Identidades en transformación,* edited by Silvia Nagy-Zekemi, 81–98. Quito: Abya-Yala, 1997.

International Labour Organization. "Indigenous and Tribal Peoples Convention, 1989." June 27, 1989. www.ilo.org/ilolex/cgi-lex/convde.pl?C169. Accessed February 15, 2014.

Jameson, Frederic. "On Jargon." In *The Jameson Reader,* edited by Michael Hardt and Kathi Weeks, 117–18. Oxford: Blackwell, 2000.

Jay, Martin. "Anamnestic Totalization: Reflections on Marcuse's Theory of Remembrance." *Theory and Society* 11, no. 1 (1982): 1–15.

Kant, Immanuel. *Political Writings.* Edited by Hans Reiss. Cambridge: Cambridge University Press, 1991.

Katz, Claudio. "Karl Marx on the Transition from Feudalism to Capitalism." *Theory and Society* 22, no. 3 (1993): 363–89.

Kaufman, Sharon L., and Lynn M. Morgan. "The Anthropology of the Beginnings and the Ends of Life." *Annual Review of Anthropology* 34 (2005): 317–41.

Keenan, Dennis King. *The Question of Sacrifice.* Bloomington: Indiana University Press, 2005.

Klarén, Peter F. *Peru: Society and Nationhood in the Andes.* New York: Oxford University Press, 2000.

———. *Formación de las haciendas azucareras y orígenes del APRA.* Lima: Instituto de Estudios Peruanos, 1976.

Kristeva, Julia. *Black Sun: Depression and Melancholia.* New York: Columbia University Press, 1996.

Laclau, Ernesto. *La razón populista.* Buenos Aires: Fondo de Cultura Económica, 2005.

———. "Why Do Empty Signifiers Matter to Politics?" *Emancipation(s).* London: Verso, 1996.

Landes, Alejandro, dir. *Cocalero.* First Run Features, Fall Line Films, Morocha Films, INCAA. December 11, 2007. Bolivia: First Run Features, 2007. Feature film.

Larson, Brooke. *Trials of Nation Making: Liberalism, Race, and Ethnicity in the Andes, 1810–1910.* Cambridge: Cambridge University Press, 2004.

Lastra, Pedro. "Imágenes de José María Arguedas." *Escritura* 17, nos. 33–34 (1992): 47–57.

Legrás, Horacio. "*Yawar Fiesta:* El retorno de la tragedia." In *José María Arguedas, hacia una poética migrante,* edited by Sergio R. Franco, 61–80. Pittsburgh: International Institute of Latin American Literature, 2006.

———. *Literature and Subjection.* Pittsburgh: University of Pittsburgh Press, 2008.

Lienhard, Martin. *Cultura popular andina y forma novelesca: Zorros y danzantes en la última novela de Arguedas.* Lima: Editorial Horizonte, 1990.

———. "La antropología de J. M. Arguedas: Una historia de continuidades y rupturas." *Revista de Crítica Literaria Latinoamericana* 36, no. 72 (2010): 43–61.

———. "Avatares del yo." Paper presented at the Congress Arguedas: Dinámica de encuentros culturales, PUCP, Lima, Peru, 2011.

Lloyd, David, and Thomas, Paul. *Culture and the State.* New York: Routledge, 1998.

López-Baralt, Mercedes. *Ícono y conquista.* Madrid: Hiperion, 1988.

Löwy, Michael. "Introduction." *Marxism in Latin America from 1909 to the Present: An Anthology,* edited by Michael Löwy, xiii–lxv. New York: Humanity Books, 1992.

———, ed. *El marxismo en América Latina: Antología, desde 1909 hasta nuestros días.* Santiago de Chile: LOM Ediciones, 2007.

Lukacs, George. *Teoría de la novela.* Buenos Aires: Siglo XX, 1966.

Lybeer, Edward. "Arguedas' Zorros and the Mimeography of Canto." 123, no. 2 (March 2008): 294–307.

MacCormack, Sabine. *Religion in the Andes: Vision and Imagination in Early Colonial Peru.* Princeton, NJ: Princeton University Press, 1991.

Mallon, Florencia. "De ciudadano a 'otro.'" Resistencia nacional, formación del estado y visiones campesinas sobre la nación en Junín." *Revista Andina* 12, no. 1 (1994): 7–54.

———. *The Defense of Community in Peru's Central Highlands: Peasant Struggle and Capitalist Transition, 1860–1940.* Princeton, NJ: Princeton University Press, 1983.

Manrique, Nelson. "Comentario a F. Mallon 'Visiones campesinas . . .'" *Revista Andina* 12, no. 1 (1994): 64–68.

———. "Una mirada histórica." *José María Arguedas, veinte años después: Huellas y horizonte.* Lima: Escuela de Antropología de la Universidad Nacional Mayor de San Marcos, 1991.

———. "Gamonalismo, lanas y violencia en los Andes." In *Poder y violencia en los Andes,* edited by Henrique Urbano, 211–23. Cusco: Centro de Estudios Regionales Andinos Bartolomé de las Casas, 1990.

Mariátegui, José Carlos. *Siete ensayos de interpretación de la realidad peruana.* Lima: Biblioteca "Amauta," 1959.

———. "Prologue to Tempest in the Andes." In *Marxism in Latin America from 1909 to the Present: An Anthology,* edited by Michael Löwy, 28–33. New York: Humanity Books, 1992.

McNamee, Eugene. "The Government of the Tongue." *Law and Literature* 14, no. 3 (2002): 427–61.

Méndez, Cecilia. "República sin indios: La comunidad imaginada del Perú." In *Tradición y modernidad en los Andes,* edited by Henrique Urbano, 15–42. Cusco: Centro de Estudios Regionales Andinos Bartolomé de las Casas, 1997.

Menges, Patricia. "Lenguaje y liberación en *Todas las sangres.*" *Texto Crítico* 9, no. 27 (1983): 112–49.

Mier Cueto, Enrique. "Las prácticas jurídicas Aymaras desde una perspectiva cultural." In *Justicia Comunitaria en los pueblos originarios de Bolivia,* edited by Instituto de la Judicatura de Bolivia, 61–84. Sucre: Instituto de la Judicatura de Bolivia, 2003.

Milstein, Brian. *Between Voluntarism and Universal Autonomy: Jacques Derrida's "Force of Law."* Unpublished paper, New School for Social Research, New York, 2003, magictheatre.panopticweb.com/aesthetics/writings/polth-derrida.html. Accessed August 8, 2013.

Miranda Luizaga, Jorge. *Filosofía andina: Fundamentos, alteridad y perspectiva.* La Paz: Hisbol/Goethe Institut, 1996.

Montoya, Rodrigo, comp. *José María Arguedas, veinte años después: Huellas y horizonte, 1969–1989.* Lima: Escuela de Antropología de la Universidad Nacional Mayor de San Marcos, 1991.

Montoya, Rodrigo. "Antropología y política." In *José María Arguedas, veinte años después: Huellas y horizonte,* compiled by Rodrigo Montoya, 17–30. Lima: Escuela de Antropología de la Universidad Nacional Mayor de San Marcos, 1991.

Moore, Melisa. *En la encrucijada: Las ciencias sociales y la novela en el Perú.* Lima: Fondo Editorial de UNMSM, 2003.

Morató Lara, Luis. "José María Arguedas: Fundación del movimiento literario transcultur-alista." In *Identidades en transformación,* edited by Silvia Nagy-Zekemi, 63–80. Quito: Abya-Yala Editing, 1997.

Moreiras, Alberto. "Freedom from Transculturation: A Response to Priscilla Archibald." *Social Text* 25, no. 4 [93] (Winter 2007): 115–21.

Murra, John. *Formaciones económicas y políticas del mundo andino.* Lima: Instituto de Estudios Peruanos, 1975.

Nancy, Jean-Luc. "The Inoperative Community." In *The Inoperative Community,* edited by Christopher Fynsk, 1–43. Minneapolis: University of Minnesota Press, 2001.

———. "Preface." In *The Inoperative Community,* edited by Christopher Fynsk, xxxvi–xli. Minneapolis: University of Minnesota Press, 2001.

———. "The Unsacrificeable." Translated by Richard Livingston. *Yale French Studies* 79 (1991): 20–38.

Nietzsche, Friedrich. *La genealogía de la moral.* Translated by Roberto Mares. Mexico, DF: Grupo Editorial Tomo, 2002.

Noriega, Carlos. "Hay más muertos." *Diario la primera,* June 22, 2009, www.diariolaprimera peru.com/online/entrevista/hay-mas-muertos_40840.html. Accessed August 16, 2013.

Noriega, Julio. *Buscando una tradición quechua en el Perú.* Coral Gables, FL: Iberian Studies Institute, 1995.

Norris, Andrew. "Giorgio Agamben and the Politics of the Living Dead." *Diacritics* 30, no. 4 (2000): 38–58.

Orellana Halkyer, René. "Prácticas judiciales en comunidades indígenas Quechuas." In *Justicia Comunitaria en los pueblos originarios de Bolivia,* edited by Instituto de Judi-catura de la Bolivia, 11–40. Sucre: Instituto de la Judicatura de Bolivia, 2003.

Orrillo, Winston. "*Todas las sangres:* Un gigantesco esfuerzo novelístico de José María Arguedas." *El Correo,* February 25, 1965, 12.

Ortega, Julio. "El discurso de suicidio." *Anthropos* 128 (1992): 61–62.

———. "*Todas las sangres.*" *El Expreso,* August 10, 1968, 11.

Ortega, Julio, and Christian Fernández, eds. *The Fox from Up Above and the Fox from Down Below,* by José María Arguedas. Translated by Frances Horning Barraclough. Pittsburgh: University of Pittsburgh Press, 2000.

Ortiz Rascaniere, Alejandro. *La pareja y el mito. Estudios sobre las concepciones de la per-sona y de la pareja en los Andes.* Lima: Pontífica Universidad Católica del Perú, 1993.

Osorio, Nelson. Interview about Arguedas in *Hermano compañero, compañero de sangre: José María Arguedas,* directed by Rómulo Franco Ruiz-Bravo. Lima: Fondo Editorial PUCP, 2009.

Oviedo, José Miguel. "*Todas las sangres* de José María Arguedas." *Suplemento Dominical de El Comercio,* February 7, 1965, 6–7.

Paredes, Julieta y Mujeres Creando Comunidad. *Hilando fino desde el feminismo comuni-tario.* La Paz: Mujeres Creando Comunidad, 2010.

Pinilla, Carmen María. *Arguedas, conocimiento y vida.* Lima: Fondo Editorial de la Pontí-fica Universidad Católica del Perú, 1994.

Portocarrero, Gonzalo. "Arguedas, sanador del Peru." *Página de Gonzalo Portocarrero* (blog). gonzaloportocarrero.blogsome.com/2013/06/14/arguedas. Accessed August 7, 2013.

Prada Alcoreza, Raúl. "La hermenéutica de la violencia." In *El retorno de la Bolivia plebeya,* edited by Grupo Comuna, 91–141. La Paz: La Muela del Diablo, 2000.

Primer encuentro de narradores peruanos. Lima: Latinoamericana Editores, 1986.

Ptacek, Melissa. "Sacrificing Sacrifice." *Theory and Society* 35, nos. 5/6 (December 2006): 587–600.

Quijano Obregón, Aníbal. "Carta del Dr. A. Quijano sobre *Todas las sangres* de J.M. Arguedas." *Boletín de Sociología* (1965): 18–20.

Rabasa, José. "Postcolonialismo." In *Diccionario de estudios culturales latinoamericanos*, edited by Monica Szurmuk and Robert McKee Irwin, 219–23. Mexico, DF: Siglo XXI Editores, 2009.

Rama, Ángel, ed. *Formación de una cultura nacional indoamericana*. Mexico, DF: Siglo XXI Editores, 1975.

———. *Transculturación narrativa en América Latina*. Mexico, DF: Siglo XXI Editores, 1985.

Reinaga, Fausto. *El sentimiento mesiánico del pueblo ruso*. La Paz: Ediciones SER, 1960.

Rivera, Fernando. *Dar la palabra: Ética, política y poética de la escritura en Arguedas*. Madrid: Iberoamericana Vervuert, 2011.

Rivera Cusicanqui, Silvia. "El otro bicentenario." In *Chixinakax utxiwa: Una reflexión sobre práctica y discursos descolonizadores*, edited by Silvia Rivera Cusicanqui, 9–18. Buenos Aires: Tinta Limón, 2010.

———. "Sociología de la imagen: Una visión desde la historia colonial andina." *Chixinakax utxiwa: Una reflexión sobre práctica y discursos descolonizadores*, edited by Silvia Rivera Cusicanqui, 19–53. Buenos Aires: Tinta Limón, 2010.

Romero, Oscar. *Homilia del tercer Domingo de tiempo ordinario*, January 27, 1980. www .servicioskoinonia.org/romero/homilias/C/800127.htm. Accessed August 17, 2013.

Rowe, William. *Ensayos Arguedianos*. Lima: Centro de Producción Editorial de la Universidad Nacional Mayor de San Marcos: SUR Casa de Estudios del Socialismo, 1996.

———. *Mito e ideología en la obra de José María Arguedas*. Lima: Instituto Nacional de Cultura, 1979.

———. "'No hay mensajero de nada:' La modernidad andina según *los Zorros* de Arguedas." *Revista de Crítica Literaria Latinoamericana*, no. 72 (2010): 61–96.

Ruiz-Bravo, Rómulo Franco, dir. *Hermano compañero, compañero de sangre: José María Arguedas*. Lima: Fondo Editorial PUCP, 2009. Film.

Salazar Bondy, Sebastián. "Arguedas e indigenismo." *La Prensa* (1954): 10.

———. "Arguedas: Fe en el hombre." *El Comercio*, November 30, 1961, 2.

———. "Arguedas: La novela social como creación verbal." *Revista de la Universidad de México* 19, no. 2: 18–20.

———. "La evolución del llamado indigenismo." *Sur* (March–April 1965): 44–50.

Salmón, Josefa. *Decir nosotros: En la encrucijada del pensamiento indianista*. La Paz: Editora Autodeterminación, 2013.

———. "La presencia indígena en la nueva constitución plurinacional boliviana." In *Decir nosotros: En la encrucijada del pensamiento indianista*, 67–81. La Paz: Editora Autodeterminación, 2013.

Salomon, Frank. "Introductory Essay." In *The Huarochiri Manuscript*, translated and edited by Frank Salomon and George L. Urioste, 1–38. Austin: University of Texas Press, 1991.

Sánchez, Luis Alberto. "El indigenismo de *Todas las sangres*." *El Correo*, August 5, 1965, 12.

Saravia, Joaquín, and Godofredo Sandoval. *Jach'a Uru: ¿La esperanza de un pueblo? Carlos Palenque, RTP y los sectores populares urbanos en La Paz*. La Paz: ILDIS-CEP, 1991.

Schmitt, Carl. *The Concept of the Political*. Chicago: University of Chicago Press, 2007.

Schwab, George. "Introduction." In *The Concept of the Political,* expanded ed., edited by George Schwab, 3–16. Chicago: University of Chicago Press, 2007.

Sheehan, Jonathan. "Sacrifice before the Secular." *Representations* 105, no. 1 (Winter 2009): 12–36.

Shirova, Klara. "*Todas las sangres,* la utopía peruana." *José María Arguedas en el Corazón de Europa,* 97–144. Prague: Universidad Carolina de Praga, 2004.

Spalding, Karen. *De indio a campesino: Cambios en la estructura social del Perú colonial.* Lima: IEP, 1974.

Spitta, Sylvia. "José María Arguedas: Entre dos aguas." *Between Two Waters: Narratives of Transculturation in Latin America,* 141–176. Houston: Rice University Press, 1995.

Spivak, Gayatri Chakravorty. "Can the Subaltern Speak?" In *The Post-Colonial Studies Reader,* edited by Gareth Griffiths Aschcroft and Helen Tiffin, 24–28. London: Routledge, 1995.

Stefanoni, Pablo. "Un nuevo mapa político de Bolivia." *Le Monde Diplomatique* 164 (February 2013): 10–11.

Stein, Steve. *Lima obrera (1900–1930).* Lima: Ediciones El Virrey, 1986.

Strong, Tracy B. "Foreword." In *The Concept of the Political,* expanded ed., edited by Charles Schwab, ix–xxxi. Chicago: University of Chicago Press, 2007.

Suetonius Tranquilus, Gaius. *Lives of the Caesars.* Oxford: Oxford University Press, 2000.

Tapia, Luís. "La densidad de las síntesis." In *El retorno de la Bolivia plebeya,* edited by Grupo Comuna, 61–90. La Paz: La Muela del Diablo, 2000.

Tarica, Estelle. "El 'decir limpio' de Arguedas: La voz bilingüe, 1940–1958." *José María Arguedas, hacia una poética migrante.* Edited by Sergio Franco. Pittsburgh: International Institute of Latin American Literature, 2006.

———. *The Inner Life of Mestizo Nationalism.* Minneapolis: University of Minnesota Press, 2008.

———. "Arguedas después de la violencia." Paper presented at the Congress Arguedas: La dinámica de los encuentros culturales, PUCP, June 23, 2011, Lima, Peru.

Taussig, Michael. *Devil and Commodity Fetishism in Latin America.* Chapel Hill: University of North Carolina Press, 2010.

Thurner, Mark. *From Two Republics to One Divided.* Durham, NC: Duke University Press, 1997.

Todorov, Tzvetan. *Los géneros del discurso.* Caracas: Monte Ávila Editores Latinoamericana, 1978.

———. *On Human Diversity.* Cambridge, MA: Harvard University Press, 1993.

———. *The Conquest of America.* New York: Harper and Row, 1984.

Urton, Gary. *At the Crossroads of the Earth and the Sky: An Andean Cosmology.* Austin: University of Texas Press, 1981.

Urbano, Henrique, ed. *Tradición y modernidad en los Andes.* Cusco: Centro de Estudios Regionales Andinos Bartolomé de las Casas, 1997.

Vargas, Raúl. "Sobre *Todas las sangres.*" *El Expreso,* March 26, 1966, 12.

Vargas Llosa, Mario. *La utopia arcaica: José María Arguedas y las ficciones del indigenismo.* Mexico: Fondo de Cultura Económica, 1996.

———. *La fiesta del chivo.* Madrid: Alfaguara, 2000.

Vidal, Ana María. "Derecho oficial y derecho campesino en el mundo andino." In *Entre la ley y la costumbre: El derecho consuetudinario indígena en América Latina,* compiled by Rodolfo Stavenhagen and Diego Iturralde, 141–53. Mexico: Instituto Indigenista Interamericano, 1990.

Vilas, Carlos M., and Richard Stoller. "Lynchings and Political Conflict in the Andes." *Latin American Perspectives* 35, no. 5 (September 2008): 103–18.

Virno, Paolo. *A Grammar of the Multitude.* Boston: Semiotext(e), MIT Press, 2004.

Walker, Charles. "Los indios en la transición de la colonia a la república: ¿Base social de la modernidad política?" In *Tradición y modernidad en los Andes,* edited by Henrique Urbano, 1–14. Cusco: Centro de Estudios Regionales Andinos Bartolomé de las Casas, 1997.

Williams, Raymond. *Marxism and Literature.* Oxford: Oxford University Press, 1977.

Žižek, Slavoj. *Violence.* New York: Picador, 2008.

Zuidema, R. Tom. *Inca Civilization in Cuzco.* Austin: University of Texas Press, 1990.

INDEX

absolutism, democracy and, 103
abuse, 59, 97, 106, 110, 123, 126–27, 129, 147n13
Adelman, Jeremy, 90
afterlife, 63, 65, 66, 71; concept of, 57, 68; death and, 49, 50, 57, 58
Agamben, Giorgio, 20, 45, 46, 61, 95, 96, 143n4; authoritarianism and, 25; community and, 2; living law and, 88; state of exception and, 87, 100, 102, 103
Albó, Xavier, 6, 131, 132, 153n6
Alianza Popular Revolucionaria Americana (APRA), 78, 79, 80, 119, 120, 151n71
Andean culture, 26, 151n77
Andean worldview, 1, 49, 132, 139n2
antagonism, 3, 4, 111, 114, 115
anticapitalism, 113, 117
antifoundationalism, 122
anti-imperialism, 112, 113, 114, 115, 117
Anto, 9, 68, 69, 71, 141n28
Apark'ora, 49, 50
Apocalypse of Saint John, 135
"Appeal to Some Intellectuals" (Arguedas), 134
appearance, essence and, 36
APRA. See Alianza Popular Revolucionaria Americana
Apus, 24, 64
Aquíles, 77, 91, 97, 151n80
Aragón, Don Bruno, 22, 24, 33, 52, 60, 63, 68, 71, 73, 87, 90, 92, 93, 109, 128; Aquíles and, 97; aura of, 44; authority and, 23; behavior of, 39, 40, 100; Chris-

tian value system of, 84; Cisneros and, 42, 43; dedication/incorruptibility of, 106; divine and, 36; Fermín and, 43, 53, 103, 106; gamonal and, 32; God of, 105; hacienda of, 25–26, 35, 45, 88, 89, 91; Indians and, 30, 31, 41; judgment of, 94; justice and, 103–4; Lucas and, 103, 105; madness of, 39–40; moral strength of, 36; neutralization of, 27; persecution of, 120; personal/political nature of, 41; physical suffering of, 37; power of, 34, 39; psychological factors of, 38–39; public sphere and, 35–36; ravings of, 40; reforms by, 91; Rendón Willka and, 106, 107; responsibility of, 41, 98; self-sacrifice of, 107; serfs and, 34, 37, 68, 69, 116; sexual behavior of, 35, 36, 106; sins of, 37–38, 106; as social subject, 46; varayok's and, 25, 26, 103; violence of, 43, 107, 108; virtue and, 37; vision of, 105
Aragón, Don Fermín, 12, 22, 38, 39, 41, 52, 56, 63, 64, 68, 69, 78, 79, 93, 97, 102; authority of, 89; behavior of, 107; Bruno and, 43, 53, 103, 106; Cisneros and, 4, 45; modernity and, 89; order/progress and, 83, 88–89; performativity and, 103; projects of, 53; Rendón and, 53–54, 71, 80; substitution and, 88; vision of, 54; wounding of, 104
Aragón, Doña Rosario, 63, 68, 69
Arendt, Hannah, 25, 45
Arguedas, José Maria: Andean perspective of, 49; antagonisms and, 9; communica-

tion/ conciliation and, 123; effective
leaders and, 129; essentialisms and, 122;
ethnographic studies and, 56, 82; horizontal destitution and, 58; indigenous
peoples and, 3, 126; law/justice and, 107;
majestic/beautiful and, 93; Marxism
and, 111; mourning by, 82; multiple
sovereignties and, 6; nonproject and, 85;
Peruvian society and, 1, 84; poem by,
134; political thought of, 2, 19; reading
of, 123; Socialism and, 110; Stalinist
orthodoxy and, 112–14; suicide of,
134, 140n7, 149n54; vision of, 119–20;
writing of, 4, 5, 14, 63, 81, 83, 112, 119,
120, 131, 132, 140n9
*Arguedas, hermano compañero, compañero
de sangre* (documentary), 12
Aryans, 48
Asunta, 104, 106, 126, 156n64
authoritarianism, 25, 45, 61
authority, 23, 34, 61, 62, 63, 89; concept of,
25, 45; indigenous, 87; power of, 46;
public, 44
Awajun, massacre of, 7
ayllu, 17, 18, 19, 22, 26, 30, 43, 45, 46, 48,
54; abolition of, 15–16; customs/tradi-
tions and, 88; death sentence of, 83;
disappearance of, 51; finitude/com-
munity and, 55–66; formation of, 31;
geographical community of, 57; judicial
structures of, 90; protection of, 89; punishment in, 93; rotational nature of, 59;
sovereignty of, 4, 23; structure of, 74, 84
Aymara, 6, 18, 76, 139n2, 151n77
Aztecs, 125

Bagua situation, 7, 141n22
Bakhtin, Mikhail, 12
Barraclough, Frances Horning, 139n4,
158n24
Bazalár, Gregorio, 13, 121–22, 128–29, 133
Beasley-Murray, Jon, 117, 141n39
beautiful, majestic and, 93
behavior, 39, 40, 100, 107; abusive, 126; ceremonious, 43; cultural/historical factors
and, 19–20; physical, 35; sexual, 35, 36
Belaúnde Terry, Fernando, 17
Bellido, 73, 101; death of, 86, 98, 102,
141n28
Benjamin, Walter, 2, 87, 97, 98, 108, 133
birth, community and, 59

Blanco, Hugo, 17
Bloody October, 9
Bodin, Jean, 24
Bolívar, Simón, 15, 19
Bosteels, Bruno, 7, 110, 111
Bourdieu, Pierre, 146n62
Braudel, Fernand, 38, 152n89
Buscando un Inca (Flores Galindo), 145n50
Butler, Judith, 66

Cabrejos, 29, 59, 61, 80, 104, 148n13; death
of, 102; obedience by, 78; punishment of,
126; Rendón Willka and, 53, 60, 70
Cáceres, Mariscal, 16
Caero, Bascopé: afterlife and, 57
Calderon de la Barca, Pedro, 103
Camac, Alejandro, 115, 120, 127
camac, concept of, 11
Camacho, Oscar Vega, 9
campesinos, 9, 131, 132
capital: accumulation of, 41, 44; transnational, 4, 52, 54, 55, 76, 78, 80, 83, 84,
151n80
capitalism, 55, 56, 81, 118; agrarian, 113, 114;
internal, 117; struggle against, 114, 115;
transitional stabilization of, 113
Cardozo, Father, 118, 128, 137; Chimbote
and, 130–31, 133; final speech of, 113;
Ramírez and, 135; revolution and, 134;
speech of, 133, 135–36
Carta Magna, 6
caste, 75, 84, 92
Castro-Klarén, Sara, 11, 149n33
Cesar Augustus, 25
Chimbote, 13, 112, 117, 118, 120, 122, 128,
136, 137, 157; described, 130–31; egalitarian future of, 130; revolution in, 133
cholos, 42, 45, 83, 84, 114
Christian mythology, 39, 41, 58
Cisneros, Don Adalberto, 27, 40, 46, 77, 91,
93, 126; Bruno and, 42, 43; collaborators of, 44; Fermín and, 44, 45; lands of,
45; Paraybamba and, 97; punishment
of, 41–42, 90, 93, 94, 97, 103, 108, 126;
social mobility and, 92; citizenship,
18–19, 89, 95, 119; full, 28; passageway
to, 19; requirements of, 15; rights to, 76;
sovereignty and, 24
civil society, consolidation of, 18
class-consciousness, consolidation of, 115
class struggle, concept of, 111

conceptual sphere of, 99, 104; effectiveness, 94; execution of, 103; law and, 105, 107; outside law, 103–7; struggle for, 119

k'achua hymns, 64, 65–66
Kafka, Franz, 133
Kant, Immanuel, 24, 25, 27
Kaufman, Sharon, 57
Klarén, Peter, 14
K'oropata, 57, 63, 64, 68, 71
K'oto, Adrian, 26, 34, 41, 65, 66, 68, 69, 70; communication and, 146n53; speech of, 38–39

"La agonia de Rasu Niti" (Arguedas), 114
labor, 18, 82, 123; alienated, 78; capitalist concept of, 81
Laclau, Ernesto, 2, 5, 62
La Convención, 17, 82
Lahuaymarca, 51, 55–56, 59, 60, 61, 154n23; citizenship and, 89; towns of, 30
land: reform, 90; struggle for, 114
language gaps, revolutionary potential of, 130–37
La Providencia (hacienda), 25, 31, 34, 40, 49, 145n38
"Last Diary" (Arguedas), 113, 119, 134; narrative voice of, 117–18
latifundio, 56, 114, 157n14
law, 24, 87, 153n8; custom and, 88, 153n8; force of, 87, 88, 102; justice outside, 103–7; life and, 91; living, 88; martial, 7, 109; modalities of, 23; national, 90; as normativity, 92; politics and, 100; positive, 46, 88, 96, 100–103; preserving, 100; private, 46, 61; state, 8; universality of, 98
legality, 2, 98, 102, 103
Legrás, Horacio, 1, 12, 14, 20, 122, 126, 128, 134, 136, 152n83
Leguía, Augusto B., government of, 17
Lenin, Vladimir, 110, 120
liberal ideology, 126
liberation theology, 1, 130, 135, 156n64
Lienhard, Martin, 12, 13, 14, 117, 149n54, 150n60
life: law and, 91; politicization of, 119
literary analysis, 14, 15
Literature and Subjection (Legrás), quote from, 1
lordship, performance of, 35

Lucas, Don, 60, 76, 91, 103, 156n64; execution of, 43, 104, 105, 107

majestic, beautiful and, 93
Mallon, Florencia, 16
manifestation, freedom of, 62
Manrique, Nelson, 6
Marcha Minera por la Vida, 9
Mariátegui, José Carlos, 6, 31, 110; national bourgeoisie and, 113; Stalinist orthodoxy and, 112–14
martyrdom, 52, 57, 58, 67, 148n28
Marxism, 81, 110, 111, 113, 114
Mein Kampf (Hitler), Nancy reading of, 47–48
memory: historical, 81; national, 84; ritual of, 66; suppression of, 81
Mesa Redonda sobre Todas las Sangres (Arguedas), 3
mestizos, 16, 36, 42, 62, 79, 114
metaphysics, 69–70
Mier Cueto, Enrique, 5, 26
Milstein, Brian, 24, 25, 28
Miners' March for Life, 9
mining, 22, 86
Miranda-Luizaga, Jorge, 72
mobilization, 18, 60, 121, 131
Moctezuma, 125
modernity, 65, 89
modernization, 77, 83, 89, 142n66
Montaigne, Michel de, 125
Moore, Melisa, 9, 32, 59, 156n64, 157n68
moral force, 65, 112
Morgan, Lynn, 57
mourning, ritual of, 66
Muela del Diablo, 9
muscle generosity, 134

Nancy, Jean-Luc, 2, 13, 59, 67, 136, 147n3, 149n47; community and, 48; essay of, 49, 50; finitude and, 15, 48, 57–58, 62, 64; García Linera and, 50; Mein Kampf and, 47–48; nationalist rhetoric and, 58; nonprojects and, 74; on political, 48; political subjectivities/ death and, 47; terminology of, 51–52; work of death and, 65
narrative voice, 16, 41, 43, 45, 66, 75, 84, 91, 98, 102, 107, 117, 119; dialectic movement of, 12–13
national community, 50, 52; heterogeneous